COLOURING OVER THE WHITE LINE

COLOURING OVER THE WHITE LINE

The History of Black Footballers in Britain

PHIL VASILI

MAINSTREAM
PUBLISHING

EDINBURGH AND LONDON

This book is dedicated to
Carrie MacArthur.
I wrote, she suffered.

First published in Great Britain in 2000 by
MAINSTREAM PUBLISHING COMPANY (EDINBURGH) LTD
7 Albany Street
Edinburgh EH1 3UG

ISBN 1 84018 296 2

A catalogue record for this book is available from the British Library

Typeset in Gill Sans and Garamond
Printed and bound in Great Britain by Butler & Tanner Ltd, Frome and London

Acknowledgements

There are lots and lots of people who've helped me along the way. I cannot name and thank them all. I'm afraid of starting in case I forget a name or two or three or four . . . dozen. Cheers. You've all been brilliant, whether as individual football nuts, club historians, club secretaries, players, ex-players, managers, (a couple of) chairmen(!), supporters, families of players, friends of players or just interested people. Your help has been invaluable.

However, I must name those that have been with me all the way on this one: my partner Carrie, children Andrea, Fionnulla, Alex and Louisa and Carrie's parents John and Anne MacArthur.

A special thanks to two very special people: Howard Holmes for writing the introduction and Shaka Hislop for writing the foreword.

A big thankyou to Colin Yates for use of his excellent charcoal drawing of Cyrille Regis.

A thankyou to Joe McAvoy and also to Bill Campbell at Mainstream for getting back to me so quickly . . . and with a decent advance!

Contents

Foreword

Growing up in Trinidad in the '70s, I guess it was strange that I chose football over cricket. It was the typical story of a boy growing up in the Caribbean, playing on poor pitches, on the streets, wherever; watching British football every Saturday morning and admiring every ball that was kicked and never thinking that I would one day grace those very pitches. Still, every Saturday there would be a race on to the local park, everyone wanting to be John Barnes, Ian Wright or Clyde Best.

After a five-year soccer scholarship in the United States, I was offered a trial by second-division Reading in July 1992. Two months later I signed a two-year contract. Words can never express the emotions that ran through me. Here I was, walking in the middle of my own dream, and loving it. I was thrown straight into the first team and life was great. After a bright start, however, things took a turn for the worse. Injury, culture shock and homesickness all took their toll. I still maintain to this day that had I not signed a two-year contract, I would not have returned from Trinidad after my first year.

My second year was a lot better. My then girlfriend and now wife Desha came to live with me. I played every game in the first team and we were promoted to the first division. That summer I signed a new two-year contract with Reading. Life was again sweet. The following season I played every game, culminating in a play-off final loss to Bolton at Wembley. That summer Desha and I got married. We were hardly back from our honeymoon when the speculation regarding my move to Newcastle began. It eventually went through for a fee of £1.5 million in August 1995. I had hit the big time!

Things started very well at Newcastle. I was playing under another of my idols, Kevin Keegan. By November we were eight points clear in the Premiership. It was during this time that I became involved with a group called Youth Against Racism and their project 'Show Racism the Red Card'. It involved my going to various schools and talking about my experiences in the game, especially the racism, which had been minimal until then.

Then injury struck again. A torn thigh muscle had me on the treatment table for six weeks after which there was a spell on the bench. I finally got my place back, but by this time we were a point behind Manchester United with seven games to go. In my second game we were away to Blackburn live on Sky's Monday-night football. We were leading 1–0 with four minutes to go when we conceded a goal for which many blamed me. To make matters worse, Blackburn snatched an even later winner. That's when it began. Extremely racist letters flooded my post. All of a sudden it seemed that every person of colour was to blame for Newcastle not winning the title. We should all know our places and go back 'home'. Although positive letters of encouragement and support far outweighed those of the ignorant and misinformed, it did cause some concern. The distinction between team support and individual blame became blurred to some.

My father was here at the time. His initial reaction was simply to laugh. These letters were to be ignored. This wasn't hard for him – he had lived in 1960s Britain. A place where 'No Blacks, No Irish, No Dogs' signposts were not only common but accepted. His experiences, as you can well imagine, were considerably harsher than anything I had ever encountered. I wouldn't have endured the experience of 1965, when he and his friend Desmond Allum were wrongly arrested by the police. After acquittal they sued and won a record settlement. With the proceeds, both attended law school. My father eventually became a magistrate and 'Uncle Desi' is arguably Trinidad's most accomplished litigator.

During one of my many talks at a Newcastle high school, one of my team-mates and co-speakers, who was White, admitted that as a young boy on the terraces he would join in racist chants. He wouldn't consider himself a racist, and I would never accuse him of such as he is truly one of the nicest people you could hope to meet. But at the time he sincerely believed he was doing his team a service by putting off the opposition, nothing more. It was only through his progression in football and playing alongside Blacks that he realised how wrong he was. In speaking to fans up and down the country you realise that many people who partake in racist chanting, or any kind of abuse for that matter, simply see it as doing their team a favour. Ironically, this abuse is never supposed to affect the Black players on their own team. Again, it is only in speaking to Black footballers and fans that they realise how wrong they are. There are, of course, some who are motivated by hate, and to these I can only say ignorance is not a virtue.

In the summer of '96 my first daughter Maalana was born and it was undoubtedly the happiest day of my life. It was during this time that a racist experience occurred which was especially saddening, but in hindsight quite amusing: I was at a petrol station opposite St James's Park when a group of six kids, no more than 12 years old, began shouting racist abuse at me, calling me every name under the sun. Then one of them recognised me. 'Hey, that's Shaka Hislop.' They all came running over and asked for my autograph! My initial reaction was one of amazement, then I was utterly dumbfounded. Without saying a word I quickly got into my car and drove off.

Later that season I was contacted by football historian Phil Vasili – who has become a good friend – to help in a documentary on the world's first Black professional footballer, Arthur Wharton, for BBC's *Black Britain*. There I was, jumping around in those nineteenth-century clothes. What a sight it was! It got me thinking though: what did he have to tolerate? How did he cope with it? Did he ever realise what a service he was doing to every Black footballer who succeeded him? I believe that every Black footballer, from the 16-year-old apprentice of 20 years ago to the millionaire Premiership stars of today, directly or indirectly, owes Arthur Wharton a huge debt of gratitude. All this for a man who died penniless and was buried in a pauper's grave.

I spent another year at Newcastle before moving to West Ham. Within 12 months I had played with or under some of the players I would race to the park to be: John Barnes, Ian Wright, Kevin Keegan and Kenny Dalglish. Playing with these stars has certainly helped me focus more on my responsibilities, not only to myself and my family, but those millions of youngsters of all 'races' who dream of one day playing professional football.

I still do a lot of work for 'Show Racism the Red Card', though admittedly since the birth of my second daughter Khazia, my time and involvement has been somewhat limited. The gist of it, though, is that things are changing for the better thanks to more people than I would ever be able to mention. I recently read an interview where John Barnes said, 'as long as there is racism in society there will be racism in football'. Truer words could not be spoken. It may seem optimistic, but I believe that if we did our bit, as footballers, to rid the game of racism, the fight against it within society would be enhanced. But, just as my father has the utmost respect and trust for the police, those in authority must 'do the right thing' and put all their weight behind everyone's efforts in what seems to be the never-ending struggle to 'Colour Over the White Line . . .'

Shaka Hislop
January 2000

Preface

Only a few of the footballers in this book were great players. Most were just ordinary professionals earning a bit more than their mates who weren't players. What brings them together is not the fact they were footballers, nor even that they were people of colour, but the common experience of racism they shared. While I enjoyed researching, meeting with and writing about the characters in *Colouring Over the White Line*, in an ideal world there would have been no need to tap away at a keyboard in my leaky shed-cum-study.

Inside these pages are stories of lives that are remarkable and ordinary. I hope you enjoy their tales.

Introduction

I'm at the top of the world, standing on a concrete grandstand in the July heat, surrounded by dancing fans singing 'Somalia, fantastica', watching the final of the 1998 World Anti-Racist Football Championships in Montefiorino, Italy.

Phil Vasili is the ringer with a team called the Somali Blades and he's told the team to call him 'Dunga'. The side from Sheffield have won all 7 games on the way to this final, including victories against Italian Ultras, Brazilian women, and the Senegalese in a penalty shoot-out. Yet, incredibly, so have the other Sheffield team, an Asian side from the Abbeydale area of the city. Both are dead on their feet. The final is goalless, title shared, both sets of players celebrating by throwing their kit to the crowd, each shirt bearing the logo 'Football Unites, Racism Divides'.

I first met Phil in April 1996, when the new-born 'Football Unites, Racism Divides' (FURD) project, backed by Sheffield United FC, invited him up to discuss the idea of an exhibition of black footballers. He was very excited that day as he was going on to Rotherham after our meeting to visit Sheila Leeson, a relative of Arthur Wharton whom Phil believed to have been the world's first Black professional footballer.

Sheila Leeson, Arthur's great niece, had come across a box of yellowing photographs whilst clearing out some cupboards. One photo was remarkable: it showed Arthur in running gear, standing alongside this huge trophy, awarded to him when he won the AAA 100-yards in 1886.

Arthur died a poor man, buried in an unmarked grave at Edlington, near Doncaster. Sheila had tracked down the exact position of his remains in Edlington Cemetery, and FURD launched an appeal to raise the money for a headstone. The next day a film production company was on the phone enquiring about the rights to Wharton's lifestory. That evening Phil decided to postpone his broader research into the history of black footballers, and dedicate his next 12 months to writing Arthur's biography.

In May 1997, with a simple ceremony at his graveside, Wharton's resting-place was marked at last after 67 years of anonymity – an 'Absence of Memory' – the subtitle of Vasili's book on Arthur, published in 1998.

FURD worked closely with the author in the telling of Arthur's tale, and we soon learnt of Phil's unfulfilled potential as a player, young hopes dashed after being on Cambridge United's books as a teenager. So it was inevitable that he managed to wangle a place in the Somali Blades to play in Montefiorino, the same team that Arthur Wharton had played for a century earlier, albeit as understudy to the incredible William 'Fatty' Foulke.

A multiracial French team had just stuffed Brazil to win the World Cup, but any romantic notions were swept aside as soon as the Somali Blades' mini-bus tried to enter French territory at the Channel Tunnel. Two of the team were stopped and told they wouldn't be allowed in, as the immigration officers refused to accept their refugee passports. I had anticipated this, and brandished a personal letter from a government minister stating that the two young men had his full backing, and requesting they be allowed to pass through France on their way to Italy. This did not impress the officials: one of them muttered that they had enough Africans in France already.

I was on the verge of losing it. The team voted to return to Sheffeld unless everyone was allowed in, and I felt a year's planning heading for disaster. It was at this point that 'Dunga' came to the rescue, first calming me down, and then agreeing to accompany Big Bob and Tino to catch the Ostend ferry from Dover. Six hours later the party was reunited and we sneaked into France at the Belgian border, Bob and Tino Iying beneath a pile of coats and kitbags. By this time Dunga had acquired another nickname – 'the Good Guy'. Where Racism had threatened to divide, football had united.

Howard Holmes
'Football Unites, Racism Divides'
December 1999

ONE

The Pioneers 1883–1918

Arthur Wharton, a Ghanaian with Caribbean and Celtic ancestry, turned out for Staffordshire football clubs Cannock and Cannock White Cross in 1883–84. Ever since there has been a consistent presence of players of colour in British soccer. Chapter one tells the story of this first generation, of the events that shaped their lives as footballers and as Black men in Britain at the height of its imperial power. Arthur played in the first division for Sheffield United in 1895. The second Black footballer to play at the highest level, Walter Daniel John Tull, was also the first Black soldier to be commissioned as a combat officer in the British Army.

Also included in this chapter are Tull's brothers Edward and William; the first players of Asian descent, Jack and Eddie Cother, who featured for Watford in the 1890s; John Walker, Scotland's first Black professional; Fred Corbett, a journeyman forward for Thames Ironworks; Egyptian Hassan Hegazi of Fulham, the first North African to play in the Football League and the enigmatic 'Costa' who appeared briefly for Southport Vulcan in 1919.

Arthur Wharton[1] was a unique Victorian sports star. Born at Jamestown, Accra, Gold Coast Colony – now Ghana – on 28 October 1865, he was the son of the Rev. Henry Wharton, a Wesleyan Methodist missionary from Grenada, West Indies. Indeed, Henry is not just the father of the son, he holds his own special place in the history of the Black Diaspora as the first African–Caribbean to hold the post of General Superintendent of the Gold Coast District of the Wesleyan Missionary Society. A biography of Henry was published in 1875, two years after his death. Henry's father, Arthur's grandfather, was a seafaring Scottish merchant and Henry's mother a freeborn African–Grenadan. His wife Annie Florence Grant, Arthur's mother, was the daughter of another Scottish trader, John C. Grant, and Ama Egyiriba, a Fante royal. The Grant family was a big noise in the Gold Coast, involved in business, politics and religion. Arthur's uncle, Francis Chapman Grant, was owner of the *Gold Coast Times* and one of the richest Euro-Africans in the Colony. Wharton therefore embodied, and was a product of, those destinations of the triangular (slave) trade route encompassing Britain, West Africa and the Caribbean; an economic, political and cultural universe known as the Black Atlantic.

As a professional footballer, Arthur was uncharacteristic because of his colour and his class. From an upper-middle-class cosmopolitan family and educated to at least 22 years of age, he attended Dr Cheyne's Burlington Road School in West London between 1875 and 1879. After returning home to the Tropics he once again sailed for Britain in 1882 to train as a missionary teacher at Shoal Hill College, Cannock – until summer 1884 – and Cleveland College, Darlington, from autumn 1884 to the academic year 1887–8. Both were Weslyan Methodist institutions. Very few paid players, if any, would have come from such privileged and educated backgrounds but Arthur loved mixing with White Trash!

While at Shoal Hill College in Cannock he played football and cricket. However, it was as a sprinter for Cleveland College, Darlington, that he forced his way on to the sports pages and into the conversation of the spectating punters. During the spring and summer of 1885, he competed in handicap races for prizes – a fruitbowl, a watch, a clock – which began to crowd his study room in the small northeastern railway town. The following season his trainer Manny Harbron entered him for the national sprint title at the Amateur Athletic Association (AAA) Championship at Stamford Bridge, London, in July which he won in a time of 10 seconds even, the first Black athlete to win an AAA championship. This later became generally recognised as the first world record in the event, although an official world record list was not published by the International Amateur Athletics Federation until 1913. After lifting the prize of the Prince Hassan Cup, he reclaimed his title and trophy in 1887. A song was composed about his success at the '86 AAA Championships – frustratingly the words have been lost – and contemporary interviews with him feature in many of the most popular national sports newspapers of the day, such as the *Athletic Journal* (26 June 1888). He was a proud, compassionate and passionate man with a fiery temperament. To some of his 1990s admirers he was a NWA.

In 1888 he became a pedestrian, a professional runner. And in September of that year he won the unofficial professional championship, the Sheffield Handicap at the Queen's Ground in the city. Thus for three seasons Arthur could reasonably claim to be the fastest man in the world. So why, for 13 seasons, did he earn his weekly wage as a goalkeeper, a position only those five numbers short of a full house would go for?

It was with Rotherham Town that Arthur first signed professional in the summer of 1889, although long before this time he may well have had his wallet swollen with numerous 'thank you' notes, anonymously given and signed only by the governor of the Bank of England. The best team and most prestigious club he kept for, Preston North End, had been renowned for ignoring the ban on paying players before professionalism was legalised in 1885. Yet when Arthur signed for the Deepdale club in 1886, it was as an amateur. Major Wiliam Sudell, the Preston manager who had been instrumental in forcing the FA to accept the right of footballers to be paid, went after Arthur specifically because he was the best *amateur* goalie around. Though the Major had won his battle to be allowed to pay players, the new rules governing their eligibility for the FA Cup had the effect of excluding many professionals from taking part in this, the only national competition. So the Preston North End Football Club and cotton-mill manager went after some top-drawer amateurs, one of whom was Arthur. However, it's a racing certainty that the Cleveland College student would have enjoyed a life of Riley on the expenses paid by Sudell. In fact the Major was jailed in 1895 for playing the role of Big Time Charlie by spending over £5,000 (which belonged to the Preston mill he managed) on expense and hospitality payments to Preston players. The Big Ron of his time did a lot for his boys.

With 'the invincibles' Arthur reached the semi-final of the FA Cup in March 1887, only to be knocked out as favourites by West Bromwich Albion. It was during this 1886–87 season that some northern football correspondents recommended Arthur for an England cap – for which he was never fitted.

Arthur left PNE in 1887–88 after playing in just two games at the beginning of the season. He missed out on the 26–0 thrashing of Hyde, which still stands as a record in the FA Cup. At this point in his sporting career, in the second half of the 1880s, his running was more important to him. And it musn't be forgotten that he was also still a student, supposedly training to be a missionary or minister. Yet Arthur preferred games of the body over those of the mind. He chose, as I'm sure most of us would have done at his stage in life, the sweat, dirt and exhiliration of triumph and glory instead of a safe and steady pensionable post. Later in his sporting career, when his status had declined from athletic star to journeyman footballer, he did apply for a postion in the Gold Coast civil service.

During Arthur's 20 years in competitive football he played for local sides Cannock and Cannock White Cross in season 1883–4; Durham County champions Darlington 1885–88; the 'invincibles' – 'the best team in the world' – 1886–88; Rotherham Town of the Midland League and Football League Division 2 1889–94 and 1895–96; Football League Division 1 Sheffield United 1894–95; Lancashire League clubs Stalybridge Rovers 1896–97 and 1899–00; Ashton North End 1897–99; and Football League Division 2 Stockport County 1900–02.

As a goalkeeper, one of his trademarks was his 'prodigious punch'. There were always two targets (yes, even when he was sober): the ball and the opponent's head, and he'd always connect with one. A number of match reports mention the run-ins he had with forwards. Goalkeepers could handle the ball anywhere in their own half and could be shoulder-charged with or without the ball. This physicality appealed to Arthur.

His combative nature could also be seen in his off-pitch dealings with the clubs who employed him. Most, apart from Preston, who could weave money at the mill, and Sheffield United, who were a big city club with large support, had financial problems. Inevitably, as part of their cost-cutting exercises, the management would dip into the players' wage packets. And Arthur, as a celebrity, would be on a higher wage than most, with more to lose. Yet he was not a man to accept such things with a shrug of the shoulder and a forced smile – at Rotherham he had numerous battles with the management committee and at

Stalybridge and Ashton the story was similar. At Stockport County, his last club as a full-time professional, the players went on strike and in one match picked the team and kept the gate money for themselves. Footballers taking control of their lives – a revolutionary situation that (unfortunately) didn't last.

Arthur's sense of his own worth, and stubbornness in his attempts to realise it, is also evident in the solitary, individualist world of athletics. At a meeting in Middlesbrough in 1885 he felt he'd won his race. On being awarded the second prize of a salad bowl he smashed it in front of the organising committee and told them to make a new one out of the bits. However it was another meet at Bradford in 1887, which drew a crowd of 15,000, that provides us with the essence of Arthur's 'diss me at your cost' spirit. The event – billed as 'The Big Boom' – had been arranged specifically so that the Gold Coaster could compete with homeboy Frank Ritchie, against whom he'd had a number of well-publicised needle races. The two were great and bitter rivals. In fact Arthur beat Ritchie in the AAAs final at Stamford Bridge when he set his record. The prize at Bradford was a cup worth 40 guineas. But Wharton wasn't toeing the line as the gun fired. He was in the crowd, having seen the trap that had been laid for him: the third and only other competitor in the race, J. Priestly, was wearing spikes that were nothing more than a pair of pit boots with the heels taken off and nails knocked through the sole. They were not for the purpose of a better grip but to puncture Arthur. However the young Fante student was too cute to get assaulted out of the duel by a make-weight dummy so he waited for the 'race' to finish and then offered Ritchie a head-to-head. Frankie went home instead.

In most eras of football there have been extrovert goalkeepers who feel it is their job to please the crowd by showcasing their athleticism. Bruce Grobbelaar is probably the most recent example. In all probability Arthur was the godfather of them all. A letter writer to the *Sheffield Telegraph and Independent* half a century after the event recalled that:

> In a match between Rotherham and [Sheffield] Wednesday at Olive Grove I saw Wharton jump, take hold of the cross bar, catch the ball between his legs, and cause three onrushing forwards – Billy Ingham, Clinks Mumford and Micky Bennett – to fall into the net. I have never seen a similar save since and I have been watching football for over fifty years.[2]

In 1997 BBC's *Black Britain* decided to feature Arthur. They asked the Newcastle keeper Shaka Hislop to dress up in nineteenth-century football kit and perform some of Arthur's legendary tricks. The filming took place at Newcastle United's training ground at Durham on a cold, windy day in early spring after Shaka had spent the morning working with his team-mates. After numerous attempts at swinging from the bar and trying to catch the ball between his legs Shaka finally trapped the leather. The big Trinidadian had revived the spirit of Arthur, while slipping slowly into a state of mild hypothermia . . .

In a game governed by passion as much as rational thought and logical argument the merits of a player are only sometimes univerally recognised. Rarely do two supporters agree on their club's best XI. While Arthur gave good showbiz value for punters' gate money, he also had his critics, in particular 'Whispers' of the *Athletic Journal*:

> Good judges say that if Wharton keeps goal for . . . [Preston] North End
> in their English Cup tie the odds will be considerably lengthened against
> them. I am of the same opinion . . . Is the darkie's pate too thick for it to
> dawn upon him that between the posts is no place for a skylark? By some
> it's called coolness – bosh![3]

Though an acrobatic athlete and showman, Wharton's comedic interventions should not cloud reality. He was grounded in his Blackness. Yet like the uneasy relationship between his agile, innate exhibitionism and his skilled, honed athleticism, his dual and contradictory status as a Man and Black Man in a Britain at the high point of its imperial power and modernity was the source of much aggravation. A lifelong battle was over his right to be accepted for what he did and not for what he was seen to be. At one athletics meeting, out of view, he overheard one competitor boasting to another that 'we can beat a blooming nigger anytime'.[4] Now facing them, the 'nigger' offered to box them if they preferred. They declined.

As Wharton became more successful, the debate over who and what he was became more politicised. His public identity, as he sought to define it and as others competed to construct it, became a contested area. The national sports press and some local and regional newspapers often highlighted Arthur's African inheritance, especially after his Stamford Bridge triumph. The new sprint champion was, said the 'referee', 'by no means a representative Englishman in appearance . . . [He was] a brunette of pronounced complexion.' The 'referee', also thought Wharton's heel was unusually long, supposedly typical of 'men of colour'.[5] The *Manchester Guardian*, 5 July 1886, described the new champion as 'South African'. Arthur's local rag, the *Darlington and Stockton Times*, 10 July, was unable to make up its mind despite its status as the mouthpiece of the sprinter's adopted home. It simultaneously labelled him a 'West Indian student' and 'Darlington youth'. By 18 September they'd generalised him as 'a coloured colonial'. The national *Sporting Chronicle*, 5 July, painted him as 'a gentleman of colour' and a 'Darkie'. However, by the autumn of 1887 the literary allusions had become a little more imaginative – but no less racialised. The *Athletic News*, 25 October, introduced 'Othello' to the stage.

This readiness to separately categorise Arthur from those around him through frequent reference to his colour was not accompanied by hard factual detail about his origins, which tended to remain ill-explored and inconclusive. Reporters of the national press, especially those based in London, often referred to Wharton as 'Darkey' or 'Darkie'. Locally, in the early stages of his career there was less inclination to colour Arthur, though by the 1890s the prefix 'Darkie' was used more frequently in regional newspapers. For instance, the move to Stalybridge in January 1896 was described by the *Northern Daily Telegraph*, on 18 January through allusion to 'new caught' game: 'Rovers have bagged a real nigger as goalkeeper in Wharton, who is none other than the 'Darkie' who used to guard the North End citadel'. 'Nigger' Arthur, a short bound and leap up the evolutionary scale from his primate cousins, was now captured for the delectation of Stalybridge football folk. (The animal analogy was used to positive effect when Arthur left Rovers. The *Ashton Herald*, 29 December 1900, told how Arthur had been 'lionised' by the football folk of Stalybridge and Ashton.)

Consciously or otherwise Arthur was often ambiguous as to his precise geographical and ethnic origins. In several interviews – to the *Athletic Journal*, 21 June 1887, the *Sheffield Independent*, 11 September 1888 and the *Ashton Herald*, 15 February 1896 – while he makes clear his West African roots, he does not refer directly to the Gold Coast by name.

This out-of-kit contest which Arthur fought between 1886 and 1902 to be defined primarily by his sporting achievements suffered a cruelly ironic twist with his application of August 1893 for a position with the Gold Coast Government Service. The posts for which he had applied were paid at £250 a year and 'entirely in the hands of natives'.[6] The wages, in terms of amount, would not have been much better than his earnings with his employees Rotherham Town Football Club, though in real terms such a sum would have had greater buying power in West Africa than in Britain.

Working for the colonial government like his brother Charles, with its pensionable security, would have been considered a respectable occupation by Arthur's extended family – who had paid for his education in Britain – and the Fante elders of his community. Arthur's fame as a face on the track and noted sticksman went largely unnoticed by his Euro-African compatriots, especially the élite of Accra and Cape Coast, among whom modern sports like football and rugby did not have the cultural significance and worth attributed to them in Britain.

Gold Coast Governor F.M. Hodgson, with the assistance and collusion of the Colonial Office in London, rejected his application. The official explanation, in a letter sent to Arthur dated 28 December 1893, cited his 'ineligibility' through lack of suitable training for the posts available, adding that there would be little chance of any similar opportunities arising in the future. A classic 'don't call us, we'll call you'. One of the positions mentioned – for which Arthur was listed as inadequate by Hodgson – was 'Schoolmaster Government School'. Yet in an interview given to the *Ashton Herald*, 15 February 1896, Wharton said his last days at Cleveland College were 'in the capacity of teacher'. Unfortunately the Public Records Office (PRO) have not made available the original application. This document would have revealed Arthur's CV in his own hand. Unofficially, for the eyes of contemporary civil servants only, three reasons for rejection were noted in the margins: his 'inappropriate' status as ex-100 yards amateur champion runner of England; the drunkeness of his brother Charles; and the 'life of ill-repute' of his sister Clara.[7] The political executive and colonial bureaucrats wanted it both ways: Arthur was condemned because some penpusher in Accra thought his brother a pisshead and sister a slag. Yet his obvious *difference* from them – as 100 yards record holder – was also used to knock him back.

Using Arthur's athletic excellence as a reason not to recruit him also flowed against the developing thrust of colonial appointment policy and practice. Odette Keun, on her travels in English-speaking Africa in the 1920s, noted that the colonial administrators were young and university educated, with 'their athletic record and their physique being taken into consideration [on appointment]. Many of these civil servants were in their time . . . well-known cricketers and football players.'[8] The Warren Fisher Committee on Colonial Service appointments recommended in 1930 that the Colonial Office should look for 'vision, high ideals of service, fearless devotion to duty born of a sense of responsibility, tolerance and above all the team spirit'.[9] Such qualities, they thought, were best learnt on the games field, preferably at public school and Oxbridge. The Gold Coast annual confidential report on political officers in the Service in the 1930s, contained the specific question: 'Is he fond of games or sports generally?'[10] Participation in sport, the colonial administrators argued, developed a distinction of character necessary for a successful career, especially valuable early on when many new appointees would be posted up-country. Between 1930 and 1939, 90 per cent of the recruits to the Gold Coast civil service had achieved excellence at sport. Though how many would have been world record amateur sprint champions; or professional runners or footballers; or Black?

Arthur's decision to run for money – to become a pedestrian – taken in spite of 'his mother and relatives [being] strongly opposed'[11] represented an attempt, unique so far, in his life to create a professional identity of his own choosing.

The timing – only three years after he vowed not to go professional – could have been due to a complex of reasons, the most obvious being the closure of Cleveland College at the end of the 1888–89 academic year. This forced Arthur to make a decision about his future. If he returned to the Gold Coast he would be captive to family and social pressures to 'do the right thing'. If he stayed in Britain and followed a sports career he would be on his own and have to earn an independent living.

From inside the Gold Coast Euro-African community, Arthur's action may have been seen as unpatriotic: turning back on his duty to 'his people' in pursuit of his own selfish desires. From Arthur's perspective there was internal pressure from his family to complete his studies, pass his exams, qualify for his chosen profession and return home; and external pressure from trainers, promoters and peers to commit himself to athletics.

Yet in practice the decision may already have been determined by expediency. His dual roles of scholar and sportsman did not sit happily alongside each other. His achievements on the sportsfield shortened the time for study, further enlarging the distance between himself and his family in the Gold Coast. While Arthur was setting athletic records for narrowing the relationship between distance and time, these achievements paradoxically lengthened the distance between himself and his family. As he became more succesful, so did he rely more on this success – spiritually, emotionally and economically.

A career in sport was chosen because it empowered Arthur. For the first time in his life he could be his own man, make decisions for himself that relied upon his own actions. The cost of this independence was that the price was always hidden. Winning, for himself, his trainer, his backers, his supporters was now everything because it would now provide everything, most crucially the means to live. Losing was not an option.

There was, almost certainly, another, hidden, underlying factor weighing on Arthur's mind at this point in his life: his fathering of one, possibly two daughters by his wife's sister, Martha. Arthur's application to join the Gold Coast Government Service in August 1893 was made before the start of his third season with Rotherham Town FC. The summer had been vexed. He was in contractual dispute with the club and had not re-signed. In addition, Martha was just five weeks away from giving birth (to Nora). He had also applied to become licencee of the Plough Inn public house at 23 Greasebro' Road, Thornhill, Rotherham – which he took over at the end of September – having recently left the Albert Tavern, his first pub, after a year's occupancy. It is clear, then, that during the summer of 1893, Arthur was actively considering alternative and secondary ways of earning a living. Why? Well, there was the face-off with his employers Rotherham Town over wages. As influential however, and possibly more so, was Arthur's inability to keep his dick inside his long johns in the presence of his wife's sister.

Arthur married Emma Lister, a local girl of 1 Rawmarsh Road, Rotherham in September 1893. As well as Martha, Emma had a brother, George. Just under eight months after Emma and Arthur's marriage at the parish church of Masbrough, Martha, in domestic service at nearby Barnsley, gave birth to her first daughter on 6 May. The baby was named on the birth certificate as Minnie *Wharton* Proctor. It is not known why she was given Arthur's surname. Indeed the fact was kept secret for generations. Two and a half years later, in September 1893, one month after Arthur's application to the Gold Coast Government Service, Martha gave birth to another daughter, Nora Proctor, leaving out the father's name on the birth certificate. Martha was already mother to Ben Marsh, born in 1882, from a marriage that did not last. The closest surviving relatives in Britain to Arthur Wharton are the three daughters of Nora, of whom Sheila Leeson lives, appropriately, directly opposite Millmoor, the stadium of Rotherham United FC.

The mystery as to why Minnie was given Wharton as her middle name; why this was subsequently erased; and the identity of Nora's father, opens up the possibility of Arthur being the father of Minnie and even Nora. Minnie was described by her niece, Sheila Leeson, as 'swarthy skinned'. Furthermore, the complex web of troubled relationhips within the extended family seems to support the view that Arthur was the likely suspect. On Emma's death – 21 April 1944 – Minnie bought the burial plot and gravestone at Masbro' cemetery and it was her wish, on her death, to be interred alongside her aunt. Emma, it has to be assumed, did not want to be buried with Arthur at his grave in Edlington, near Doncaster; nor did she make any provision for a headstone to be placed at her husband's grave in the 13 years between their deaths. Was this bond of loyalty between Minnie and her aunt Emma based upon a shared understanding of being wronged by the same man? In contrast Minnie's sister Nora 'had no time for Aunt Emma'.[12] Was this because Emma refused to confirm with Nora the identity of her father, and so prevent a (loving) relationship? Nora, in her turn, refused to talk to any of her children, including Sheila Leeson, about the identity of their grandfather.

Arthur had two causes of death recorded on his certificate: epithelioma, a form of cancer, and syphilis. Further proof that he'd been putting it about as a young man? Before the effects of his cancer began to show – an enlarged nose and growth on one side of his face and neck – he was physically attractive, well travelled, confident and with money in his pocket and his celebrity status and exotic allure would also have made him attractive to some women. The fit athlete would have needed a great deal of self-restraint not to have been sexually active outside his marriage. A case of easy come . . ?

For whatever reason, Emma had no children while Arthur's parents had ten. Did this outward appearance – embarrassment – of infertility affect his sexual behaviour? Did he feel his identity as a (virile) man undermined by the absence of young Whartons? In the Gold Coast, with its numerous cultural influences – indigenous, Islamic and Christian – being sexually active outside marriage would not have been considered as grave a cultural violation of morality as in Britain, dominated as it was by a bourgeois moral code obsessed with repressing, diverting and inhibiting sexual urges and erotic behaviour.

A number of suggestions have been made linking Arthur to Martha and her daughters. The firmest is the middle name of Wharton on Minnie's birth certificate. It is also the most intangible. Further, it seems to be corroborated by the oral history of the family which has passed the intrigue down through successive generations of the Lister-Wharton-Proctor-Leesons. The Leeson family until 1996 did not know that Minnie had the name Wharton; or that Nora had a blank space under 'father' on her birth certificate. Only in the course of research into their family history, by various members of the family, were these skeletons in the cupboard revealed. Nora's attitude to Emma leaves the feeling that some have taken their secrets to the grave with them. Sheila Leeson feels confident that 'swarthy skinned' Minnie was the daughter of Arthur. She is less certain, though still persuaded, that her mother was Arthur's daughter. To add to this catalogue of circumstantial evidence, in the winter of 1997, Sheila's grandson Liam became the South Yorkshire schools under-13 cross-country champion!

Wharton played professional football until at least 1901–02. After that he continued to play professional cricket although around that time he began to fade from public view. The (incomplete) picture that emerges is of a proud, confident, emotional and reckless man exploiting his talents to earn a living. The unanswered question is why he was so quickly forgotten.

A sporting contemporary of Arthur's was K.S. Ranjitsinhji; an Indian prince who used the cricket bat to produce fleeting moments of wonder and lasting memories of beauty. During the summer of 1899 he beat the scoring record of the legendary W.G. Grace by piling up 3,000 runs over the season. In *Beyond A Boundary*, Trinidadian Marxist C.L.R. James leaves the reader in no doubt as to the elevated status and place 'Ranji' held – and still holds – within the sport. He was revered by followers of cricket throughout the British Empire, irremovable from the pantheon of Great Names of Cricket.

Why can the same not be said for Wharton in football? While his achievements in athletics do feature to a limited extent in the histories of that sport, the reasons for his absence in histories of the ball game seem almost conspiratorial. A present day historian has suggested, laughably and quite seriously, that Arthur was nothing more than a local hero, a 'regional sportsman'.[13] A list of over 1,000 players in *Football Who's Who* for both 1900–01 and 1901–02 omit Wharton, as they do the Cother brothers, Fred Corbett of West Ham United and John Walker of Hearts and Lincoln City, all 'Coloured' players. The *Book of Football* (1906) focused on a number of leading clubs. In its treatment of Preston North End there is a section on goalkeepers which names four of those who either pre- or pro-ceeded Arthur – but not the man himself. In separate discussions of 'Good Goalkeeping' and the longevity of career of some footballers in *Football and How to Play It* (1904) there is no mention of Wharton although he played professionally until he was 36 years of age. From the 'Table of Leading Goalkeepers 1872–1949' in *The Official FA Yearbook 1949–50*, Wharton is absent because he failed to play for England, feature in an FA Cup final or play for the Football League representative XI. Nick Hazlewood, author of *In the Way* (1996), a recent book devoted to goalkeepers, again did not find space to include Wharton. Other writers – Cashmore (1982), Hamilton (1982) and Woolnough (1983) – who dealt specifically with Black footballers and sportsmen either ignored or dealt with him in passing.

Both Ranjitsinhji and Wharton were labelled by British sports commentators as 'coloured'. This is what united the two sportsmen: they were both the object of colour-coded – racialised – appraisal. Racism took a variety of forms, however. The ethnicity and culture of the individual or group had also to be categorised. Once these three factors – colour, ethnicity and culture – had been dissected, the Asiatic – yellow – peoples were placed at a more advanced position along the continuum of civilised/uncivilised, than the African. According to this ordering of society, 'Ranji', as an ethnic Indian, was of a less barbaric, more evolved culture. The justification for this assertion was premised on the view of the South Asian sub-continent as having had a history conveyed from generation to generation through the base language of Sanskrit. Since at least the eighteenth century, some European scholars maintained that Sanskrit and the classical languages of Europe, Latin and Greek, had a common source. Indeed some, such as William Jones writing in 1786, argued that Sanskrit was the linguistic base from which all Indian and European languages had originated. A little later Friedrich Schlegel developed the notion of an ancient Indian 'race' from whom the Aryan 'race' evolved. The Aryans – Caucasians – had moved from their homeland of the Asian Caucasus and peopled Europe. For Schlegel, the Indian Aryans were responsible for the ancient civilisations of Pharaonic Egypt. This interpretation of the past in effect de-Africanised Egypt. Schlegel felt that the production of sound in a language betrayed the evolutional state of the people who spoke it. Indo-European languages were 'inflectional', noble languages able to transmit sophisticated thought; African 'gutteral' languages were animalistic and therefore unable to facilitate the transmission of civilised, progressive thought and ideas. Therefore Africans were the least evolved, most animalistic of humans, especially those south of the Sahara Desert where written languages didn't exist, leaving cultures and peoples without history, having accumulated nothing of worth – only a void of Barbarism.

In respect of social class it could be argued that both Ranjitsinhji and Wharton came from aristocratic backgrounds, although the public perception of Wharton's class as a young athlete was that he was a 'gentleman', a bourgeois. This perceived difference is important. Ranjitsinhji was accepted by his peers, the public and the press as upper-class. He played as an amateur for Cambridge University, Sussex and England. While Wharton, a resident of the industrial north of England, played professional football for working-class clubs and ran for money. As such he could not be classed as an amateur 'gentleman' athlete.

It was much easier to forget Arthur because the people among whom he played his sport, lived and died, did not have the means to ensure his name and reputation survived. Working-class communities do not generally write their own histories, own printing presses, have editorial control within newspapers, commission art, erect statues or have power over mass communication. While celebration of the defeat of the enemies of the ruling-class – Remembrance Sunday on 11 November, for instance – is seen almost as a social duty, working people do not in a similar manner remember their victories, as a class, in a manner defined and constructed by themselves as a class. The Peasants' Revolt 1381; Kett's Rebellion 1546; the Tolpuddle Martyrs 1834; the Chartists of the 1840s; the Mutinies on the Western Front 1917; the Bolshevik Revolution of 1917; the 1919 Rebellion of Red Clydeside and Revolution in Europe; Cable Street 1936; and the smashing of the National Front at Lewisham in 1977 are just a few examples of events, movements and battles that are not celebrated by the majority of workers in a carnival of joy. Where are the prominent statues to honour these historic events of working-class action?

If momentous and inspiring working-class acts are suppressed, erased or forgotten it is not surprising that the achievement of one individual is airbrushed out of the contested and congested space called 'History'. Wharton was made invisible because he became both Black and working-class.

The place, as in geographical situation, of their achievements is also important. Ranjitsinhji was an aristocrat who played cricket within the heart of the empire. He was selected for England but did not *represent* England; rather just the glory of England as an imperial force. He was a cricketing colonial who stood testimony to the justice of the imperial mission; he was surrounded by individuals and institutions of enormous power and this power included the means to produce memory as a cultural commodity. Yet while Arthur was on the margins of influence and power, his proletarianisation – the act of his becoming working class – provides the essential clue as to why he was so quickly forgotten. His career was fashioned and shaped by opposing forces that at the same time raised and lowered him. He was elevated by his achievements on the sports field to the status of 'celebrity', while his occupational status as a professional runner, footballer and northern leagues cricketer lowered his social class. This is not a value judgement, just a description of the social consequences brought about by his decision to become a professional sportsman. 'Ranji' was remembered because of his talent and ability but equally because those with whom he mixed socially, of whom he was a part – the élite of cricket and society – wrote about their lives and times. He also published a book on cricket from which C.L.R. James quotes. Wharton did not mix in such company. If he did put pen to paper his writings have been lost, disappearing with his other personal belongings save a bible and a small collection of photographs which came to the notice of Sheila Leeson via an individual collector who had bought an album disposed of by an elderly member of the Leeson family houseclearing on the death of a relative.

Yet the careers of the South Asian cricketer and the Black African footballer throw light on to areas of sport in late-Victorian-pre-First World War Britain that have been shaded from view. Other Black footballers and runners have been mentioned already. In Rugby, James Peters, a Black man born in Manchester, played for England between 1906 and 1908; African–American racing cyclist Marshall Taylor beat British and continental opponents in 1902; in 1907 African boxer Andrew Jeptha won a world title in London. Ex-slave Bobby Dobbs fought in Britain in 1898 and returned in 1902, staying for eight years. People of Colour were kitted-up all over the place: at the crease; on the field; on the track; at the velodrome; and in the ring.

The whipping of White supremacist ideology by the triumphs of Black athletes, in particular boxers, vexed racists. Public appeals were made for the best scrappers of the White 'race' to come forward to defeat and subdue the animal threat occasioned by these triumphs. The sports editor of the New York *Sun*, Charles Dana, raged:

> We are in the midst of a growing menace. The black man is rapidly forging to the front ranks in athletics, especially in the field of fisticuffs. We are in the midst of a black rise against white supremacy . . . Less than

a year ago Peter Jackson could have whipped the world – Corbett,
[Robert] Fitzsimmons . . . but the white race is saved from having at the
head of pugilism a Negro . . . There are two Negroes in the ring today
who can thrash any white man in their respective classes . . . Wake up you
pugilists of the white race! Are you going to permit yourself to be passed
by the black race?[14]

The success of African–American Jack Johnson in becoming the first Black world
heavyweight champion in 1908 – he was forced to wrap the belt around him in
Sydney, Australia, unable to find a venue in the United States – would no doubt
have triggered editor Dana into another bout of racial fury. In fact the journalist's
tirade merely lifted the lid – but with a public audience – on the latent prejudice
that bubbled to the surface when notable White athletes were defeated by Blacks
in significant sporting competition. The bruising caused by each jab, hook and
upper-cut in Johnson's taunting, smiling demolition of White contenders was felt
many times over by racist Whites, whose suffering was further intensified by the
boxer's pride in himself and delight in his blood-spilling achievements. White
hostility to Black prowess created an atmosphere in boxing – and other sports –
of heightened racism. Johnson's win led to numerous lynchings and attacks upon
Blacks throughout the United States. If the future of the White 'race' could not
be assured in the ring, the futures of some Black men would be terminated
outside it. The defeat of Johnson by a 'Great White Hope' became a burning
passion. For others, such as the Rev. Meyer, the mere matching of Black and
White was unfair. He campaigned to stop Johnson fighting 'Bombardier Billy'
Wells in London in 1911:

> The present contest is not wholly one of skill, because on the one side
> there is added the instinctive passion of the Negro race, which is so
> differently constituted to our own, and in the present instance will be
> aroused to do the utmost that animal development can do to retain the
> championship, together with all the financial gain that would follow.[15]

The bottom line in Meyer's explanation for Black success on the sports field – the
animal in the Black – was to become the common feature of the excuses offered
by the supremacists for defeats of Whites on track and field. The agility, physical
dexterity, instinctive endurance and unfeeling durability of the Black athlete,
derived from their animalism, made contests between Black and White unfair.
The former would always be at an advantage when human competition included
only a physical dimension. Thus it was because Whites were more evolved and
civilised, at a more advanced stage of human development, that they were
incapable of inflicting those kinds of comprehensive defeats on Blacks in sport
that had been achieved by Whites in business and politics. The animalist
argument represented an attempt to rubbish Black athletic success by devaluing
the victory – and, therefore, the social significance of defeat: unequal bodies in

unequal contests. Black boxers were not allowed to fight for British titles during much of the inter-war period. It was not until 1948 that a Black British middleweight, Randolph Turpin, was allowed to contest a domestic title with a White Briton.

Racism invests Black athletic achievement with great symbolic value. In such a politicised sports environment, the erasure from collective memory of Black triumph was profound. For those Europeans and Americans with an interest in maintaining the status quo, to accept Black success at face value would have undermined the crucial notion of natural White superiority. If this ideological keystone was shifted, would not other ideas underpinning the hierarchical structure of society, such as those justifying class and gender inequality, also come crashing down? Of course, in reality, sporting contests between Black and White were anything but equal. The opportunity for most White athletes to develop their skill and talent was far in excess of that to Blacks. The operation of the colour bar, official and unofficial, whether in Britain, its empire or indeed any part of the globe dominated by Europeans, sustained inequalities across the board.

Martin Offiah, a Black rugby player for the England international team is nicknamed 'Chariots' by his team-mates. It refers to the film *Chariots of Fire*, the last two words of the film's title having a phonetic harmony with the player's surname. It is the closest association any Black athlete has with the film about athletics, among other things, in the decade after the First World War. One of the greatest sprinters in Britain during this time was Harry Edward, born in British Guiana in 1895. Wearing the vest of the Polytechnic Harriers club, he ran 200 metres in 21.7 seconds in Berlin in June 1914, following this up with a time of 22 seconds for the same distance in Budapest in July. While the outbreak of war shortened the duration of his career it did not dull his astonishing speed. In 1920 he won the AAA's 100 yards title with a time of 10 seconds – equalling Arthur's 1886 record – and also ran the 220 yards in 21.6 seconds. At the Olympics of that year he won the bronze in the 100 and 200 metres. It was said that his faltering start in the shorter distance deprived him of the gold (and silver). In 1921 he beat Harold Abrahams – a British Jew and one of the two central characters in the film – in both the 100 and 200 yards. At the 1922 AAA championship, Edward won the 100, 200 and 440 yards titles *within an hour*. His outstanding performances won him the Harvey Memorial trophy, presented to the best athlete of the championship. Abrahams thought the young Guianan 'one of the most impressive sprinters I have ever seen'.[16] That the two runners featured – the other was Scot Eric Liddell – in *Chariots of Fire* both came from ethnic minority backgrounds adds poignant irony to the exclusion of Edward. Furthermore, it was trainer Sam Mussabini's excellence in nurturing the talent of Edward that propelled Abrahams to invite the Arab–African–Italian coach to try and work his magic on him. (Mussabini also coached another Black runner, Jack London, who won the AAA 100 yards title in 1929 and was an Olympic silver medallist.)

The film is a selective, arbitrary and unimaginative interpretation of British athletics in the 1920s. The nation is white, overwhelmingly anglo-saxon and ruled by the fathers of God's children. The only perceived threat to this 'natural' supremacy comes from the Jewish Abrahams. (Liddle, though a Scot, is doing the work of God's chosen Englishmen as a missionary in China.) It won an Academy Award as the best film of 1981. However it was the picture's unspoken and missing dialogue – its silence – that was most eloquent. It pronounced British athletics in this inter-war 1920s to be White yet egalitarian where, upon the track, anti-Semitic racism could be pounded to dust underfoot.

Yet while *Chariots of Fire* addressed contemporary social and political tensions it did so in a timid, limited and one dimensional manner. Where were Harry Edward and Jack London? Indeed Liddle's record of 9.7 seconds for the 100 yards at the 1923 AAA championships was only the second time Wharton's 'even time' – set 37 years earlier – had been broken (South African G.H. Patching broke Arthur's record in 1912 with a time of 9.8). Liddle, incidentally, buried in China far away from his birthplace, like Wharton, was not remembered by a gravestone until after his resuscitation in the film.

One Black athlete whose career has not been forgotten, the detail reverberating through time and across cultures, is USA sprinter Jesse Owens. Hitler had intended the 1936 Berlin Olympics – the first to be televised – to be an athletic showcase for Nazism. But Owens packed his own script on leaving Ohio. He won four gold medals, Blacking-out the sunrays of Aryan success. His defeat of 'superior' German – and other White – runners in an illusion of effortless grace re-choreographed Hitler's intended dramatisation. According to Nazi ideology, racial struggle was the motivational force of history. Competition at its most naked was not over the control of material wealth and the means by which a society creates that wealth, but between 'races' for purity, survival and dominance. Only the unadulterated and non-miscegenised races – those that had fucked themselves – would endure. The salvation of the human 'race' – in effect, for Hitler, the biological struggle for Aryan domination – was only possible through the elimination of all other (sub-)species. Thus the apparatus of racial oppression and destruction so characteristic of Nazism: official denigration and separation of minorities; their forced, slave labour in ghettos and concentration camps; and eugenic and ethnic cleansing which was genocidal in scale. Owens, as a Black 'auxilliary' of the United States was an 'Untermenschen', accorded the same racial status as Jews and Gypsies and the same social status as communists. All would be bound for the gas chamber upon the triumph of the Nazi will.

These triumphant Black sportsmen, Owens in 1936 and Wharton in 1886, were united by not only their colour but the wider significance their excellence represented. Their athletic success broadcast comparable messages, rubbishing simplistic ideas of Black inferiority. In both Nazi Germany and late-Victorian Britain, ideas about 'race' – in effect the relationship between physical appearance, behaviour and evolution – dominated and literally coloured any discussion of nations and peoples. 'Race' was used as an instrument of separation: to divide the working class from uniting in pursuit of their common interest.

It would be foolish to argue that the quality of life for minorities was similar in the two countries. An obvious difference was in the respective role of the State. While the Nazis tried to enforce racial and political purity through decrees of law and active brutality on the part of its 'security forces' the British government did not force minorities and political opponents to shower in a gas chamber. What is argued is that the ruling class of both countries invested a great deal of worth in the concept of 'race'; it was at the core in any discussion about the social health and well-being of the nation. In this sense both were highly racialised societies. This was how a Black resident in London at the turn of the century described the experience of a fellow Black:

> Recently, three white men of gentlemanly appearance . . . [were] going in
> the opposite direction to that of a coloured man . . . [when] one of the
> company . . . called the attention of his comrades to the presence of the
> coloured man, and then said 'Look at that thing' . . . This laceration of
> the feelings of coloured people, which has now become a practice in
> England, is partly due to the fact that Englishmen, having adopted the
> notion that they are superior to coloured men, have found rudeness and
> incivility to be the best supports of the imposture. [17]

The difference between the racial universe of Britain in the 1880s and '90s and that of Germany in the 1930s was the degree to which the lesser 'races' were allowed a place in the New Order. Eugenics – effectively the science of racial purification – was relatively new in the 1880s, while in Nazi Germany it had reached an influential, genocidal maturity. Yet both societies were dominated by a ruling class that viewed themselves as a superior 'race'. And, while Wharton and Owens confounded these ideas by their athletic skills, the animal-in-the-Black argument was used by supremacists to escape from the contradiction the excellence of the two presented.

The career of Owens after Berlin did not have the slip and slide of Arthur's after-sport life. In 1950 Jesse was named 'Athlete of the Half-Century' by Associated Press. Twenty-two years later his old college awarded him an honorary doctorate. And in 1976 he received the Presidential Medal of Freedom, ranked as the highest civilian 'honour' in the USA. The reason for this elevation is explainable. While Wharton's achievements had undermined the ruling ideas of his age, Owens's four Olympic golds affirmed the meritocratic ideals at the heart of Democratic America. The symbolic message was trumpeted to the German masses to the sound of the USA anthem while Owens stood on his winner's podium and spoke of less inequality, less hatred of others and more individualism. Owens's success became wonderful propaganda material for the marketing forces of Liberal Democracy. Despite being a willing supporter of the American Dream, Owens, especially in the post-1945 Cold-War period, was still considered a suspect 'Nigger' by Hoover and his FBI. (Any running Negro was a suspect to these suited defenders of the 'American Way'!)

Looking from the inside out – from the perspective of the runners as Black individuals – the major difference between the two was the public treatment their excellence attracted. Wharton's success was quickly forgotten because, ironically, of its importance. This is not to suggest a conspiracy of silence: many who have achieved, in all walks of life, have been forgotten while, in contrast, many who have achieved little when judged solely in terms of their own efforts and once the privilege of birth or wealth are factored out of the evaluation, are remembered. (Princess Diana being the most obvious example.) Historical memory is not arbitrary; this is recognised by those on the left in politics. Indeed the key function of any socialist party is to act as the memory of the working class, celebrating confidence-inspiring victories and learning from defeat. In late-Victorian Britain, with the unashamed theft of Africa speeding up, it was not convenient to trumpet the doings of a son of Africa conquering those sons of conquerors in their own backyard, on their own turf. Arthur's achievements as an African in Britain stood in opposition to what was being said to justify Britain's 'achievements' in Africa. For Owens, it was the opposite. In many ways his Olympic success flowed with the current of international politics. The Nazis were an economic and imperial threat to the leading capitalist nations, including state-capitalist USSR, the empire Hitler most wanted to destroy. Probably more than any other state in history, and that includes the Soviet Union, Nazi Germany was constructed around a particular body of ideas. As such it was vulnerable to practical refutations of its ideology by contradictory action and events. Owens should not have happened. His public, physical denial of the superior race ideas of Nazism, on the track of the Nazis and, to their deepest embarrassment, in front of thousands of Germans, provided immense propaganda material to the opponents of Fascism. These Defenders of Democracy, the USA, Britain, France, conveniently put aside the racism and inequality so obvious and profound in their backyards – a contradiction analysed by George Orwell in his 1939 essay 'Not Counting Niggers' – to proclaim the success of Owens. His medals were held up as not so much a victory for racial equality – if this message was taken up seriously by the Homeboyz it could have dangerous repercussions for mainstream America – but rather a defeat for the particular variety of racialism practised and propagandised by the Nazis.

A generation later, Cassius Clay, as he was then known, replied to similar hypocrisy by throwing his Olympic gold medal into the river in his home town of Louisville, Kentucky. 'With my gold medal actually hanging around my neck I could not get a cheeseburger served to me in a downtown Louisville restaurant.'[18] This individual response to racism by one Black champion took a collective form eight years later at the 1968 Olympics. Against the background of growing Black anger and hostility to the war in Vietnam, where African–Americans were disproportionately filling the bodybags, Black athletes John Carlos and Tommie Smith black-fisted their way through the 200-metres medals ceremony. At the 400-metres equivalent, their colleagues Larry James, Lee Evans and Ronald Freeman wore black berets, headgear of the revolutionary

Black Panther movement. The lesson of Owens and Clay/Ali had been learnt. These Black athletes were determined not to allow their performances to be stolen from them. If they were to stand for something larger and more meaningful let everybody know about it:

> I wore a black right-hand and Carlos wore the left-hand glove of the same pair. My raised right hand stood for the power in black America. Carlos's raised left-hand stood for the unity of black America. Together they formed an arch of unity and power. The black scarf around my neck stood for black pride. The black socks with no shoes stood for black poverty in racist America. The totality of our effort was the regaining of black dignity.[19]

Sport reflects global circumstances, in so doing sport and politics become intertwined and inseparable. While the geographical backdrop to Carlos, Smith, James, Evans and Freeman was the Estadio Olimpico, Mexico City, the political backdrop was one of Black revolutionary activism. (Interestingly, Rodney Pattison and Iain Macdonald, British winners of the Flying Dutchman yacht competition, also wore military caps and saluted when receiving their medals. Unlike Carlos and Smith, they were not sent home.) Prior to the Olympics, Black athletes in the United States had formed themselves into the Olympic Project for Human Rights (OPHR). Carlos and Smith were both supporters of OPHR. The project had originally intended a Black boycott of the Olympics. A revision of this plan resulted in the adoption of a policy that aimed to question and undermine the nationalism characteristic of the Olympics as a whole. They were determined that the Stars and Stripes would not be wrapped around their bodies. While the dead Black soldier in Vietnam had no choice as to what covered him, the athlete did. The conscript had been forced to give his life in service of the State. No such 'honour' would be forced upon Carlos and the others. Their wins were for 'Black America'. The Olympics was an opportunity to reinterpret the United in United States and proclaim the virtues of Black consciousness. (These two occasions also provided an ideal platform upon which Black, USA athletes could vent their anger at the racist head of the USA Olympic Committee, Avery Brundage. The hostility of these athletes towards the Chicago millionaire was historic, stemming from his 'fact finding' tour to Nazi Germany in 1935 from which he returned clueless. He had been sent by the American Olympic Committee to assess the suitability of Berlin as the Olympic venue, and in particular the treatment of Jewish sports people. He found no evidence of the mistreatment of Jewish athletes.)

The USA in 1968 was certainly not united. Many Blacks felt that the FBI had a hand in the killing of Martin Luther King in April. And in the death of Malcolm X in 1965. Rioting and rebellion by Black Americans in over one hundred cities followed the murder of King. Those killed in the suppression numbered 39, 34 of whom were Black. The struggle of African–Americans for liberty, justice and equality nearly two hundred years after these principles had been inscribed in the constitution of the country was the struggle against systemic rascism and poverty. It was poverty, this common enemy with a common cause that linked and united Black and White during the 'Poor People's March' on Washington in May 1968, representing 30 million destitute Americans. It culminated in 'Resurrection City', a canvas township put together by the marchers in the (cold) heart of the capital(ism). After five days the leaders were imprisoned and the shanty town destroyed.

Mexico City itself was the site of an uprising by students and workers against the government of President Gustavo Diaz Ordaz in the months before the Olympics. Just a week before the opening ceremony, soldiers with fixed bayonets charged a crowd of over 15,000. In the stabbing and shooting by the military that followed, more than forty protesters were killed. Indeed 1968 was a year in which the poor and pissed-off in many different parts of the world walked and fought together in the streets: in Ecuador, France, Brazil, Czechoslovakia to name some of those most prominent. The struggle for Black emancipation in the USA was at the forefront of a global dissatisfaction with capitalism. The times really did seem to be changing.

Arthur's known political activity was small-scale when compared to his sporting achievements, though he was a member of the Miners Federation of Great Britain, forerunner of the NUM, during the General Strike in 1926. His contribution, as a Black man, to the struggle of British labour for emancipation was not unique. There is a long history of self-activity by Black Britons and Black residents of Britain: in 1780 Charlotte Gardiner was hanged for daring to confront the authorities through her part in the Gordon Riots; in the same decade Olaudah Equiano began campaigning against slavery. His daughter Anna Maria is buried in the grounds of St. Andrews church, Chesterton, Cambridge. She died in 1797, aged four. A plaque was erected on the outside wall, the words and the sentiment expressing respect and tolerance of difference:

> Should simple village rhymes attract thine eye,
> Stranger, as thoughtfully thou passest by,
> Know that there lies beside this humble stone
> A child of colour haply not thine own.
> Her father born of Afric's sun-burnt race,
> Torn from his native fields, ah foul disgrace!
> Through various toils at length to Britain came,
> Espous'd, so Heaven ordain'd, an English dame,
> And followed Christ; their hope two infants dear.
> But one, a hapless orphan, slumbers here.
> To bury her the village children came,
> And dropp'd choice flowers, and lisp'd her early fame;
> And some that lov'd her most as if unblest.
> Bedew'd with tears the white wreaths on their breast;
> But she is gone and dwells in that abode
> Where some of every clime shall joy in God.

During the nineteenth century William Davidson, a Jamaican, was hanged in 1820 for his part in the Cato Street conspiracy. The conspirators were seeking revenge for the Peterloo Massacre of 1815 in which 11 demonstrators had been killed by the militia; William Cuffay was a leader of the Chartist movement in London; Henry Sylvester Williams formed the African Association in 1897, to encourage pan-African unity. (In 1900 the first ever Pan-African Conference was held in London. Its ultimate objective was to bring about the end of colonialism.)

The black gloves and berets of 1968 were the African–American expression of a movement against oppression that had flowered with Toussaint Louverture's victorious slave rebellion in San Domingo – Haiti – in 1797. Yet from the anti-slavery campaigns of the eighteenth and nineteenth centuries to the Black Panthers of urban America and beyond, the characteristic feature has not been the ethnic exclusivity of the participants, but their common class background. Leader of the Panthers, Malcolm X, came to acknowledge the necessity of unity between peoples – after they had achieved unity amongst themselves – if any were to stand any chance of destroying capitalism:

> You have whites who are fed up, you have blacks who are fed up. The whites who are fed up can't come uptown [to Harlem] too easily because the people uptown are more fed up than anybody else, and they are so fed up it's not easy to come uptown . . . when the day comes when the whites are really fed up with what is going on – and I don't mean those jive whites, who pose as liberals and who are not, but those who are fed up with what is going on – when they learn how to establish the proper type of communication with those uptown who are fed up, and they get some coordinated action going, you'll get some changes. And it will take both, it will take everything that you've got, it will take that.[20]

Arthur owed a debt, as do all sports people, to those who fought to improve the lives of Black and working people. Without pressure from ordinary people to change their lot, they would not have had the small amount of leisure time and money for relative luxuries that did exist. They forced those above, in parliament, in the boardroom, in the courtroom to change laws, working practices and conditions. In Britain it was activity by individuals and groups, such as the Chartists and trade unions in general, that won improved social and economic conditions which enabled men and to a much lesser extent, women, to pursue a living in sport. Activists in the workplace, street and meeting hall created the space for Wharton to perform.

Once Arthur stopped playing football professionally in 1902, though his cricketing exploits continued to be publicised, little else about him was. Even though his name is synonymous with numerous firsts, as Black professional footballer, Black Football League player, 'gentleman' professional, Black AAA's 100-yards title holder – the list could continue – a list of factual achievements could only provide an incomplete picture.

His private relationship with Emma was left unresolved in the sense that the difficulties created out of living together and having separate lives – Arthur's being very public – was not underpinned by mutual love and respect. It was a journey neither would have chosen had they known the route beforehand. The birth of Minnie and Nora to sister-in-law Martha, assuming that they were Arthur's children, would have created anguish for Emma, Martha and Arthur – for obviously different reasons. For all three the world may have taken on a surreal feel from 1893. Arthur, the nationally known celebrity ever willing to encourage adulation of himself by others yet unable to give himself fully to his most enduring fan, the woman with whom he had chosen to share his life. Public acclaim versus private grief. For a man so used to winning physical contests, this emotional conflict may well have overshadowed his public triumphs with its deep, lasting, cutting impact. Once he shut the door on the outside world, how much worth did his feats of time over distance, of combining agility and strength, carry when faced with the turbulent emotions of his marriage?

What of Martha and Arthur's anguish of lovers doomed? Enveloped and roused by a love that produced love but was nevertheless inevitably destructive; a haunting, secret and unacknowledgeable bond. How did they cope with the impossibility of their affair? What was the burden of Emma and Arthur's barren marriage compared to Martha's life-long torment of dual denial: of being the mother to her children and partner of her lover?

For a man who was the focus of so much positive attention, who brought excitement into the lives of many, it was surely not lost on Arthur how negative his physicality could also be. Prevented from openly – and therefore fully – loving his children? And them from loving him. And he from loving himself.

While it could be argued that Arthur had a fair amount of power in determining the course of his personal relationships – marriage, his affair with Martha – he had little influence in deflecting or ducking the power of systemic, institutional racism. We can assume from his application to join the Gold Coast Government Service that he would have swapped his role as northern working-class hero with that of an anonymous West African civil servant. Here we find one of the greatest paradoxes in his life. His elevated status as sporting icon in Britain unwittingly involved, as part of the deal, not being able to return to West Africa on his own terms. As an unnamed official of the Colonial Office commented, his sporting excellence was 'inappropriate' training for the career of a bureaucrat. Thus his success, in the sweep of the hand of a pen-pushing official, became transformed into a handicap the burden of which was measured in years rather than yards. Though Arthur was not alone. To end a glittering sporting career in poverty is not unusual for working-class athletes, especially when they are Black. Boxer Joe Louis and footballer Albert Johanneson, who features later, are two tragedies that spring to mind.

But racism in and of itself does not automatically bring about hard times. Its impact is dependent upon the power of the firer and the body armour of the receiver: the relation of power between the parties involved. A telling example is the experience of Trinidadian Learie Constantine who played first-class cricket in Lancashire 20 years after Wharton. A West Indies international, he was invited, in 1928, to play professionally for Nelson in the Lancashire League. His family – his partner and their daughter Gloria – were later joined by another Trinidadian and family friend, C.L.R. James. According to James there was one other person of colour in the small cotton town who collected rubbish in a pushcart. After some tense moments early on the Trinidadians became accepted by the working class of Nelson. No doubt Learie's success at the wicket – Nelson won the Lancashire League seven times in Constantine's nine seasons with the club – helped just a fraction. James recalls one incident that Constantine interpreted as a sign of acceptance:

> Early one morning a friend turns up, has a chat and a cup of tea and rises to leave. 'Norma, I am just going to do my shopping. If you haven't done yours I'll do it for you.' Later Constantine said to me, 'You noticed?' I hadn't noticed anything. 'Look outside. It is a nasty day. She came so that Norma will not have to go out into the cold.'[21]

In 1943 Constantine booked rooms for himself and his family at the Imperial Hotel, Russell Square, London. He was in the capital playing for the West Indies against England at Lords. On arrival, the manager, mindful of the effect a Black family would have upon his trade, and fearful in particular of the response of some White American soldiers staying at the Imperial, reluctantly agreed to honour Constantine's booking for one night and no more. The family went immediately to another hotel and Learie sued the Russell Square hotel. He won £5 in damages. The aptly named Imperial had picked on the wrong man, a public figure with a high profile, who had the economic means, social status as a civil servant and the social contacts to fight back 'against the revolting contrast between his first-class status as a cricketer and his third-class status as a [Black] man'.[22]

The sports career of Wharton was distinguished by two essential characteristics: his abilities as an athlete – skills that were the coalition of innate talent and applied toil – and the social reaction to his colour and ethnicity. In respect of the first characteristic, he achieved fame but no lasting material benefit for his physical prowess. In respect of the second, responses to his colour were conditioned by a national and imperial backdrop that held 'race' to be as important as social class in determining one's place in the world. Arthur's burden was not his colour but the dual identity forced upon him because he was a man of colour. As a sportsman, he lived in two co-existing but different worlds: in one he was acclaimed and 'one of us'; in the other he was racialised and categorised as an 'other'. The *Athletic Journal* interview, 26 June 1888, told of two personas, the public and the private. 'Arthur is a most sociable fellow when you know him, "but you have to get to know him first" . . . taken all round he is a straightforward good natured chap.'

The words 'when you get to know him' can be rewritten as 'when you get to know him as a man, an individual' – an unintended revelation that within Arthur was two identities. It also suggests a tension between the public and private images of the man. There was a distinction between Arthur the Athlete and Arthur the 'Black Man'. The athlete was big and tall, the Black man small and made to crawl.

For the last 15 years of his working life, Arthur was a colliery haulage hand at Yorkshire Main Colliery, Edlington. He died on 12 December 1930 at Springwell House sanatorium near Edlington, Doncaster after a 'long and painful illness'.[23] He was buried four days later in a third-class grave in the municipal cemetery of the pit village. There is an absurd symmetry between Arthur finishing his working days underground, being smothered in coaldust beneath the surface and out of view, and the slow but steady erasure of his achievements from collective memory. In 1996, Sheffield-based 'Football Unites, Racism Divides' launched the Arthur Wharton Memorial Fund to provide a headstone to mark Arthur's burial plot. Fittingly, the largest donation came from the Professional Footballers Association. It was laid in place on a rainy, overcast day, on Thursday, 8 May 1997. The dust was once again being kicked up from below.

As Arthur was blackening underground, Second Lieutenant Walter Daniel Tull's body, like countless others, was decomposing on a battlefield near Favreuil, France, a victim of the second Battle of the Somme in March–April 1918. Fighting with the 23rd Battalion (2nd Football) of the Middlesex Regiment, he was the first Black soldier to be commissioned as a combat officer in the British Army. Leicester Fosse goalkeeper Private T. Billingham, along with another soldier, attempted to carry their dead comrade back to their lines for burial. However German soldiers were closing ground on them and the instinct of self-preservation kicked in. Walter had been shot through the head on 25 March, aged 29. He has no known grave, only an inscription on the memorial wall, bay 7, at the Fauborg–Amiens War Cemetery, Arras, France. The National Army Museum, which holds the records of the Middlesex Regiment, responded with a blank expression of ignorance when asked about Tull.

His obituary in the *Rushden Echo*, 12 April 1918, entitled 'Famous Footballer Killed', included a photograph of Walter smiling in military fatigues. It recalled his transfer to Northampton from Spurs for 'a heavy transfer fee' (undisclosed at the time of signing), his 'fine physique', his commission and the mentioning of his name in dispatches. The closing sentence read: 'The deceased sportsman was an officer and a gentleman every inch of him, and the news of his death will come as a great shock to his many Rushden friends.' His older brother Edward, to whom he was very close and had as next of kin on his army application form, was devastated: 'the worst moment of my life'. His death was reported in regional and national sporting and football newspapers from Manchester to Folkestone.

Walter's father, Daniel, was born in St. Thomas parish, Barbados. He was the son of Anna and William Tull, both born into plantation slavery. Educated by

Moravian missionaries, Daniel became a carpenter and, seeking a better life, left for St. Lucia around 1873. This wasn't uncommon. Wages were often higher on other islands such as Trinidad, British Guiana and St. Lucia, as much as four times the average Barbadian day rate.

A law passed by the Barbados legislature – the slave owners' parliament – in 1676 forbade the teaching of Christianity to Blacks for fear of spreading ideas about equality and self-improvement. This left the soul-saving market to small religious sects such as the Quakers, Methodists and Moravians to preach, convert and 'educate' the Black and Coloured population. Although the island had more schools per square mile in 1834 than any other British colony, only five accepted Blacks. With his portable skills, Daniel emigrated following in the wake of 16,000 other Barbadians who left the island between 1838 (abolition of slavery) and 1870. His third and final island destination brought him to Folkestone, England, during the summer of 1876 (a time of conflict and revolt in Barbados) and within five years he had married Alice Palmer, a Kent woman whose family were agricultural labourers. Very probably Daniel met his wife at Grace Hill Wesleyan Chapel which both attended. Instead of raising their Victorian noses to the Black migrant, the Palmers welcomed him to their family. He was a religious man, he could read and write and had a trade as a carpenter – altogether a good catch for Alice.

The 1891 census lists the Tulls as living at 51 Walton Road, a working-class neighbourhood in the fashionable seaside town. On 14 April 1895 Alice died from cancer at the age of 42 leaving Daniel with their five children. Shortly afterwards, Alice's cousin Clara became his second wife 'largely to mother the children'.[24] When Daniel died two and a half years later from heart disease, it was to the Methodist community that Clara turned for help. And she desperately needed it. The birth of Miriam in September 1897, three months before her husband's death, meant Clara now had responsibility for six children. The resident minister of Grace Hill Wesleyan Chapel, the Rev. George Adcock, recommended Walter and his elder brother Edward to the Children's Home and Orphanage (CHO) in Bethnal Green, east London, a Methodist institution run by the Rev. Dr Stephenson. Placing the two school-age boys in the home, it was hoped, would prevent the family becoming destitute. The eldest son William was working, and could therefore make his weekly contribution to the family pot, while Alice's two girls – Cecilia, 13 and Elsie, 6 – could help Clara with baby Miriam and the domestic chores. In this set-up, Edward and Walter were liabilities: extra mouths to feed and bodies to clothe.

Adcock knew Stephenson and reminded him, when supporting the boys' application, of the financial assistance Folkestone Methodists had consistently provided for the CHO. While both Adcock and Stephenson were keen to see the boys enter the Home in Bonner Road, Stephenson was anxious that the Elham Union – the Poor Law parish upon which the Tull family relied for money to survive – should continue to contribute towards the boys' upkeep once they had entered the Home. An exchange of letters between Lonergan (clerk and superintendent registrar of Elham Union), Stephenson and Adcock resulted in the Folkestone Poor Law Guardians eventually agreeing to subsidise the living expenses of the boys at the rate of four shillings each per week (plus a suit when they reached 21). This was more than double that paid directly to Clara when the boys were living at the family home in Walton Road! Mindful, perhaps, that Elham Union could be paying out even more money for Walter and Edward once they'd moved to Bethnal Green in a letter of 22 January 1898, Lonergan pointed out to Stephenson that 'the father of these children was a negro and they are consequently coloured children. I do not know if you are aware of this or whether it will in any way affect the application?' So what? replied Stephenson. Edward and Walter carried their trunk through the doors of their new home on 24 February. Adcock had made arrangements to cover travel expenses for Clara to accompany her 'two dear sons, the little dark boys'.

Subsequent letters from Clara, William, and Cecilia – 'Cissie' – requesting to see the boys reveal a family determined not to let the seismic emotional upheavals break them. Worryingly, their love had legal limits to its expression, imposed by the 'Agreement' signed between Clara and the Home. There was to be no 'interference in any way' by Clara while the children were under Stephenson's care. The CHO had the right to send the children abroad. And many, scandalously, were sent. If Clara weakened and decided to ask for Walter and Edward to come back, eight shillings (40p) per week times the length of duration in the Home would have to be repaid. This fine was, no doubt, meant to be prohibitive in the sense that, in effect, it prevented Clara – and other guardians to whom the same rules applied – from reclaiming their children even if they wanted to. These conditions had to be agreed before the children could even be considered for acceptance into the Home.

Stephenson had three aims for children placed in his care: to teach them a moral code based upon Wesleyan Methodist principles; to provide a basic, elementary education; and to equip boys with a trade and girls with domestic skills, which in Walter's case meant an apprenticeship in the Home's print shop. In pursuing these aims, the CHO could play its part in the mission of empire-building by providing human resources for use at home or in the colonies. By 1909, the NCHO – the 'National' prefix was added in 1908 – had sent 2,000 children to Canada alone. Many of these were not told by the NCHO that they had living relatives in Britain.

Fortunately the Tull boys were not part of Britain's human export trade to the New World that was the plight of many poor orphans. Instead, in November 1900, aged 14, Edward was adopted by a Glaswegian family, the Warnocks, after they had seen and heard him on a money-raising CHO singing tour. (The wandering choirboys pulled in around £66.) The co-ordinator of the adoption application in Glasgow was J.W. Butcher, minister of the Claremont Street Wesleyan Church (which later erected a memorial scroll commemorating members of the church who had died in the Great War, with Walter's name inscribed). He supported the Warnocks in their request for 'Eddie', whose name was changed to Tull-Warnock on completion of the legal formalities. Mr Warnock, a dentist 'whose clientele is mainly among the poorer people' promised to educate him in dentistry and 'treat him as a son'.[25] Clara – now Mrs Beer – delighted that her lad was out of the Home and in an environment where he could get a start in life, sent a basket of food for a celebratory last supper at Bonner Road.

Edward's departure was hard on Walter. By nine years of age, the youngest of the Tull boys, he had lost both parents and was forced by circumstance out of the family home. Now the person on whom he relied most was gone. At best he was a long way off. However, both he and Edward were determined to remain close in spirit. In fact the Warnocks actively encouraged their relationship. In July 1903, the Glaswegians sent 52/- (£2.60), an enormous sum, for Walter's fare up to Scotland.

The death of Mr Warnock during the First World War compelled Edward to take a leading role in the Warnock family. The adopted son took full responsibility for the dental practice in St. Vincent Street, Glasgow, and arranged for his sister Cissie to look after Mrs Warnock at her second house in Girvan, on the west coast of Scotland. He also invited his first stepmother Clara Beer, her second husband Bill Beer and sisters Miriam and Elsie to Girvan during the war. And he was instrumental in securing Walter for Rangers FC, for whom his – Edward's – close friend James Bowie played. (Bowie later became the club's president and held a similar position with the Scottish FA.) Edward met him while both were playing for Girvan Athletic.

Walter spent seven years at Bonner Road, within an environment described by his brother as 'harsh and disciplined' but not unbearable. While playing for the Orphanage football team at left-back a friend, recognising his talents, suggested he write for a trial to Clapton, a successful East London amateur club. By October 1908, some ten weeks from posting, he was in the first team. The 1908–09 season turned out to be a wonderful introduction to senior competitive football: Clapton won the Amateur Cup, the London Senior Cup and the London County Amateur Cup and Walter was described by *The Football Star*, 20 March 1909, as Clapton's 'catch of the season'. [Playing at inside-left] 'our dusky friend' [was soon noticed by Tottenham Hotspur for] 'his clever footwork'. Up to that date Tull had not played in a losing Clapton side. His excellence led to an invitation to play for Tottenham's 'A' and Reserve teams and eventually the first team on their close season tour to Argentina and Uruguay. It was a meteoric rise for the 20 year old, just four months after making his début for Clapton's first team.

In a letter written while *en route* to South America, 26 May 1909, Walter reveals his mixed feelings towards professionalism. It wasn't coincidence that he'd joined Clapton, an amateur club in an area of London that was extremely fertile hunting ground for professional clubs in the production of both players and supporters. He had rejected an offer from an amateur club in the Midlands to play for money – there may well have been pressure from the home, family and friends to remain an unpaid player and pursue a career in printing. The Amateur Cup winners, a club with 'faithful followers and a fine *esprit de corps* (team spirit)'[26] would, like any successful team, have wanted to have remained intact. Clapton had given him his chance in senior football and, no doubt, friends and colleagues would be distanced by his leaving. At the CHO he would have been trained into the Methodist ethos of Muscular Christianity – playing games to develop a fit body and compliant attitude of mind – a doctrine that inferred that being paid to play any sport misses the point of what playing is all about. Muscular Christianity, for the Methodists, was about character building. To play football for wages would change the nature of the game and its players, making profit/winning the ultimate objective rather than the development of a moral character.

Despite these ethical difficulties over professionalism, the practical reality of making ends meet, in the wider context of the desire to be one's own man, led him to join Spurs on 20 July for a £10 signing-on fee (the maximum allowed). Two months earlier, while travelling to the Argentine, it was still in his mind to 'get a place on one of the newspapers' as a printer.

Social developments such as urbanisation, rises in real incomes, better nutrition and a reduction in the working week, freed time and energy that could be used for recreational pursuits. A realisation that money could be made from football – and, more generally, the games people play when they are not working – was swiftly exploited. New, bigger stadia able to hold more paying spectators were opened, such as Tottenham Hotspur's White Hart Lane and Everton's Goodison Park, the first purpose-built football stadium. While football was not a profit-maximising business, men with money and little else, through their investment in the business of football, could become faces in the community.

During the middle part of the Edwardian decade, corruption within clubs had became a public issue. A maximum wage of £4 per week had been imposed by the Football League in 1901. A little later in the decade they began to probe 'under the counter' payments and other such creative and necessary ways of beating the cap on wages. Yet the Football League's self-righteous posturing stuck in the throat of many of those who played the game for a living. Hadn't they, the game's administrators, created the opportunity and motivation for corruption by allowing clubs to draw up feudal employment contracts and imposing the maximum wage? The rapid commercialisation of football during the last decade of the nineteenth century – an era which echoes today's environment – and the industrial relations climate it produced contributed to a sense of class consciousness amongst a number of players, leading to a wider debate on their overall rights and conditions. While Tull agonised over the morality of taking wages, others, such as Billy Meredith of Manchester City and Charlie Roberts of Manchester United, fought for the right to form a union and earn an uncapped wage. However the intensely competitive nature of football and its small-workplace environment militated against the mass of footballers becoming active in the cause. This inaction stood in contrast to the world outside where British workers – the 'Great Unwashed' to the élite of society – were entering a militant phase known as the 'Great Unrest'.

While Tull had pressure from those close to him not to turn professional, the decision to do so (with the capital's leading club) was the act of a rational man. He did it in circumstances not of his own choosing, to paraphrase Marx. Quite simply Tull knew that he could earn more from football than from printing. And as a Black man in a predominantly White society, the respect of the community and the potential for fame that was almost guaranteed by signing was too good to refuse, whatever the doubts raised by those non-Black Britons of comfortable means.

With the benefit of hindsight most historians of sport recognise that the labels 'amateur' and 'professional' were metaphors for class division. It was another tactic, employed by those who played the same sports as the 'Great Unwashed', to keep the dirty majority in their place. The formation of the Amateur Football Association in 1907 – initially called the Amateur Football Defence Federation – over the issue of admittance of professionals to county football associations, was essentially a southern based, public-school alumni reaction to the growing might of northern, working-class professional clubs. For the southern toffs, allowing the muck and brass brigade into the privy council of football was akin to asking the moneylenders back into the temple. Such cleavages had occurred in other sports, most notably in rugby, with the split in 1895 between southern, bourgeois Union and northern, working-class League.

The amateur/professional debate was characterised by hypocrisy. The élite, amateur Corinthian Football Club, almost exclusively ex-Oxbridge, often charged more in expenses to play than the weekly wage bill of their professional opponents; amateur cricketers could receive unlimited income from benefit matches. And, crucially, the majority of amateurs didn't depend on their sport for a living. They played to fill time, pursue and enjoy their pleasures or seek excellence. If they played badly, the disadvantages were a loss to ego and pride, not to the pocket. For the amateur, sport was not the only source of nourishment for the spirit. And those who excelled and chose to remain unpaid did so, primarily because they didn't need to go professional. They had other dimensions to their lives that provided the means to live and nourish the ego. Loss of form wasn't the demon-with-material-consequences that shadowed the exploits of the working-class professional.

Complicating the issue were the 'shamateur' clubs like the one in the Midlands that wanted Tull's services and were prepared to pay under-the-table. They wanted it both ways: to use the same device – money – as professional clubs to build a successful team; but at the same time remain unsullied by the grubby practice of *openly* paying to beat opponents. The economic and social conditions that produced the amateur, produced the shamateur. The Amateur FA wanted to disown the Frankenstein of commercialism and moral indiscipline that football had become. Their formation represented an attempt at social cleansing, roping off their sanitised playing field from the 'oiks' with whom they would no longer fraternise. Yet, in 1914, their project of football apartheid no longer sustainable, they asked to rejoin the FA.

Tull was not a well man for part of the trip to Argentina and Uruguay, suffering from 'sunstroke and [feeling] very queer for a few days'.[27] He and another forward, J. Curtis from Gainsborough Trinity, were new signings to a young team that had been promoted to the first division in their inaugural season in the Football League. The transition in football culture that Walter would have undergone by going on tour with 'the first truly great professional side in southern England' would have been profound.[28] The next six months represented the best days of his football career.

The tour to Latin America was arranged by the FA and the Committee of the Sociedad Sportiva, Argentina. Along with Everton, Spurs played the top club sides and representative teams of the Argentine and Uruguayan Football Associations – twelve games in all. (Two professional clubs, Nottingham Forest and Southampton, had already visited the continent; Spurs and Everton had toured Austria together four years earlier, as guests of First Vienna FC.) To accommodate the visit, the first round of the Argentine FA Cup had been postponed. Though neither team lost to their South American opponents, some players acted as spoilt *prima donnas* complaining about the quality of their accommodation on arrival in the Argentine capital: 'None of the waiters spoke English . . . the aspect of the bedrooms was anything but cheerful'. It was also cold and there were no fires or easy chairs![29] Proof that spoilt footballers are not unique to the modern game. However what caused the greatest aggravation was the difference in cultural attitudes to the game, despite the British influence in founding and developing football in that part of the world.

This difference showed itself in the first game between Spurs and a representative Argentine League XI. It was more of a maul than a match. An off-the-ball foul on Tottenham forward, D. Clarke, was 'the filthiest charge in the back it is possible to imagine'. Another forward, Minter, was sent off unfairly, according to the sports correspondent of the English-language daily newspaper the *Buenos Aires Herald* (*BAH*). After protests by the Spurs team and the intervention of the chairman and other club officials, who came down to the pitch from the stands, Minter was reinstated. Play was held up for three minutes. The *BAH*, 17 June 1909 (p.9), never slow to assert the superiority of anglo-saxons over their gaucho hosts, continued indignantly, 'It shows one what kind of a sporting spirit the native has, when I say that they laughed and clapped their hands with joy when they saw Clarke reel.' These 'fine chaps from London' had been 'treated very badly'. The matches, said the *BAH*, also illustrated the gulf in tactical awareness that the Latin Americans still had to bridge, a major weakness being their positional play. The visitors were much better organised and more fluid in their co-ordination and movement, especially in running off the ball.

Action by players over wage capping and unionisation meant tourists had left behind a highly charged political environment in England, yet had ironically come to one of equal intensity. Two hundred thousand workers had been on strike in May, a strike which was eventually crushed by the army. The first match of the tour between Everton and Tottenham – the first time two Football League clubs had played each other in Argentina – was attended by the president of the Republic, Figuerón Alcarta. At half-time he met the teams. The clubs' visit held national importance for the development of the game in that country and it provided an opportunity for the president to cultivate a superficial relationship with the masses, to do a bit of grandstanding.

The tourists were surrounded by people and institutions who wanted to make political capital out of their presence: the Argentine president; the football establishment of Argentina and Uruguay but, most shamefully, the mouthpiece of the British colonial settlers, the *BAH*. Quite simply they argued that Spurs and Everton were better because Britain was better and Britain was better because it had an empire and one of the reasons it had an empire was because Britons were better at sports, and therefore war, than other nations. The editorial message broadcast by the *BAH* was explicit: game playing, nation building and war were complementary activities. They were an inseparable trio. This vision was explained in its 'Mission of the Athlete' address welcoming the tourists:

> A little while ago we saw an illustration of a football match somewhere near the Bight of Benin. The sable Africans were there shown kicking with barefeet, the sun-bleached skulls of their slaughtered enemies . . . a mere replica of the game played when the noble savage first found grim solace, in his piping intervals of peace.
>
> From kicking empty craniums to scoring a sensitive shin is, after all, a mere transition, but the step is one of considerable extent. However, we must not allow natural speculation upon origin to lead us away from our theme . . . football [is] an international link, one of the many links that connect the human family.
>
> We look upon [the footballers] as men with a mission . . . Every unit in a football team is a missionary who teaches the gospel of sport by strenuous example. Sport is essential, exercise is vital, to the well-being of nations and individuals alike. The people who do not love field sports will not take kindly to field campaigns. War is best waged by those nations who have learned the absolute truth of the saying 'unity is strength'. Disciplined unity, which involves instant and cheerful obedience to even unwelcome orders, is the secret of success, not merely on the football field but on the field of Mars.
>
> Our 'missionaries' then, are here today to preach the gospel of individual fitness, and demonstrate the value of their teachings. They are here, too, because in Argentina there is a growing willingness to learn the game in order that the Argentines of the rising generations may, in their turn, play the game. The youth of Argentina are finding out that the sensuous life, the life of the sybarite, is not conducive to glory, or even commercial pre-eminence. Politics and cigarettes may round off a feast,

but they will not extend a territory, or keep the flag flying proudly.

England was fated to bear a great part in the building up of the nation . . . On the battlefield of old, the foundations of British enterprise in Argentina were laid, and on Wednesday next we may go down and see yet another of the long series of great efforts made by Britain to develop Argentina's resources.[30]

There were no tears and waving hankies at the dockside when the teams left. The tempestuous matches had resulted in a rush of correspondence on the letters page of the *BAH*, with editorials questioning the 'adaptability of the Latin races to strenuous games such as football'. The newspaper thought it would be 'some time' before other British clubs visited. However, it did note that trouble at a Celtic–Rangers match a month earlier limited its authority to:

moralise . . . when the canny Scots set such an example it seems hardly just to think too harshly of the warm blooded 'criolle' players and spectators who are unable to keep their excitement and enthusiasm within rational limits.[31]

Personally, Tull had mixed fortunes in his football rite of passage to Argentina and the Big Time. It was stern and harsh, yet an exotic and unique introduction to the game at élite level. Though suffering a bit on the journey over (added to by the discomforts of the hotel!), his enthusiasm to play seems not to have been affected. In his first game he'd 'installed himself as favourite with the crowd'.[32] Unfortunately, the Spurs management were not as impressed with Tull as the *BAH*. He was left out of the next game. When selected, he played at centre or inside-forward, Spurs attempting to find the right front-line combination after the departure of England international centre-forward (and amateur) V.J. Woodward to Chelsea. (He also joined the Football Battalion of the Middlesex Regiment.) The sum total of his performances, however, did earn Tull selection for Tottenham's first-ever game in the First Division in September.

The historic double of Walter's football league début and Spurs' initiation into first division football was deflated by the result, a 3–1 defeat away to Sunderland. If any game proves the truth of the maxim 'pride cometh before a fall', it's football. (At one level this was an eerie repeat of history: Wharton also made his football League début at Sunderland and his team, Sheffield United, similarly lost by two goals.) This was followed by another defeat, 4–2, to their scouse mates Everton in front of 20,000 at Goodison. Yet over 32,000 paid to watch Spurs' first home match against FA Cup holders (and Players' Union strikers, the self-proclaimed 'Outcasts') Manchester United. They shared the points in a 2–2 draw, 'Darkie' Tull having been brought down for a penalty. Walter was on top form, just like watching a Brazilian:

Tull's . . . display on Saturday must have astounded everyone who saw it. Such perfect coolness, such judicious waiting for a fraction of a second in order to get a pass in not before a defender has worked to a false position, and such accuracy of strength in passing I have not seen for a long time. During the first half, Tull just compelled Curtis to play a good game, for the outside-right was plied with a series of passes that made it almost impossible for him to do anything other than well.

Tull has been charged with being slow, but there never was a footballer yet who was really great and always appeared to be in a hurry. Tull did not get the ball and rush on into trouble. He let his opponents do the rushing, and defeated them by side touches and side-steps worthy of a professional boxer. Tull is very good indeed.[33]

He scored his first goal against Bradford City a week later and continued to receive more praise than criticism for his performances. Despite being 'a class superior to that shown by most of his colleagues',[34] Tull was relegated to the reserves by the end of October having played just seven first-team games. He played 16 games for the 'Stiffs' – the reserves – during the remainder of the season. Quite why Tull was never given another chance in the first team that season remains open to speculation, so I will. All that's certain is that he was good enough, when on form, to have merited selection. And there is nothing in the contemporary match reports to suggest a sustained loss of confidence. Wider social pressures may have played a role, especially if the racial abuse Tull received at Bristol (discussed below) was unnerving ambitious directors.

The 1910–11 season was worse. He played only three first-team games and scored once, against Manchester City. His third game against Arsenal in April was to be his last. His outings with the reserves totalled 27, with 10 goals scored. They won the South Eastern League, Tull playing for its representative team against Chelsea at the end of the season. He may have gone to Heanor Town for a period on loan, although this cannot be confirmed. His career with Spurs that began on such a high ended frustratingly and unsatisfactorily. By October 1911, when Tull signed for southern League Northampton Town – winners of the competition in 1909 – 'for a heavy transfer fee', he was not a chirpy cockney. (The deal included the exchange of R.C. Brittain to the North Londoners.) The 'Cobblers' manager was former Spurs player Herbert Chapman, who later became uniquely successful with Huddersfield Town and Arsenal. So revered is he, in fact, that a bust of the South Yorkshireman greets visitors to Highbury. A cockerel astride the gun carriage. It seems Tull caught Chapman's eye while playing against the Northampton reserves the previous season. Additionally, former colleagues at White Hart Lane may have put in a good word on Walter's behalf. Also competing to sign the Black Briton were Aston Villa, Leicester Fosse and Clapton Orient. Chapman's relative open-mindedness in signing a player of colour may have been the result of his own experience as a young footballer with Stalybridge Rovers in 1896, where he may well have been signed by Arthur

Wharton, then the player/coach of the mill-town club. Chapman was originally from Sheffield, while Arthur had played for Sheffield United. (In fact, apart from a six-year spell over the Peninnes while employed by Stalybridge Rovers, Ashton North End and Stockport County between 1896–1902, Wharton had lived in South Yorkshire from 1888 to his death in 1930.) Another potentially important factor in linking Tull, Chapman and Wharton is that all were practising Methodists, or from Methodist backgrounds. These congregations acted as networks of social welfare as much as religious communities. It was the Methodists, that employed Henry Wharton and educated Arthur, who ensured the Tull family was not left destitute once the children were orphaned and, indirectly, set Edward and Walter on career paths by enabling them to live in institutions – the Warnock household and Bonner Road – that acted as springboards for their future careers.

Walter's opening games for Northampton did not show the form of his first season at Spurs. He didn't explode on to the scene, but rather took the stage quietly and acted shyly. His début against Watford didn't inspire a great deal of talk or writing. By the end of November he was in the reserves. However, a conversion to wing-half from inside-forward led to a revival in form. 'Tull has now settled in the half-line in a manner which now places him in the front rank of "class" players in this position.' He played over 110 first-team games, scoring nine goals, including four in one match and became, in the process, a 'favourite with the crowd'.[35] On 21 December 1914, he became the first Northampton Town player to join the 17th (1st Football) Battalion of the Middlesex Regiment. It was commanded by Major Frank Buckley, Boer War veteran, ex-Manchester United and Aston Villa, a legendary disciplinarian who later became famous as manager of Wolverhampton Wanderers.

Tull's mercurial rise from orphanage team to First Division carried with it echoes of Arthur's celebrity status: that of Black working-class hero. Walter grew up in a Britain whose rulers were arrogant and self-assured, believing they were divinely destined to recast those 'uncivilised' parts of the world in their own image. In his first year in the home the South African Boer War broke out. The press was awash with stories about the brutish Boer and why it was in the natives' interest not to side with the Dutch-speaking settlers. The war was presented to the British public as a moral crusade. Not so oddly, the establishment media, national politicians, religious leaders, captains of industry and other spokesmen for the ruling class didn't dwell on the diamond and gold mines British capitalists vowed never to give up.

At Earls Court Olympia in London, an exhibition opened entitled 'Savage South Africa'. A review in the *Illustrated Sporting and Dramatic News*, 23 May 1909, headed 'Briton, Boer and the Black', stated that the purpose of the enterprise was to show 'life, chase and warfare from the Cape to Cairo . . . The most striking episodes in the wild life of Savage South Africa . . . [and illustrate] the "pride, pomp and circumstance of glorious war."' The review spoke of the 'magnificent black men from the Zulu country'. However, London County

Council officials forced the 'native kraals' in which the Zulus were exhibited to be sectioned off so that the public couldn't fraternise with the 'heathen warriors' and their 'ebony babies'.[36] It was a compliment followed by a know-your-place slapping down. Or perhaps the officials were just trying to authentically recreate what would soon be seen on the South African veld: enclosed areas otherwise known as concentration camps.

In a game at Bristol City on 9 October 1909, Tull was racially taunted by 'a section of the spectators (who) made a cowardly attack upon him in language lower than Billingsgate'. The reporter was clearly upset by the abuse of Spurs' 'most brainy forward' whose 'tactics were absolutely beyond reproach'.

> Let me tell these Bristol hooligans (there were but few of them in a crowd of nearly twenty thousand) that Tull is so clean in mind and method as to be a model for all white men who play football whether they be amateur or professional. In point of ability, if not in actual achievement, Tull was the best forward on the field.[37]

The history and political geography of Bristol as a port whose wealth and growth owed much to the slave trade may explain, in part, this prejudice. A further factor, the growing influence of the ideas of scientific racism, should also be considered. Its fundamental notion that Blacks were naturally inferior to Whites, a fact which could be proven by science, was a sentiment that was becoming commonplace.

Sport as preparation for war was a consistent theme of British imperialists as we have seen with the 'mission' statement of the *BAH*. Yet by embodying these two pursuits, Tull burnt the straw house of these patriots by undermining the ideology of scientific racism from which they dredged for their fantasies. Incredibly, his achievements as a sportsman were equalled by his exploits as a soldier in a war he came to hate.

According to *The Manual of Military Law*, Black soldiers of any rank were not desirable. During the First World War, military chiefs of staff, with government approval, argued that White soldiers would not accept orders issued by men of colour and on no account should Black soldiers serve on the front line. Forty-four years earlier the War Office argued that the army should be wholly White, despite the presence of Blacks in the army since at least the sixteenth century, an African trumpeter being part of Henry VII's court in 1507. In fact Britain had been ruled by an African Roman, Septemius Severus, during the third century. In that century a 'division of Moors'[38] was stationed at Hadrian's Wall. While the Romans could accept a rainbow army, the British élite, sixteen hundred years later, could not. At the War Office in 1886, a veteran of the Anglo-Asante War of 1873–74, Lord Wolseley, pleaded: 'Let us keep our British Regiments strictly British . . . If ever we begin to fill our ranks with alien races our downfall will most surely follow.'[39] But Black soldiers did enlist and fight in the First World War. Laura Tabili, in *We Ask for British Justice – Workers and Racial Difference in*

Late Imperial Britain (1994) has argued that there was a 'Coloured' unit of UK Blacks in the British Army . Tull's brother William was a sapper in the Royal Engineers, the same regiment as Charles Augustus Williams, the Barbadian father of Doncaster Rovers centre-half Charlie Williams. Eugene and John Brown, the Nigerian father and uncle of Roy Brown, a club colleague of Stanley Matthews at Stoke City in the late 1930s, served in the 5th North Staffordshire Regiment while attending college in Britain. Eugene was killed in action, while John ended his war days in hospital. There were numerous other Blacks that also broke the colour bar. However, it was not until 1918, a time of severe manpower shortage, that the Army Council *officially* allowed British and colonial Blacks to sign up in the UK.

The British Expeditionary Force (BEF) fought nine principal battles between August and October 1914. At the end of October, Secretary of State for war Lord Kitchener issued another call for volunteers to both replace those killed and enlarge the BEF. Pressure to suspend league and cup professional football gathered momentum:

> Football is an excellent thing, even in time of war. Armies and navies can only be maintained so long as the community fulfils its function of producing means for their support; and healthy recreation is essential for efficient production. A man may be doing his duty in other fields than the front. But there is no excuse in diverting from the front thousands of athletes in order to feast the eyes of crowds of inactive spectators, who are either unfit to fight or else unfit to be fought for . . . Every club who employs a professional player is bribing a needed recruit to refrain from enlistment, and every spectator who pays his gate money is contributing so much towards a German victory.[40]

The FA took up the call, urging all those involved in football that were single to enlist. And though war propagandists were given permission to bang the drum and offer the king's shilling at half-time, the campaign was a disaster. Very few recruits succumbed. The Manchester-based *Athletic News*, 7 December 1914, was outraged by the crude attempts to portray football, and those civilian workers that had anything to do with it, as pro-German conspirators:

> The whole agitation is nothing less than an attempt by the ruling classes to stop the recreation on one day in the week of the masses . . . What do they care for the poor man's sport? The poor are giving their lives for this country in thousands. In many cases they have nothing else . . . There are those who could bear arms, but who have to stay at home and work for the army's requirements, and the country's needs. These should, according to a small clique of virulent snobs, be deprived of the one distraction that they have had for over thirty years.[41]

Eventually, of 5,000 professionals, 2,000 joined the military services. It isn't clear how many of these footballers were conscripted. Young, single, gifted with his feet and Black, Tull volunteered for the 17th (1st Football) Battalion of the Middlesex Regiment made up almost entirely of players. Corporate recruitment was a ploy of military recruiting. Getting workmates, friends, relatives, neighbours to join up together had two purposes: generating peer group pressure to conform to the will of the majority and delivering a ready-made bond between the recruits. This in turn created a collective discipline better able to withstand and hold firm against an extraordinary physical, emotional and psychological bombardment.

Shortly after guesting for Fulham in Autumn 1915, Tull arrived in France from Salisbury Plain as part of the 33rd division, 100th Brigade, on 18 November 1915. They were initially billeted at Les Ciseaux, 16 miles from the front line. Their accommodation in December was the 'Collège des jeunes filles' (Young Women's College!) at Bethune. What an up-and-down start to the war – by the 9th, half the Battalion was on the front line.

Tull was a member of 'A' company. After a break from dealing and receiving death, they were sent back to the front at Festubert, 'a pestilential part of the line on 20 January, together with 'B' company'.[42] Two days later Vivien Woodward, the ex-Spurs forward whose transfer to Chelsea prompted Spurs to sign Tull, was wounded. Front-line duty often lasted a month or more. A letter of relative innocence from Walter while in France early in 1916 spoke of the boredom in waiting to be sent up the line:

> For the last three weeks my Battalion has been resting some miles distant from the firing line but we are now going up to the trenches for a month or so. Afterwards we shall begin to think about coming home on leave. It is a very monotonous life out here when one is supposed to be resting and most of the boys prefer the excitement of the trenches.

Yet a reading of the war diaries of the Regiment, held at the Public Records Office, provides a different impression. Away from the intense warfare of the trenches, the Battalion escaped with football match after football match, interspersed with tug-of-war and other athletic competitions. Sometimes there would be matches on consecutive days. Officially, at least, life was full-on and being redefined, reappearing as a fantastical chimera amidst the slaughter.

Tull was sent home on hospital ship St. Denis on 9 May 1916 suffering from 'acute mania'/shell shock, or what is now recognised as post-traumatic stress syndrome. (One of the military hospitals was at Sandgate, Folkestone, although it is not known if he was a patient there.) He returned to France, fit to kill and be killed, on 20 September.

The 1st Football fought in the Battle of the Somme, July–November 1916. There were over 60,000 killed on the first day, the greatest numbers ever in British military history. At the close of this mass slaughter in mid-November, the total death toll for all combatants stood at 1,115,000. In one of the last major actions by the 17th, the Battle of Ancre, they were ordered to capture the German Z-Z trench at Pendant Copse. The attack began at 5.15 a.m. on 13 November. According to the War Diary entry:

> All ranks were extremely cheerful and success seemed inevitable. [They] went over in waves, 'B' and 'D' Companies playing mouth organs. [By 7.20 a.m.] a certain amount of confusion existed . . . Various units were all mixed up in 'No Man's Land' . . . [and] the machine guns were causing a lot of trouble . . . The enemy killed heavily various parts of our line.

Only 79 men returned from over 400. In his report, the commanding officer of the 17th put the decimation down to 'fog', 'uncut wire' and the added disorientation caused by the movements of the Royal Scots and West Yorkshire regiments, which confused his men. Some casualties were almost certainly the result of fire from the Battalion's own machine-gunners and those of the Scots and Yorkshire regiments. Such an apocalyptic scenario was also compounded by gas – first used in 1915 – blowing back in their faces. In fact, the attack had been constantly postponed because of the weather and there were officers who believed it should not have gone ahead. However, General Sir Douglas Haig thought success would help morale at home and on the Russian and Romanian fronts. General Gough gave the order to proceed, despite visibility being down to 30 yards the morning battle commenced. Is it any surprise troops later mutinied after witnessing and feeling such a callous disregard for their lives by their commanding officers?

> The real explanation of the fury felt by the soldiers, which invested the war with a more savage character, is to be sought elsewhere. In the face of gas, without protection, individuality was annihilated; the soldier in the trench became a mere passive recipient of torture and death. A final stage seemed to be reached in the whole tendency of modern scientific warfare to depress and make of no effect individual bravery, enterprise and skill.[43]

His period of duty completed, Tull arrived back in England on Boxing Day. The next six weeks was a time to forget, catch up with William and his sisters who were still in Folkestone, and visit Edward and the Warnocks in Glasgow before reporting to the 10th Officers Cadet Battalion in Gailes, Scotland, to begin his training for a commission on 6 February. On being made 2nd Lieutenant in May 1917, Walter became the first Black combat officer in the British army. (There had been Black medical officers.)

The recruitment in the UK of Blacks into the British army was a matter of luck and gradation of colour. Some recruiting officers were not too fussed about accepting brown men, while others followed regulations to the letter. The question still remains as to how Walter got accepted for a commission and at a time when officers were supposed to be of 'pure' European descent. His official military record gives no clues, although the practical reason is pretty obvious. He was good at his job, respected by his footballer/soldier comrades and was a comparative veteran compared to the conscripts that were now being drafted. And the army was desperately short of officers.

In respect of being accepted into the army in the first place, the policy of recruiting friends, workmates and neighbours into geographical and vocational regiments worked in Tull's favour. The 17th and 23rd Battalions of the Middlesex Regiment in which Walter served were made up of footballers, many of whom would have known and played with or against each other. They had joined the Battalions because they were made up of players between whom, it is assumed, relationships had developed of self and mutual respect. Such an environment would have allowed Tull freer expression to his character and personality as man, soldier and footballer. Amongst footballers Tull had nothing to prove – the field of play is a great leveller. Strengths and weaknesses are exposed and exploited. There is no hiding place. He was as good as them, as they and the thousands of others who played professionally or watched, knew. Whatever his colour signified in the wider sense, if Walter could give of his best on the sportsfield, and take the worst that players and fans could throw, he could do it as an equal in this other form of conflict.

While he was training at Gailes, the 17th were involved in the Battle of Arleux and received over 462 casualties. The lives stolen were literally irreplaceable. New conscripts were younger. (Most of the 70 that arrived at the end of January 1918 'had just turned 19 years old'.)[44] The pioneering 1st Football Battalion – the first of its kind – was disbanded on 10 February, the remnants divvied out to other Battalions.

As second lieutenant, Tull was posted back to the 23rd (2nd Football). Almost immediately he was in action at the Battle of Messines, where the Battalion lost half its men. The objective was to capture the village of Messines and its ridge from which the Germans had a vantage point over their enemies' positions. Using mines and heavy bombardment, the British succeeded. The irony for Walter was that the recapture of Messines by the Germans in their Spring Offensive of 1918 cost him – and others – his life. Seven weeks after the Battle of Messines, at the end of July, the 23rds were thrown in at the Battle of Ypres, otherwise known as Passchendaele. This offensive by British, Australian and Canadian troops sought to take control of Belgian coastal ports. Lasting three months, eight kilometres of territory was gained at the cost of 300,000 casualties. No doubt Haig, the British commander-in-chief, considered the campaign a victory.

After the killing fields of Flanders, the 23rds were posted to the relative quiet and beauty of northern Italy, although it was just as cold. The casualty rate here was one in twenty-one, compared to five out of nine on the Western Front. Their task was to assist the Italians, alongside the French, in defending this gateway into northern Italy – in particular the river Piave – from invasion by Austrian and

German troops. On New Year's Eve, Walter officially defied army regulations by leading men and issuing orders, something an 'alien' officer should never do. He broke the colour bar and was mentioned in dispatches by Major-General Sydney Lawford for his 'gallantry and coolness' in doing so:

> You were one of the first to cross the river Piave prior to the raid on 1–2 January 1918, and during the raid you took the covering party of the main body across and brought them back without a casualty in spite of heavy fire.[45]

Shortly after, Tull returned to France to die in the second Battle of the Somme.

As an orphan from childhood, as a footballer and as a soldier, Tull's life had witnessed extremities of tragedy and heroism. As such, even the day-to-day simplicities of living carried extra burdens. As the Bristol reporter said of Tull's dignity in the face of racist hostility, his behaviour was a lesson to the White men on the pitch. Perhaps he should have said 'to all men' and left it at that. His death in battle was poignantly poetic in the sense that it encapsulated those two opposite but entwined essences of life, heroism and tragedy: 'Killed [on the battlefield] instantaneously with a bullet through the head'.[46] Billingham, who tried to rescue him, says he lived for two minutes. Walter had soldiered virtually the duration of his war; he was a veteran of numerous campaigns; awarded the 1914–15 Star and British War and Victory medal, and recommended for a Military Cross. Perhaps that should now be awarded.

It could be argued that Tull was politically naïve. He served in an army that didn't want him, an army whose chiefs of staff argued Black soldiers were a threat to discipline and accepted the findings of science that he and his kind were throwbacks. (Once the war had ended the colour bar was re-imposed, lasting until the 1940s.) He fought for a country who, almost immediately the war had ended, responded to 'race' riots in Liverpool, Cardiff, Newport and London by setting up repatriation committees in Hull, South Shields, Glasgow, Cardiff, Liverpool, London and Salford. In an example of breathtaking hypocrisy, Black people who had fought in the war *were* repatriated.

Yet, despite and because of this it seems Tull became aware of who and what he was. In a letter from the front he wrote to Edward that he had asked for a posting to the British West Indies, a regional post that was radicalised in 1919 by the experiences of its returning soldiers and sailors. The mutinies – the British West India Regiment rebelled in Italy in 1918 – strikes, demonstrations and riots that swelled in the wake of peace were a loud and unmistakable testament to the growing self-confidence of Caribbean workers, veterans and anti-colonialists. Had Walter palled up with fellow Black soldiers serving in the BWIR?

Arguably 1919 is the closest Britain has come to revolution in the twentieth century. Whether the war created the mood of rebellion amongst workers – this sometimes taking a horribly distorted and misguided form as we saw with the 'race' riots above – or merely speeded up a process that had already been years in fermentation is not for debate here. The fact is it happened. People were changed by the conflict. Tull was changed: his eagerness to enlist soured to a hatred for the carnage.

Did Walter recognise that he was a pioneer? Perhaps the most compelling evidence that he was aware of the social significance of his achievements is in the continuity of the achievements themselves. His days at Tottenham and Northampton brought pressures unknown to his White team-mates. As a soldier he was the only Black combat officer in the British army until the Second World War. (The colour bar has only recently been raised in the élite Guards Regiment which, in the 1990s, had its first Black recruit.) His dogged persistence in not accepting the pre-determined roles reserved for people of his class and ethnicity has left a solid and inspiring legacy. Through his actions, Tull ridiculed the barriers of ignorance that tried to deny people of colour equality with their contemporaries. His life stands as testament to a determination to confront those people and those obstacles that sought to diminish him and the world in which he lived. It reveals a man, though rendered breathless in his prime, whose strong heart still beats loudly. On Sunday, 11 July 1999 Northampton Town erected a sculpted memorial to Walter in a dedicated Garden of Remembrance and chose to use this epitaph. It was a proud and moving moment.

Even if Walter had managed to survive the war and fulfil his pledge to Rangers, he would not have been Scotland's first Black footballer. This honour goes to left winger John Walker who grew up in the port of Leith, now part of Edinburgh. It is *Trainspotting* territory and when he was playing for his first adult team, Leith Primrose, the steam locomotives were still pulling into Leith station. In the year (1898) that Sudan was colonised by the British and the Scottish TUC was formed, 'Walker, the darkey' signed for neighbours and betters Leith Athletic of Scottish League Division Two. Making his début against the Edinburgh–Irish club from across the Links in Easter Road, First Division Hibernian, he scored 'making an excellent impression'.[47]

The local youngster continued his good form at the beginning of the following season, so much so that the *Leith Observer*, 8 October 1898, now referred to him as the:

> 'Black Jewel' [whose] consistent and brilliant play won for him fresh laurels and new friends. It also gave him one enemy . . . R. MacFarlane, the Airdrie right-back. So often did he outwit the latter that the back . . . deliberately struck Walker.

Edinburgh's other First Division club, Heart of Midlothian, fancied parading the jewel on their turf, signing him at the end of October for an £80 transfer fee. However, the sparkle didn't mesmerise. His individualist style did not endear him to the Tynecastle committee who preferred to select David Baird or John Blair in his position, though Walker did play in the East of Scotland Shield final in March 1899, where they defeated great rivals Hibs 1–0. A few months later, after Hearts had finished the season as runners-up to Rangers, Walker was on his way to Lincoln City of Division Two of the Football League. He didn't settle in Lincolnshire and made only six appearances for the 'Imps'. One of the reasons may have been the racist comments made about him in the local press. He returned to Scotland in January 1900 and died prematurely eight months later.

John William 'Jack' Cother and younger brother Edwin 'Eddie', though born in Uxbridge, Middlesex in the 1870s, were the first professional footballers with Asian antecedence. In fact they were Eurasian, or what was later termed Anglo-Indian, because they had a British mother and an Indian father, William, who may well have been Anglo-Indian himself. This would not have been unusual. Many British men working or serving in the military in India married local women. Indeed so common was the practice in the late eighteenth and early nineteenth centuries that the colonial authorities in India did everything in their power to end it. The descendants of both still live in the Watford area.

Jack was the more successful footballer. His first recorded club was Colne Valley in Lancashire but he played virtually all his career in and around Watford after this excursion north, officially turning professional in 1897. It was rumoured he was being paid at Colne, though it was never admitted. However if he wasn't being paid, why go so far from home just to play as an amateur? With a reputation as a hard, robust full-back he made over 140 appearances for Watford first team, scoring three goals. Once his career had ended in 1905, he continued his association with the club, selling programmes and helping out on match days. He died in 1946, aged 73, and is buried, fittingly, at Vicarage Road Cemetary, close by the Watford ground.

While Jack was the model of consistency, dedication and, given his continued attachment to Watford FC after his career ended, commitment, it is his brother Eddie who captured my imagination. Five years younger, his professional career was short, officially lasting only one season (but maybe longer given the practices of the time). His clubs, for whom he played in the mid- to late 1890s, included Watford Athletic, Watford St Mary's, West Herts and Watford. At his best, he was a formidable half-back (midfield). 'With any amount of dash and go, he combines ability to find the net, and is a worker for the whole 90 minutes' (*Watford Observer*, 14 January 1899). Yet by 1900, his professional career was over. This is where his story turns more interesting and touches upon issues that many of today's Black youth would recognise.

In 1907 Eddie was in the dock at Watford Police Court (WPC). He was charged with assaulting Albert Russell when trespassing while cutting watercress from a stream. Eddie counter-charged Russell with assault. The ex-footballer had one witness and Russell six, including a policeman who said Eddie was 'under [the] influence [of alcohol] and excited'. Unsurprisingly, Cother was fined 10/- (50p) or 7 days' hard labour. He was also ordered to pay £1.4/- (£1.20) costs for having his counter-assault charge dismissed. Many other court appearances followed. He may have turned out at WPC more times than he did for WFC. While he may not have been man-marked as a player, it seems one law officer, Police Sergeant Morley, followed Eddie around as a virus looks for a home. Morley was the arresting officer on a number of occasions, including those that led to court summonses for gambling in 1909 and assault on the Police Sergeant himself in 1911. (Interestingly, also in 1911 and at the same court, a William Tull was convicted of poaching and fined £1 with 3/6 (18p) costs. Walter Tull's older brother had lived temporarily in the London area before the First World War.) Most of Eddie's run-ins with the law were for gambling (often while drinking), with the odd assault charge (justifiable in the PS Morley case). His troubled life included spells in St. Alban's Workhouse in which he eventually died in 1951, his destitution causing him to be buried in a pauper's grave at St. Alban's Borough Cemetery.

While all the men so far discussed were undisputed footballers of colour, a similar assertion cannot be made for Fred Corbett. He has been included, however, because of his appearance in team photographs, the final judgement resting with the reader. His first professional club was Thames Ironworks, later West Ham United. The team, made up of workers at the Canning Town shipbuilders, was formed after a strike at the yard. The unspoken aim of the newly created 'Hammers' was to foster better relations between management and workers after a period of great militancy in the docks of East London.

Thames Ironworks turned professional in 1898 and joined Division Two of the Southern League for the start of the 1898–99 season. The total number of new players signed at this time was thirty, only three being retained from the previous campaign. Corbett, an 18-year-old goal-scoring right-winger, was employed the following season, at the end of which the club changed its name to West Ham United. He played a total of 39 games and scored 12 goals – including a hat-trick against Wellingborough – before moving to Bristol Rovers in January 1901–2. He also signed for Bristol City, Rovers again (twice), Brentford, New Brighton and Merthyr Town in 1912–13, which was to be his last club. In 14 seasons of senior competitive football in the Southern and Football Leagues, Fred played over 280 games, scoring 101 goals – a good rate for a winger.

Black amateur footballers also played at senior competitive level during this period. From 1904 to 1912, while training to be a dentist, Walter's brother Edward Tull appeared for Ayr Parkhouse of the Scottish League Division Two, Girvan Athletic and junior club Ballantrae and was characterised as 'a tricky inside-forward and a menace in the goal area'.[48] A member of the Turnberry Golf Club, he won three trophies in one season walking the greens. Given the notorious reputation of golf clubs – coloured clothing that stings your eyes, yes please; people of colour, no thanks – how Edward became a member would probably be a story in itself.

Edward's aptitude and inclination for ball games may have been honed and encouraged while he was a pupil at the innovative Allan Glen's school in Glasgow, where he was a member of the football team and where sport was an integral part of the curriculum. He later became president of the Old Boys Association – which may partly explain why Turnberry allowed him to be swinger at their club. A socialist and admirer of Paul Robeson, Edward, like the latter, was renowned for 'his rendering of Negro spirituals'.[49]

Edward and Walter's eldest brother, William, a sapper in the Royal Engineers during the First World War, is also reputed to have played for local league teams in the Dover and Folkestone area. He died in March 1920 at the age of 37 from the effects of gas attacks suffered in the war.

The most prominent amateur footballer of colour of this period is forward Hassan Hegazi, the first Egyptian to play in the Football League when he appeared for Fulham in November 1911. Though he scored on his début in a 3–1 win over Stockport County – Arthur Wharton's last professional club – he did not play for the 'Cottagers' again. He had come to the West London club's notice when he turned out for amateurs Dulwich Hamlet, for whom he had signed earlier in that 1911–12 season. The 20-year-old Cairo-born student attended London University or Dulwich College, depending on which local newspaper is used as source, having graduated from Saidiq Secondary School in Egypt. The *Fulham Observer*, 17 November 1911, commented that while 'it was apparent the Egyptian was playing out of his class . . . with persistence something might be made of him . . . Hegazi has the makings of a League player.' (They labelled him a student of 'London University'.) He did sign for Southern League Millwall in 1912 and played one game but soon returned to Dulwich Hamlet. Never one to allow himself the luxury of a relaxing moment, he enrolled at St Catherine's College, Cambridge University in 1913 to study Arabic and history. He stayed just long enough – two terms – to play in the annual match with Oxford, earning his Blue in a 2–1 win.

'Costa, who figures intermittently on the Southport left-wing, has the characteristic pace and lack of robustness of the black. But he is more of the Red Indian than the African-Negro type, with long black hair and copper coloured skin' (*Sports Special – The Green 'Un*, Sheffield, 9 November 1918). Not much more is known about this Southport Vulcan player who appeared in a few games in the Lancashire Regional Tournament at the beginning of the 1918–19 season. (The Football League resumed the following season.) The *Southport Guardian*, 7 September, reporting Vulcan's 3–0 win over Blackburn Rovers, thought him 'the most dangerous man on the home side . . . cleverly he dribbles, and then centres accurately'. Yet a month later Southport signed former Preston North End winger George Barlow and no more was seen or heard of Costa, possibly the third Asian footballer to play at senior level in Britain.

This first generation of players of colour in Britain number at least ten. Three of these, Arthur Wharton, Walter Tull and John Walker, played at the highest level, the First Division of the English and Scottish Leagues respectively. The following chapter discusses the careers of those who comprise the second generation, so defined because their careers began in, or spanned, the period 1919–45. During these 26 years we find the first Black British international making his début and learn of the disappointment of a Black Briton allegedly told he had been picked to play for England, only to have the offer rescinded.

TWO

Batman and the Barrowboy

The Second Generation 1919–45

While second-generation Black footballers in Britain were plying their trade in relative isolation and obscurity, men of colour from the élite footballing countries of Brazil and Uruguay were becoming world renowned. Uruguay made the football world take notice in the 1920s by winning the Olympic gold medal in the 1924 and 1928 games, and the first World Cup in 1930. The star of their team was African–Uruguayan José Leandro Andrade. In fact this small but successful country selected the first Black internationals to play for a non-African nation when Isabelino Gradin and Juan Delgado wore the blue shirts of their country for a tournament in Argentina in 1916.

Yet it is Brazilian football, source of the world's greatest Black footballer, Pelé, and best ever team, the predominantly Black 1970 World-Cup winners, which is seen from the outside as a model of integration. Such a representation hides the struggle Black players had for many years to be accepted. Arthur Friedenreich, of European, African and Brazilian origin, the first star of the Brazilian game, did whatever he could to de-Africanise his appearance, such as straighten his hair under a towel and cap before a game. The star of Brazil's World Cup-winning team of 1938 was African–Brazilian Leonidas da Silva. That Black footballers from Brazil should become *world* stars in the 1930s should not have been surprising in a country which has one of the biggest Black populations of any country anywhere in the world, including Africa. It took time and struggle, however, before recognition was won.

While Black footballers had been a presence in the British game from the 1880s, changing the attitude of the FA toward issues of national identity and pigmentation took a long time. It wasn't until the 1940s that a player of colour, Hong Y 'Frank' Soo, was selected for England and only then in unofficial wartime internationals. Although it could be argued that a Black player – who wishes to remain anonymous – played for England at senior level in 1969, it wasn't until nine years later that the FA officially selected a Black footballer, Viv Anderson of Nottingham Forest, for the full England side.

Just after Andrade had starred for hosts Uruguay in the 1930 World Cup, London-born centre-forward Jack Leslie, a prolific scorer of over 400 goals for Plymouth Argyle between 1921 and 1935, was told by his manager Bob Jack that he'd been selected for England. He never made the team: 'They must have forgot I was a coloured boy,' Leslie told journalist Brian Woolnough half a century later. At the time of the interview with Woolnough, 1982–83, Leslie was working on the backroom staff at West Ham. The Hammers had missed the Canning Town youngster of a Jamaican father first time around while he was playing for Barking FC. Ironically, the Boleyn Ground at the time of Woolnough's interview with Leslie was notorious for its racist abuse of Black players. Brendan Batson, deputy chief executive of the PFA, experienced it as one of the most threatening arenas for an opposing Black player to perform in. Yet West Ham have selected Black players since 1899 and employed Leslie.

The FA of Wales, however, did play a contemporary of Leslie's – Welshman Eddie Parris of Second Division Bradford Park Avenue at outside-left against Ireland on 5 December 1931. In so doing, Chepstow–born Parris, at 19, became the first player of colour to represent a British national representative XI. At the time of his Wales début, he was leading scorer for his club with 7 league goals, finishing in the same position at the end of the season with 13 in 36 games. However there were considerations other than Parris's brilliant form which influenced the Welsh selectors. There was – and still is – no full-time professional Welsh League. Because of this the FA of Wales (FAW) could not, like the FA of England, demand the release of players from English Football League clubs for international matches. It seems that the secretary of the Welsh FA, Ted Robbins, had difficulty in getting many of his first-choice players released. Indeed, he complained to the *New Chronicle*, 4 December 1931, 'The reason given for the refusal [by clubs to release players for international duty for Wales] in some cases has been childish . . . The sporting element in the game appears to have gone, and on every hand a purely selfish, businesslike atmosphere seems to prevail.' Clubs argued that they paid the players' wages so they had first call and refusal. But Robbins had a case. The previous season the FAW had to pick a virtual scratch XI – labelled the 'Unknowns' – for the Home Championships because of English clubs' resistance to calls on their players.

All the other Football Associations of the British Isles had formed their own leagues and had the right to call upon nationals who played in these leagues. Wales was the only FA that had most of their players and all their first-class clubs playing 'abroad'. Since 1898 the FAW had argued with the FA the issue of parity: if the English FA could have unrestricted access to its players at Football League clubs, why not the FAW? The FA consistently and stubbornly refused to allow an equal playing field. While Parris's achievement as an international footballer should not be devalued, he probably would not have been chosen had the FAW the same rights of access enjoyed by the FA of England. Wales lost to Ireland 4–0 with Parris making little impression.

Two weeks after he won his one and only international cap he played against Jack Leslie of Plymouth Argyle. Before the game, the two shook hands for the crowd of press photographers eager to exhibit the 'colonial' contribution to the domestic game.

The winger, who could shoot hard and accurately with both feet, made a total of 142 league and cup appearances for Bradford, scoring 39 goals. At the close of the 1934–5 season, after making just 21 appearances and scoring three goals, Eddie left Park Avenue and moved to Bournemouth AFC on the south coast. The contrast between the Avenue, situated in the heart of the West Yorkshire textile industry, and the 'Cherries', a booming tourist mecca, could not have been greater. Bradford had finished fifth in the Second Division and missed promotion by three points, while Bournemouth had concluded their season second from the bottom of Division Three South. On leaving the 'Cherries', he travelled east to Luton Town and then on to Walter Tull's former club, Northampton Town, both of these East Anglian sides having a proud history of signing Black players.

When Eddie signed for Bradford PA in the autumn of 1928 as a 17-year-old trialist, a young Trinidadian, Learie Constantine – who was later knighted and joined the House of Lords – was rounding off his first season as a professional with Nelson Cricket Club of the Lancashire League. Eventually, joining him from the Caribbean, was his wife, their daughter Gloria, writer/revolutionary C.L.R. James and, in 1932, another Trinidadian, Alfred Pious Charles, described as Constantine's 'batman'. Charles arrived with the West Indies cricket team, his responsibility being to act as Learie's gofer. A year later Alfred decided to run after others and joined Second Division Burnley FC as a two-footed inside-forward. He never made the first team and left a year later for Nelson FC, no doubt watched by the town's Caribbean cricket hero. Yet this Trinidadian couldn't settle, meandering around Lancashire to Darwen FC, then to Stalybridge Celtic FC, where memories of another Black sporting icon – Arthur Wharton, who played for and managed Celtic's forerunners, Stalybridge Rovers, in the 1890s – may have been alive in the minds of the older residents. Sandwiched between Charles's spells at Celtic, 1936–39, was a brief interlude with Second Division Southampton where he made his Football League début against Bradford City in January 1937. It was his only first-class appearance in seven seasons as a full- or part-time footballer, a career that was played out alongside his other profession as a magician! Like his more well-known friends and compatriots, James and Constantine, Charles stayed in Britain and died in Burnley in January 1977.

Another Black Briton whose skills and consistency led to calls for international consideration was Anglo-Nigerian centre-forward and half-back Roy Brown. Like his more illustrious club colleague Stanley Matthews, he joined the ground staff of Stoke City on leaving school at 14 (in 1937) where one of his duties included barrowing hot coals to braziers installed on the Victoria Ground pitch during freezing weather. He made his début for the first team in the 1941–42 season. The war prevented Brown from beginning his First Division career until the resumption of the Football League in 1946–47, during which season he played four times. (Also at the club was the first player of Asian descent to play for England, Hong Y 'Frank' Soo. His career is examined in chapter six.)

Roy was born at Stoke on 20 December 1923 to a Nigerian father, Eugene Brown, and an English mother. Eugene had travelled to Britain in 1912 with his brother John. They came as students but full-time study was interrupted by the First World War. Instead they enlisted in the 5th North Staffordshire Regiment. Eugene was invalided out of the war and John was killed: both thus graduated in the science of inhumanity. Eventually, Eugene succumbed to his war injuries leaving Roy and brother Dougie to be raised alone by their mother.

Like many professionals whose careers spanned the Second World War, Brown's potential may never have been fully realised. He began as a half-back but the presence at Stoke of England international Neil Franklin prevented him from capturing a regular first-team place in that position and he switched to centre-forward. Although he spent the greater part of his playing career at the Victoria Ground, he started in just 74 League and FA Cup games over seven seasons, scoring 14 goals. The 1946–47 season was the most successful to date in Stoke's history. Had they won at Sheffield United in their last game they would have won the First Division Championship. In compensation the club made £32,000 profit. (The players would have seen little of this.) In July 1953 he transferred to Watford FC of Division Three South, playing 142 league games and scoring 40 goals. Joining him later at Vicarage Road were Black Britons Tony Collins and Sammy Chung. Roy's wife and family still live in the Watford area.

The second Egyptian to play in the Football League after Hassan Hegazi was Tewfik 'Toothpick' Abdallah. The inside-forward arrived in England in 1920 and made his way to Derby and the Baseball Ground where he argued for a trial with manager Jimmy Methven. Anton Rippon and Andrew Ward in *The Derby County Story* (1991) retell how the 24-year-old was nearly sold a season ticket by a confused Methven, unable to understand Abdallah's English. The Cairo-born First-World-War veteran had previously played for the National Sporting Club of Cairo and the International Sports Club of Cairo as well as an Egypt XI.

It seems he chose Derby because of his contact with a County player, Tommy Barbour, during the latter's wartime posting to Egypt. Abdallah was serving in the Egypt Expeditionary Force and played football against the British Army, which included Barbour. However the North African did not come to Britain just to play professional football. In an interview with the *Derbyshire Football Express*, 25 September 1920, he said he hoped to learn 'something about the engineering trade', a key industry in this Midland city.

After impressing in a trial game with the reserves in a Central Alliance fixture – his inclusion drawing an unusually large crowd – 'Toothpick' had his period of appraisal extended for a month. And, before the month was up, he made his First Division début at inside-right against Manchester City on 9 October, 1920. In that game Abdallah is supposed to have taken the field and asked a team-mate, 'Where's me camel?'[1] What he meant was where's Mick Hamill, the City player who was also making his début, and whom he was supposed to be marking! The combination of changing-room banter, difficulties in communication with his

Arthur Wharton, Rotherham
Town 1894.

Arthur's gravestone
at Edlington, placed
8 May 1997 after
an appeal by Football
Unites, Racism Divides.

ABOVE: Dr Stephenson's Children's Home and Orphanage football team 1902. Walter Tull, front row, second from left.

RIGHT: Walter and Edward Tull 1916.

LEFT: Walter Tull, Tottenham Hotspur 1909.

BELOW: Tottenham Hotspur Football Club 1910–11. Walter Tull, front row, far right.

C.D.ROBERTS Eq   A.COLEMAN J.OVER W.STEPHENSON J.JOYCE T.LESLIE T.H.LUNN   A.W.TURNER
                                                                                                          SECRETARY
M.P.CADMAN Esq   B.ELKIN H.MIDDLEMISS E.BIRNIE E.BULLING J.KENNEDY A.GOSNELL E.CODDET F.WILKES T.A.DALDOCK Esq F.J.BRENNAN
                  W.MINTER E.NEWMAN R.HUMPHREYS D.STEEL R.STEEL A.WILSON F.BENTLEY T.MORRIS
                                                          CAPTAIN
J.NIE   A.STEEL J.CURTIS D.BROWN   I.BROWN   R.McTAVISH J.DARNELL W.TULL   J.WARREN
TRAINER   ASST TRAINER
                          TOTTENHAM HOTSPUR FOOTBALL CLUB. 1910-1911.

Alfred Charles, Southampton 1937.

SALIM BACHI KHAN
Glasgow Celtic Reserves
1936–37

HONG Y SOO
Stoke City
1933–45.

Salim Khan played all his matches barefoot. Gil Heron, winger and poet is the father of 'Gil' Scott Heron the revolutionary jazz musican. 'Frank' Soo was the first man of colour to play for England in the unofficial Internationals during the Second World War. Roy Brown played alongside Frank Soo and Stanley Matthews.

GIL HERON
Glasgow Celtic
1951–52.

ROY BROWN
Stoke City
1938–53.

OPPOSITE PAGE – TOP: Football: the White Man's burden. Southampton 'welcomes' the Kaffirs on their tour of September 1899.

LEFT: Pobee, the flamboyant goalkeeper, psyching-out the ball on the Gold Coast tour in 1951.

ABOVE: The Nigerian goalkeeper checks out the team's 'footwear' and centre-back Onwudiwe puts in a heavy challenge despite having no boots on during the Nigerian Football Association tour of 1949.

ABOVE LEFT: Steve 'Kalamazoo' Mokone, Torino 1955. Steve was South Africa's first Black professional.

ABOVE RIGHT: Shaka Hislop playing Arthur Wharton for BBC TV's *Black Britain* 1997.

BELOW: Lindy Delapenha, Middlesbrough 1950. Lindy is seated front row, second from right.

team-mates and time has probably honed that exchange to what it is today. However any urge to take the piss soon evaporated once the game got underway for 'in some finer arts of the game [Abdallah] can give points to many first-class players'. Older supporters were reminded of the inimitable ex-Ram and England forward Steve Bloomer. 'I heard this opinion reiterated more than once, and it certainly was a revelation to note Abdallah's footwork and ball manipulation. All things considered he did remarkably well. He got Derby's first goal . . . has speed . . . [and] is a brainy player. The Egyptian's superior technique was too much for the City full-back Fletcher who, near the end of the game, deliberately tried to injure Abdallah, much to the crowd's anger.' (Echoes here of Airdrie full-back McFarlane's response to the runaround John Walker gave him. Did full-backs – or any other White player – feel it was their duty to slap down Uppity Niggers?) 'It was an incident full of significance . . . Abdallah had shown . . . what he was capable of.'[2] A début goal inside the first 20 minutes; a 3–0 win; their first £2-win bonus of the season; a welcome supply of much needed 'beer vouchers'; and comparison with a Derby legend – not a bad day out!

There were only four more win bonuses in the League that season, with the 'Rams' finishing second from bottom of the First Division and relegated. Despite this, Abdallah was retained. However, the legendary Steve Bloomer was soon employed as Methven's replacement and the ghost really did come back to haunt. Bloomer, disagreeing with the fans' assessment of the North African, indicated to Abdallah that his days were numbered at the Baseball Ground by dropping him and signing another inside-forward, R. Stewart. He was then loaned out to Cowdenbeath of the Scottish League Division Two. The following season, 1923–24, he joined Bridgend Town in South Wales, returning to the Football League with Hartlepool in March 1924 (making 11 appearances and scoring 1 goal). Later he coached in the USA.

The following decade another Egyptian signed for a Scottish League club when Mohamed Latif, a student at Jordanhill College, Glasgow, joined Rangers. He had been recommended to the club by James McCrae, a former Clyde and Manchester United half-back who was coaching in Egypt. Latif, a winger, played all but one of his games for the Ibrox club in the reserves. His single first-team outing was against Hibernian, 13 September 1935. He won some over and wound up others: '[Rangers'] attack was weakened by the inclusion of Latif, who was too impetuous.' (*Govan Press*, 20 September 1935); 'The Rangers were the first to get going, and Latif, their Egyptian player, was one of the first to come into prominence.' (Edinburgh *Evening News*, 14 September 1935.) However, the general consensus seems to have been that he wasn't up to playing first-class football. His greatest hour came in the 1936 Berlin Olympics as a member of the Egyptian team (which implies he was an amateur with Rangers).

M. Mansour, a reserve goalkeeper for QPR in 1938–39, completes the trio of Egyptians playing in inter-war Britain, though Mohamed el Guindy and Abdul

Kerim Sakr were two Egyptians who signed as amateurs with Huddersfield Town in the 1940s while studying at Leeds University after recommendation by McCrae. Neither made the first team, however. It isn't surprising that this North African country – a British colony between 1882 and 1936 – was the source of the greatest number of African players to League clubs in England and Scotland. The colonisation of Egypt introduced modern British sports such as association football quite early on in the development of the game. Egypt entered a team for the 1920 Olympic Games, a year before its Football Association was formed. Two years later it joined FIFA, the only African representative until its neighbour Sudan affiliated in 1948. In 1922 a national competition, the Farouk Cup, began. By 1949 there was a national league. It even played in the World Cup before any of the British national sides, entering a team for the 1934 competition in Italy, where they were defeated by Hungary 4–2. Within Africa, Egypt dominated country and club competitions in their early years. The national side won the inaugural African Cup of Nations in 1957, retained the trophy in 1959 and were losing finalists in 1961. Between 1964 and 1991, Egyptian clubs reached the final of the African Cup of Champion Clubs on 12 occasions, winning ten. Of these clubs the most successful has been Al Ahly Cairo who've played in six finals and won five.

If Egypt produced the most foreign-born Black footballers to play in Britain during this period, forward Peter Baines was probably the most unique of this second generation. A native Australian of Aboriginal descent, he played for Oldham Athletic in 1937–38 but not in the Football League. During the war he guested for Grimsby Town, Halifax Town, Hartlepool United, Liverpool and Middlesbrough. In April 1943 Wrexham of Division Three North signed Baines from Oldham of the same division. Although he scored 27 league and cup goals in the wartime League West competition of 1944–5, Baines made just six Football League appearances – scoring two goals – for the North Wales club once the normal League programme was resumed the following season. The first of these was his début, away against Rochdale on 3 September 1946, a First Australian first in the Football League. Yet by November he'd been off-loaded to Crewe Alexandra where he added another seven League games to his appearance record for that season. During the summer break, two-footed Baines moved across the Pennines to Hartlepool – for whom he'd guested during the war – where he played nine games for one goal. Next stop was Merseysiders New Brighton for a two-game trial in November 1947, then further north to Carlisle for another trial period. He failed to impress and dropped out of League football.

After the First World War, those British expatriates that ruled the Commonwealth of Australia and administered the state territories developed a Make Australia White policy. It is a programme that we'll come across again when discussing the careers of Charles Perkins and Yorkshire comedian Charlie Williams who played for Doncaster Rovers in the 1950s. One of the instruments used was the forced removal of Aboriginal children who looked as though they might have a hint of White in their ancestry from their parents. They were herded off to religious institutions, usually funded by the state, where they were 'civilised' – made to think and act as White children. But not made to feel White. That would be going too far. As Perkins, the second Black Australian footballer to play in Britain during the 1950s cuttingly observed, this separation of mother and child also forbade the victim access to their culture which had evolved unbroken and uninterrupted over thousands of years. It was a process of denial and degradation of the history and lifestyle of the original people of Australia that the dictators of Apartheid South Africa would have been comfortable with. While the children were being made into different people, they learnt to play football. Real Aussies played rules football, the kick-and-catch game with ball-bustin' shorts. In fact soccer was called 'wogball' because it was seen as an immigrant sport. While the stolen generation of children learnt to play football their parents were confined within reserves, often cut off from the significant places of religious and cultural importance such as dreaming sites. They too, like their children, were being made into different people.

From 1883 players of colour became an established feature of the game in Britain. This second generation of the period 1919–45 had consolidated their presence through Eddie Parris and Hong Y 'Frank' Soo's international recognition, and Abdallah's career in the top flight. We can also acknowledge the continuing obstacles illustrated most obviously by Leslie's belated omission, which carried echoes of a denial to Wharton of an international cap some 44 years earlier.

In South America, as we've discussed, players of colour were starring at top international level, in particular Uruguay, Brazil, Peru and Chile – these last two countries sending a combined touring party to Britain in 1933 which comprised a large number of Black players. The following chapter discusses tours to Britain by Black teams from Africa and the Caribbean.

THREE

Touring Teams 1888–1959

PART ONE: THE 'KAFFIRS' 1888–1948

The first Black football team to visit Britain was the 'Kaffirs' of the Basuto tribe in what is now Lesotho, Southern Africa. They arrived at Southampton dock in September 1899. Never before had a Black African squad played outside that continent. Indeed, they may well have been the first African football tourists – even if we include White South Africans. The Basutos' trip to Britain was organised by the Orange Free State Football Association (OFSFA) which was controlled by administrators of British origin. (The president was a Mr Hudgson, chairman of the Rangers FC of Bloemfontein.) Afrikaners favoured rugby. G.A.L. Thabe's history of Black football in South Africa *It's a Goal: 50 Years of Sweat, Tears and Drama in Black Soccer* (1983) makes reference to an Orange Free State Bantu soccer club which was 'active' in 1898. This may have been the 'Kaffirs' themselves or Oriental FC for whom the captain of the visitors, Joseph Twaji, played.

The reason for the tour may have been in its novelty value, raising funds for OFSFA who, it seems, were determined that the team's visit to England would pay its way and more. Thirty-six games had been arranged against the best teams of England and Scotland. The punishing schedule was to have begun on 1 September against Aston Villa, the current Football League champions, but the liner *Gaika* on which the footballers had sailed berthed nine days late, eventually arriving on 2 September.

In fact, the 'Kaffirs' were not the first Black footballers to visit Britain. This status goes to the Maori tourists of 1888. The 26 New Zealanders – including 5 Whites – played 74 games under the rugby code and, although they did play a few practice matches under association rules, these were relatively insignificant extras. For a short while, however, in the late autumn of 1879, many believed a Zulu team who played at Brammal Lane in Sheffield (among other venues) to be authentic. It wasn't long before the hoax was exposed. Under the smeared layer of burnt cork and head-dress of feathers were white-skinned and well-known footballers raising money for the dependents of those British soldiers killed in the Zulu War of 1878–9. Yet so popular were these 'Zulus', that they toured for a further year before the football authorities effectively banned them.

The rearranged programme of the Basutos had them kicking off in northeast England on 5 September, rather than the Midlands, pitching them against First Division Newcastle United at St James's Park. There was much pre- and post-match publicity, in language used to describe the physical characteristics of the visitors which hinted at, and subtly exploited, the European obsession with the (relatively unrepressed) sexuality of the African. 'The visitors [are] a fine lot of men . . . reputed to possess remarkable staying powers. [They are] clever at the game . . . Some of them remarkably good looking, and of an intelligent cast of features.'[1] A large crowd of 6,000 assembled with 'a sprinkling of the fair sex'. Some inquisitive folk had even gone to the Central Railway Station to welcome them. Compared to their opponents, the 'Kaffirs', wearing orange shirts with dark blue collars and shorts, were not good footballers. The Geordies coasted to victory (6–3), as did all but one of the teams the Africans faced. (The final statistics read: played 36, won 0, drawn 1, lost 35, with 235 goals conceded.)

Other northeastern opponents were Sunderland – Big Boys of the region having won the First Division three times in the 1890s – to whom the 'Kaffirs' lost 5–3, and Middlesbrough, who won 7–3. In all three games the Black footballers were treated patronisingly, as overgrown children: 'They are a very heavy lot and caused a great deal of amusement' (v Newcastle United); 'The delightful darkey returned to the centre line as proud as the proverbial dog' (v Sunderland); 'From a corner just on the interval, the Kaffirs, amidst loud laughter, were permitted to score' (v Middlesbrough). Without irony it also reported that 'the darkeys played a very gentlemanly game, and it says much for their good temper – which must have been sorely tried – that they did not utilise their obvious strength of body and cranium.'[2]

The various quotes illustrate confused attitudes towards the 'Kaffirs'. They were big and strong, handsome yet excruciatingly naïve and honest. However, while it would have been simple, literally, to portray the 'Kaffirs' as freak-show footballers for the amusement and entertainment of the master race, matters became complicated by the unfolding tragedy of the political and military crisis in Southern Africa, which descended into the Boer War in October 1899. A feature of the political debate surrounding the crisis was the allegiance of the Black – or 'Kaffir' and 'Bantu' as they were often disparagingly labelled – populations. Basutoland, the homeland of the 'Kaffir' footballers, was sandwiched between the Orange Free State, which was a Boer Republic and Natal, an English-speaking colony. The issue of who the Basutos would side with was a live question in British newspapers. Not unexpectedly, but certainly unenviably, the Africans found themselves on a tour organised by administrators of British descent in a country at war with the Afrikaans-speaking government and population of the Orange Free State. This political dimension created a dilemma for reporters and editors, some of whom continued to work the tourists as malleable raw material with which to stir up public prejudice. Southampton's *Football Echo and Sports Gazette* informed its readers of the Kaffirs' arrival – 'Up come eleven little nigger boys from savage South Africa' – via a cartoon situated centrally on its front page, featuring a sturdy but shaken John Bull reminding readers of Kipling's description of Britain's Black colonies as the 'White Man's Burden'. The *Athletic News* followed in similar vein. Like the cartoon in the *Football Echo and Sports Gazette*, it was placed so readers could not miss it. Instead of a group of Africans, it had an individual in a football kit but wearing only one boot, holding a spear and tomahawk, with a ring through his nose and feathers in his hair, kicking a ball. Underneath is the caption: 'Jeeohsmiffikato the crack Kaffir centre-forward thirsting for gore and goals.'[3]

Others were more sensitive – to the political needs of imperial Britain. During war-scare September there were fears expressed in the press that 'Boer spies' were inciting the Basutos to rise up against Natal. In light of this, should not the tourists be used in the anti-Boer propaganda offensive? If so, dismissing them as savages was unwise as they and their peoples may well be needed as allies should the emergency kick off into a South Africa-wide war.

Much of the ambivalent language used in the reporting of the 'Kaffirs' reflected the environment of naked, competing propaganda that all war scares generate. The zeal with which some scribblers tailored the ideological content of their output to suit pressing military and political demands and sensitivities sometimes overrode and contradicted 'common-sense' notions previously held. Thus, during the war scare period the Afrikaners became light-skinned savages, a redefinition that contributed to the justification of their imprisonment in concentration camps.

Many events have unintended consequences. The Boer, or South African, War as it was more commonly known, was one such event. Because such a high proportion of the men volunteering as recruits to the British Army were so puny and underdeveloped, the government established the Committee on Physical Deterioration in an effort to literally build up Britain's manhood. One of the solutions offered was more exercise. This was the first time the government took an official interest in sport and it probably marks the beginnings of the use of sport for unashamedly political ends. And, to compound this irony of the world's most affluent and powerful country defectively reproducing itself, 'several of the [Basutos were] over 6ft high and proportionately built'.[4]

As the war escalated over the winter of 1899–1900, Boer became Black and Black became something else. An example of this contradictory and confused state of affairs is the description of the human exhibits of the 'Savage South Africa' exhibition at Earls Court as the 'magnificent men from the Zulu country'. Yet, so 'magnificent' were these men that soon after the opening, London County Council officials instructed the exhibition manager Mr Edwin Cleary to section off the 'native kraals' in order to prevent the public – particularly nubile young women – from fraternising with the 'heathen warriors'.

The boys from Basuto, bombarded by goals, also succumbed to the propaganda barrage. In their rescheduled fixture with Aston Villa, gate receipts went to a Boer War fund. And it would have been more than a blanket full of ha'pennies because, despite their inability to match the organised teamwork of their opponents, the Southern Africans attracted large crowds. Against Tottenham, the best-supported club in the south, gate receipts totalled £89. Christmas Day was 'celebrated' with a 3–2 defeat by Brentford at Griffin Park. And against Sheffield United, the legendary Billy Foulke, perhaps the only footballer who could match the Basutos for size, played at centre-forward and scored two goals.

Hopefully the Basutos would have gone back to South Africa better footballers, though, with the war raging, there was probably little opportunity for them to apply the knowledge they had gained from their experience of playing the best teams in Britain.

PART TWO: AFRICAN AND AFRICAN–CARIBBEAN TOURING TEAMS 1949–59

During the summer of 1994 Britain's prime minister, John Major, visited post-apartheid South Africa. His purpose was to repair damage to political and economic relations between Britain and the new South African government caused by the covert acceptance of apartheid by past UK governments, in particular his predecessor Margaret Thatcher. Among Major's travelling circus was Bobby Charlton, who had some credibility on the continent because of his genuine interest in African football. His legitimacy as an authoritative, internationally renowned public figure who would be listened to by many Africans was not lost on the Foreign Office. Such use of football to further political objectives is nothing new. Indeed, in colonial Africa football was much more than a game. It was often the symbolic battlefield between the colonised and the coloniser. (Charlton's reputation may be a little less legendary now, given his involvement in England's campaign to host the 2006 World Cup, in direct opposition to South Africa.)

After the Second World War the march towards independence among Africans sped to an unstoppable momentum. For the colonial powers, most notably Britain and France, the preoccupation was with a peaceful and sympathetic transition. Uppermost in the minds of European diplomats and politicians was the need to maintain and continue, as far as possible, profitable economic relations. The necessity of not alienating Africa's ruling class, a delicate and difficult task during the Cold War era, demanded a diplomatic offensive on many fronts. Sport, in particular football, was one. Between 1949 and 1959 there were five football tours to Britain from colonial countries and a Commonwealth region: Nigeria in 1949, the Gold Coast 1951, Trinidad 1953, Uganda 1956 and the Caribbean 1959. While the footballers may have seen them as great fun and invaluable learning curves, the football administrators in Africa and the Caribbean, and the football and political Establishment in Britain, were aware of their wider significance. In the UK the tourists were treated as VIP guests, as

72

minor politicians or diplomats. But these were no ordinary footballers, trainers and managers. The agenda, all ways round, was as political as it was sporting: to instil in the mind of the African and African–Caribbean an attitude that was sympathetic to capitalism and western ideas; to illustrate how superior the British political and economic system was to the alternative (Eastern European) model on offer.

WEST AFRICA: THE NIGERIAN AND GOLD COAST TOURS OF 1949 AND 1951

The successful struggle against German and Italian fascism of 1939–45 aided the already vibrant and active nationalist movements within Nigeria and the Gold Coast (now Ghana) that were pushing for independence. Within these broad political movements were cultural organisations such as football and sports clubs, including Lagos-based Zik's Athletic Club founded by Nnamdi Azikiwe. 'Zik', who was to become a leader of the nationalist cause in Nigeria, recognised that unity among ordinary Africans of different ethnic origins could be built, among other places, on the sportsfield. The colonial administrators were aware also of the need to battle for the hearts and minds of its subject peoples in this changing, post-war, colonial world. In an address to Achimota College (Gold Coast) students in 1944, Tory peer Lord Swinton, conscious of the new mood invigorating West Africans, was eager to dampen down expectations of political freedom:

> There must be no dominating race exploiting others for its own benefit. But that does not mean that the strong and victorious nations must not lead. They must. They will have to enforce disarmament of the aggressor, to create a secure peace, and to lead in planning and reconstruction. That is not domination but natural leadership, which men and women will always look for, and to which they will always respond.[5]

Post-war colonial governments were obsessed with the management of change – the loss of direct political control – and the accommodation of nationalism. Among the many different devices and approaches adopted to cope, was sport. If the comradeship and bonding developed through sport at the public schools and Oxbridge worked to produce politically dependable colonial administrators running the European régimes in Africa, why not try the same approach with those Africans who would soon become the ruling élite and bureaucracy of their emergent nations? And football was the most popular sport among Africans.

The second half of the 1940s saw Black workers hitting out at their bosses in Nigeria and the Gold Coast. In Nigeria there had been a 44-day general strike, starting in June 1945. Four years later there was a strike on the railways (see below) and the fatal shooting of 20 miners at Enugu, with many more injured. The previous year in the Gold Coast there had been serious rioting which 'took the Colonial government by surprise . . . the prevailing emotion among us British administrators . . . was rather one of bewilderment that nice friendly people like Ghanaians should behave like that'.[6] Even 'football matches between Europeans and Africans are [now] constantly producing incidents'![7] Something had to be done to befriend those Africans worth befriending.

THE NIGERIAN TOUR 1949

The visit of Nigerian footballers to Britain in September 1949 was the first by a Black African team that represented their national Football Association. Its success acted as the catalyst for the Africanisation and modernisation of the Nigerian game. Organised football in the Lagos area was controlled by middle-class Whites, mainly civil servants who were there to service the needs of European business. Whites living in Nigeria tended to be administrators and traders, not settlers looking to stay for generations.

One man who did make it in the West African colony was trader Francis Baron Mulford (aka 'Baba Eko' translated as 'respected elder of Lagos'), viewed by many as the person most responsible for the development of soccer in the country. He had been arranging matches between Kings College school and European teams in Lagos from as early as 1914. In May 1916 there was a competitive match between civil servants and European merchants on the Kings College school ground. A second match was arranged in October to raise funds for the Red Cross. Mulford is credited with donating the War Memorial Cup in August 1919 for Lagos clubs to compete for. This probably represented the first formal, organised competition between teams in the city. Mulford played at right-back for Diamonds FC, a mixed European–African team that included Azikiwe, when they won the Lagos League in 1923. Inter-colony matches were also played with the Gold Coast during the inter-war period. In 1931 the Lagos and District Amateur Football Association (LDAFA) was established and created the Mulford Cup in recognition of the formative role played by the former racehorse owner and agent for Lagos Stores Ltd. By 1945, the year in which the Nigerian Football Association was formed, the Lagos League had three divisions, the last being split between 'A' and 'B', mirroring the structure in England.

Captain D.H. Holley, chairman of the Labour Advisory Board and Nigerian Football Association (NFA) was the 1949 tour-team manager. He was also president of the Nigerian Amateur Athletic Association (NAAA). (Two other civil servants-cum-football administrators, G.A. Henderson and T.B. Welch, also spread their administrative tentacles into the field of athletics, being members of the executive of the NAAA.) Two further civil servants involved in realising the tour were P.A. Courtney, chairman of the LDAFA and R.B. 'Darby' Allen, treasurer of the NFA during the 1950s and, respectively, director of posts and telegraphs and government printer. The NAAA had sent an athletics team to Britain in 1948 to watch the Olympic Games and compete against clubs. No doubt this provided those involved in both sectors of sport – athletics and football – with the knowledge and experience to ensure a well organised affair for the soccer players a year later.

The power held by these colonial civil servants was reflected in the composition of the 18-member squad that travelled to England. The men selected weren't necessarily the best players but the most suitable ambassadors for colonial Nigeria. This aspect of the work of the NFA officials was certainly not lost on the British dignitaries on show in the 'mother country' to lubricate the wheels of colonial diplomacy. At a civic reception held in Leytonstone Town Hall, after the Nigerians had played the Amateur Cup holders of the previous two seasons to last, Mr Rees-Williams, Under-Secretary of State for the Colonies, praised the work of Holley, Courtney and Allen in producing a team of the right kind of fellows:

> Now it says something for the activity and energy of Government servants in the Tropics that no fewer than fourteen of the players are civil servants, and there are two school teachers in addition.[8]

This activity and energy was not admired by everybody in the colony. African teams in Lagos, such as ZAC (Zik's Athletic Club), Bombers, Spitfires and Hurricanes and the Muslim Eleven FC were angered at the way those Europeans in positions of power used that power to build strong teams at the expense of Africans with lesser means.

> [Should] the Locomotive Branch of Nigerian Railways not now be called the 'Railway Institute of Football Technology'? We say so because we have yet to learn where those at the head of affairs could use public time, public funds, public materials and public vehicles so liberally in order to foster football.

This attack from the sports page of Zik's voice of Pan-African socialism, the *West African Pilot* (*WAP*), 9 February 1945, alluded not only to continuous poaching by Railways FC of ZAC's best players but also to industrial unrest on the railways, the inference being that time and energy should be spent on easing tensions there rather than creating them elsewhere. Via the pages of *WAP*, Zik debated the power structure of Nigerian football:

> If the Nigeria Railway is not efficiently run today, the fault does not lie with the Nigerian worker; it is those at the top who mix up railway work with football . . . we say that with the glaring inefficiency which is so apparent in our railway administration . . . Who would condone what your department has been doing in order to foster football at the expense of railway efficiency?[9]

However, the practice of mixing the running of a colony with the running of football wasn't confined only to civil servants in the Locomotive Branch of Nigeria Railways. 'Certain high officials . . . make it their regular pastime to dismantle certain teams and . . . virtually misuse public funds in making appointments in their departments to be dependent on the ability of an applicant to play football.' The political organisation of the game in Lagos (and Makurdi) 'where the African is not in full control of amateur football' replicated the political organisation of Nigerian society as a whole, he argued. The question of who ran the game and how power was exercised had a wider significance: 'Through the avenue of sports, the stranglehold on the African by alien peoples is strengthened and the control of the thinking processes of the African is thus assured for a long time yet.' This comment clearly recognised the ultimatum which, consciously or unconsciously, the colonial administrator presented: play the game our way or suffer the consequences. Zik felt that they were out 'to destroy ZAC' and create an environment where 'no African-managed club can thrive successfully in Lagos football'.[10] The better players of the civil servant-managed teams were treated effectively as semi-professionals in that they were rewarded with jobs and other privileges that would otherwise have been out of reach. Fifteen railway employees, for example, were given time off and travel passes to play football in Port Harcourt. A job in the civil service was a prized position for many urban Africans, the majority of whom were forced into manual labour or had no work at all. Playing football for a White-managed team offered them a way into a colonial world of 'relatively high prestige . . . non-productive employment'.[11]

This preoccupation of the footballing members of the colonialist élite with constructing a winning team in practice meant, in large part, ignoring their self-proclaimed values of fair play and an even playing field. The obsession with winning had as much to do with beating the African and keeping him in his place as it had with internal civil service rivalry between the marine, railway, public works, posts and telegraph, lands survey, police and town council divisions – and competition between the civil service and businesses such as the United Africa Company, a subsidiary of Unilever.

> Clearly those who enthrone themselves as Czars of Lagos football . . . have
> come all out in order to destroy all that is fine in the nature of the African,
> and to provoke him. Yes, the African has a keen sense of justice and . . .
> he will fight and destroy the forces of greed, envy, jealousy and injustice
> even in the realms of sport.[12]

This reference to dictatorial Russian rulers of the pre-revolutionary era was no doubt intended to trigger the democratic nerve of the (African) reader. In his autobiography Zik explained his sports philosophy. At ZAC, sportsmanship was encouraged rather than winning at all costs. 'To make these ethical precepts in sport worthwhile, prizes are awarded to those few who stick to the code of behaviour stipulated for all contestants in a particular type of sport.'[13] This ethos, formulated originally by the colonialists and held up as a symbol of their cultural superiority, was now used by Zik and his press as a gauge to illustrate the colonialists' decadence and unfitness to rule.

The teams of ZAC and the Muslim XI relied on ex-schoolboy players to replace those lured by civil servants for their teams:

> The competition between government departments . . . has assumed rather frightening proportions – to the extent that transfers and appointments . . . are made in the interests of football rather than efficiency.

This practice was also used by businessmen.

> Complaints have been made also to the Nigerian Football League to the effect that players have been seduced from one commercial firm to another because they've been good footballers and more recently it has been inferred that political influence is trying hard to take hold of the game.[14]

ZAC teams offered ethnically mixed sport and liberationist ideas rather than jobs. Unfortunately the warming thoughts of Pan-African socialism and fraternal cross-tribal unity did not meet the immediate material needs of dispossessed Nigerians. One of the stated objectives of the NFA was to foster love and friendship amongst football players. The *WAP* felt ideals such as this were not being translated in practice. There could be no 'love and friendship' while government departments and White-run businesses haemorrhaged the young life-blood of the African clubs. T.B. Welch, Co-manager of the Railways teams and his compatriots, 'were people who have not the slightest conception of what true sportsmanship is . . . Some of them are very poor sports indeed – they must win at all cost, by hook or by crook.' Far from improving the moral character of the young African footballer, they were a corrupting influence. The latter should:

> . . . take heed and get out of the tentacles of these despoilers of the character of the youth of Africa. Oh, football, what despicable crimes are committed in thy name, in Lagos, even by those who claim to be paragons of perfection and repository of all knowledge . . . what they call 'civilisation' and which I call barbarism![15]

The selection of players for the tour, therefore, could never be based on footballing ability alone. The class and ideological status of the player was an important factor in the minds of the administrators. They wanted the players to present, collectively, an image that was both acceptable to the British public and Establishment and went some way in dissolving those negative stereotypes with which Europeans had veneered Africans. This would, in turn, show what a good job the expatriates had done, thereby confirming the legitimacy of the imperial project itself. What the tour was not was a celebration of things (West) African.

Tensions surfaced when lobbying began for inclusion in the team. Of the final 18 selected, only four – Chukura, a teacher at Abeokuta Grammar School; Ibiam from Port Harcourt; Dankaro from Jos and Akioye, a teacher from Ibadan – came from teams outside Lagos. The squad that was selected represented not so much the best 18 players but the Lagos-centred balance of power. 'It . . . seemed that the selectors were keen on picking many players who were well educated . . . two such players were Akioye and Chukura, (both) schoolmasters.' Kanno was another example of how class and cultural credentials were seen as just as important as a player's form. A polished, intelligent half-back or centre-forward, he was 'just past his peak'[16] in 1949. However, the player/secretary had been educated for a while in England, and the selectors therefore trusted he'd acquired the refinements necessary for the public engagements and appearances his position would demand. Pressure was also exerted by club officials for the exclusion of certain players. Friday Okoh and Enugu, players who many Africans felt merited a place, were left behind after pressure from G.O. Urion, the European manager of Railways FC.

The official uniform of players and administrators was, for public occasions, grey flannels and a green blazer with a badge carrying a large 'N' with 'FA' in the background and 'United Kingdom 1949' woven underneath. For matches, the strip was olive-green shirts, white shorts and green socks. (A concession that was made to the players' ethnicity was in the food supplement brought to rationed Britain, 'yams, hams and jams, oils, rice, red peppers and dried shrimps'[17] which, when in London, was prepared by a Nigerian cook.)

Concern with the correctness of public appearance – traditional African robes were not acceptable – caused friction between the players and the manager, particularly the suitability of wearing football boots. All but two of the players preferred to play in bandaged feet. Only European teams wore boots in Nigeria. Africans felt such clumsy items inhibited close control and sureness of touch, great strengths of the tourists' game. Nevertheless, on disembarking from the liner *Apapa* at Liverpool, a team member said they would play in leather if the ground was overly soft. The debate over whether to put the boot on or not resurfaced in the match with the Athenian League, where the pitch was very muddy. During a first half of slipping and sliding around, the possibility of humiliation by double figures led manager Holley to try and strongarm his 'boys' into lacing-up. 'Pangloss', amateur football correspondent for the *News Chronicle*, thought he'd gone over the top. 'I do not think their morale was improved by the hectoring manner of their team manager when the half-time argument arose as to whether they should play with or without boots.'[18]

The conflict between live, bandaged skin and dead skin and laces was settled by a duo of converging forces: one, the excellence of the team and the resulting thirst for international fixtures; And two, the desire by FIFA for conformity in footwear. Andy Ralston, FA Council member for London and the Nigerians' UK organiser and co-ordinator, said in his report to the FA that 'they will never reach international class until they play in boots'.[19] However, before the NFA ruled on the matter the organising committee of the 1950 World Cup, at a meeting in Paris in February 1950, decreed that barefoot playing would be banned. This, in effect, meant the Nigerians (and other Africans and Asians) would have to adopt boots if they wanted to play at the highest level.

Some writers have argued that the cultivation of (British) sports, especially team games, by expatriate colonials allowed the British Empire to transform itself into an amicable Commonwealth of Nations through the ethos of 'playing the game': learning a common set of values. Chief Anthony Enahoro recalls his time at Kings College, Lagos, 'the Eton of Nigeria', where Mulford had, for a while, been games master and where inter-school sports competition was an important part of the curriculum:

> Mungo Park, Denham, Clapperton and the first voyagers from England to Nigeria were not 'invaders' or 'imperialist agents' but heroes, and we did not identify ourselves with the 'barbarous natives' whom they had 'discovered'. Love of country had included pride in England – the Empire was no less ours than Britain's.[20]

Empire Day (ED), when schools throughout the colony would 'celebrate' the doings of the 'mother country', showcased this making British of things African. Prior to ED, children would practise singing *Rule Britannia, God Save the King* and saluting the Union Jack. ED was a cultural transplant which undermined African traditions and culture and elevated the ways of seeing and doing of the colonial. Thus games, modernised and regulated in the British public schools and Oxbridge, replaced indigenous pratices such as dance, stick fighting and wrestling which dramatised long-cherished African themes and experiences.

Access to these new competitive, transplanted sports was through school, itself an institution of privilege as most Nigerians didn't attend. The missionary schools in particular were the nurseries of aspiring footballers. And they were the first destination of clubs looking for promising new players. The civil servants who ran football in Lagos knew this. To prevent the freeflow of African school graduates to African-managed teams, the LDAFA had a ruling which prohibited schoolboys from playing club football. Zik's *WAP*, 23 July 1949, carried a cartoon showing the office of an 'employer'. Adorning the walls are football championship shields. The European boss is standing over a young 'Nigerian school graduate' who holds his Cambridge School Leaving Certificate. The boss, clutching a sheet of paper entitled, 'Next year football season: recruitment for a super team', says, 'I have jobs for boys who can use – not necessarily their brains – but their legs.' In consequence, for Zik, his newspaper and West African socialists in general, the tour provided useful ammunition. The trip, though not theirs in conception and realisation could, with welcome irony, become another weapon in the struggle towards independence.

In pre-colonial African societies, athleticism was an important feature of culture. Organised, ritual contest – in wrestling, dance, jumping, theatre – was a device often used to unite a community. These activities would reflect the predominant concerns of that community and offered a symbolic, rehearsed resolution through play. The central place of dance in West African cultures provided a channel of communication through which celebrations, generational rites of passage, victories in war and other activities and events could be transmitted.

Such a history of games and play in West Africa gave football an inevitable political dimension that ensured it could never be just a game – in the same way, for instance, that legitimate, physical assault between Black and White in the boxing ring, in the first half of this century, was never allowed to be merely a 'contest'. Thus, the struggle for control in sport was being waged by actors aware of its wider implications and resonance. It was a struggle that complemented, and was part of, the movement for liberation in African colonial societies as a whole. Hogan 'Kid' Bassey, who won a World Featherweight title three years before independence in 1960, was fully aware of the political significance of his victory. 'I was fighting for my people, for Nigeria.'[21] Tribal loyalties had to be put aside for the greater goal of national unity. Others have developed this 'out of Africa' consciousness, arguing that the African competitor abroad is an African first and a nationalist second. An editorial in *WA*, 17 August 1949, summarising the achievements of the tourists, recognised that amongst its successes 'it has also made a small contribution to Nigerian nationhood by focusing the attention of Nigerians on "our" team.'

'Our team' left behind a Lagos that had been riven by industrial unrest on the railways, where the Station Staff Union had called out its members. The General Manager of Nigeria Railways was T.B. Welch who, with G.O. Urion, represented the managerial team of Railways FC. Welch took a hard-line attitude to the workers' complaints, acting the hard-nosed boss. 'The General Manager of the Nigerian Railway turned down an agreement for a truce which seemed to have been accepted by his representatives at a parley (with the unions) that morning.'[22] Urion and Welch's intolerance of dissent and opposition seems to have been a feature of their way of working in most areas where they exercised power. For instance, their influence over the selection of players for the tour resulted in seven Railway employees being chosen for the squad (and the exclusion of specified others).

A press conference outlining the social itinerary for the tour was held (suitably) at the Labour Department in Lagos by Holley. The team would practice at Bellefield, Everton's training ground, and at Highbury Stadium, home of Arsenal. They would also meet the Mayors of Liverpool, Manchester, London and Leyton. Various trips had been arranged to Buckingham Palace, the Guildhall and Mansion House amongst others.

The party sailed from Lagos on 16 August, sent off by a large crowd along with the Bishop of Lagos and 'many important European and African personalities', with a message of support from Governor Sir John McPherson. The players, travelling third class, ran around the deck four times each morning to keep fit. Disembarking at Liverpool 13 days later, they were greeted with a message from the Duke of Edinburgh and interviewed by the BBC for *Radio Newsreel*, (recorded in both English and West African languages) for broadcast back home to the Tropics. Television and film crews also captured their arrival. Holley said his team came as 'ambassadors of friendship'[23], a term that was to be echoed by future tourists.

A hard and strenuous fixture list against some of the top amateur teams, including the FA Amateur Cup holders and one professional side, stretched before them. Their first opponents were Marine FC at Crosby in Liverpool, in front of 6,000 spectators.

The choice of Liverpool as the city in which to kick off the tour was practical, convenient but also symbolic: it was the Nigerians' first port of call; the British Council, who were looking after the tourists' accommodation arrangements, had a regional office in the city; and Merseyside also has one of the oldest black communities in Britain, dating back to the eighteenth century if not beyond. In 1948 its population stood at 8,000, swelled in number by those who had come to Britian to fight Hitler and fascism. In the same year, they suffered terribly from attacks by White racists whose motivation was shamefully legitimised by the National Union of Seamen's divisive and destructive policy of a colour bar on British-owned ships. Thus for some Black scousers of Liverpool and beyond, and anti-racists generally, the tourists' trouncing of Marine 5–2 was a needed boost to damaged morale. The *Liverpool Echo* acclaimed them as 'wizards in bare feet'. Without boots the Nigerians still put 'astonishing power . . . behind their kicking'. The speed and brilliance of Titus Okere at outside-left was quickly spotted, who 'given the experience could find a place in most English League sides'. The return of the 'wizards' a month later to play their parting game against professional South Liverpool FC, reaffirmed the suitability of the analogy. Their phenomenal speed was compared to that of the legendary Moscow Dynamo side that had captivated Britain's entertainment-hungry footballing public immediately after the war. 'Fastest since the Dynamos' ran the headline in the *Echo*, 29 September. 'To see them give five yards in fifteen to a home player and beat him to the ball was to witness something new in football speed.' A record crowd of 13,007 saw these footballing 'MacDonald Baileys' (a contemporary Black sprinter) play out their tour with a 2–2 draw.

The game had the added significance of being under lights, the first at the ground. Under the gaze of the media, the occasion also unveiled the contradictory nature of cultural attitudes in immediate post-war Britain. The Saturday edition of the *Echo* played up the dark–light theme with a cartoon. First man: 'Is that a Nigerian flying down the wing?' Second man: 'No, I think it's a bat.' This conversation was held under the caption: 'Floodlight was necessary because it's always difficult to find a black man in the dark.' The readers' entertainment at the expense of the 'darkies' was rounded off with an excuse for the lack of goal attempts made by the home-team forwards. 'I think Liverpool were instructed not to shoot until they saw the whites of their eyes.'[24]

While in Liverpool, the tourists were guests at a reception hosted by the British Council to which colonial African students were invited, but not other Black residents of the city. It was poorly attended. In Manchester, the tourists were received by the Mayor and entertained by G.B. Ollivant and Co., though they didn't kick a ball in the city. In fact, the social schedule was so busy that players complained they didn't have enough time to train. Three games in total were played outside London, against the two Liverpool clubs at either end of the tour, and in the north east against Bishop Auckland, the top amateur club of the region. This was the Nigerians' second game after Marine. This time BA won by 5–2 in front of a record crowd of 13,000. *The Times*, 5 September 1949, felt the Africans were tired: 'Two games within six days of arriving in England proved too much for the Nigerians who, while giving an attractive display, lacked the dash and stamina of their opponents.'

Amateur Sport, 10 September 1949, the house journal of amateur football in England, saw things a little differently. 'The speed and footwork of these Nigerians were amazing and the crowd were thrilled by 70-yard clearances from the bare-footed lads.' The visitors' strength, accuracy and confidence when shooting also left its mark. 'Bobby Davison [of BA] swore after the game that Henshaw [captain of the tourists] knew he would score as he walked to take the [free-] kick. It went into the net as if jet-propelled.' The journal urged all who could to 'see these fine sportsmen from Nigeria'.

Fans had greater opportunities to do this in the south where they played six games, three against amateur league representative teams, the others against top amateur club sides. In London, the Nigerians trained at Highbury: the ground of the team of the works that supplied guns for the conquest of Africa! The first game of their 'London season' – their coming out – as 'Pangloss' of the *News Chronicle*, 9 September 1949 put it with courtly metaphor, was against Leytonstone. The East London club were 'probably the most outstanding English amateur side of the last three seasons',[25] winning the FA Amateur Cup twice in that period. In the metropolitan capital of the Empire, the Nigerians were officially welcomed by the British political Establishment. Present at the Leytonstone game were A.G. Bottomley MP, secretary for overseas trade, David Rees-Williams, Under-Secretary of State for the colonies, Stanley Rous, secretary of the FA and Sir Adeyemo Alakija of the Nigerian Legislative Council. There were also other minor politicians and administrators at the game including representatives of London boroughs and further members of the FA. A notable feature of the crowd of over 10,000 was the number of Africans (and those of African origin). Leytonstone scored in the last minute to win 2–1. The Nigerians had 'impressed' with their 'fast, quick thinking', bringing the 'best out of Leytonstone'.[26] Edgar Kail of the *Daily Graphic* eulogised upon their performance:

> Their ball control is . . . uncanny and is a form of caress that is helped by
> the spreading of the toes . . . Okere is worth £15,000 and a row of houses.
> Their artistry is superb, their deportment and their behaviour exemplary,
> and they will beat more of our leading amateur sides than will beat
> them.[27]

A reception was held in the evening at which Mr Rees-Williams praised the team
and those who'd arranged the tour. He announced that Henshaw would be
staying behind to study marine engineering and that if the tour was successful,
Britain may send a Nigerian team to the next Olympics. What relevance the
'success' of the footballers had to Nigerian athletes' suitability as Olympians
wasn't made clear. For those who read between the lines, the message was both
loud and plain: do right by us and we'll do right by you. Yeah!

Two days later the tourists met the Isthmian League. Such was the Nigerians'
reputation by now that Arthur Salter of *Amateur Sport*, 17 September 'was quite
prepared to see the Isthmian League beaten'. And some commentators – *WA*, 17
September – even thought that playing in bare feet gave the West Africans an
unfair advantage because their Isthmian League opponents were 'reluctant to
play a full-blooded tackling game'. However, this consideration didn't last long as
'several Nigerians were hobbling towards the end'. Despite losing 6–1, Salter felt
the West Africans 'whatever the result . . . are good box-office-value footballers
who enjoy their game'. His report picked out the strengths and weaknesses of the
tourists' game, speed being their number-one asset and covering and positional
play the areas they needed to improve on. Individually they had some fine players
with Okere the pick of the forwards and Ottun (right-back) and Ibiam
(goalkeeper) standing out as defenders.

Prior to their third match in London, against the Corinthian League, the
visitors were entertained by the United Africa Company (UAC). UAC had a
team in the Lagos League and had donated £500 to the tour fund. The company
was a historic exploiter of Africa's natural resources. The outstanding feature of
their performance, according to 'Pangloss', was the 'superb passing of the
Nigerian left-wing pair Anike and Okere'. Unfortunately the partnership could
not conjure a win. It ended on level terms, 2–2. So ended the first half of the
Nigerians' sojourn in the 'mother country' of the Empire. The results – one win,
a draw and three defeats – had not been spectacular but their general
performance, integrity, athleticism and agility had created many friends.

The pace off the pitch had been almost as frantic as on it, with the programme
for the following week 'full of social engagements, including a tea party at the
Colonial Office, visits to parliament, Westminster Abbey, Kew Gardens and
Wembley Stadium'.[28]

The final week in London saw the Nigerians play three matches: against
Dulwich Hamlet, the Athenian League – rated the strongest of the amateur
representative teams – and Amateur Cup winners Bromley. Reporting on the
Nigerians' first match which resulted in a 1–0 defeat, *WA*, 24 September,

noted:'The Nigerians produced all their tricks . . . but luck was never on their side'. Their worst defeat of the tour followed, 8–0, by the Athenian League. Arguably it had much to do with the weather (see the boots controversy above), the rain and muddy pitch which literally messed up the Africans' barefooted play. The adoption of boots by some in the second half merely swapped one inconvenience for another, depriving the players of their primary instrument of ball control, their toes. This was the only match where the weather had been unkind. September 1949 was the warmest since records began in 1871 and the driest for 20 years.

Their last game in London and penultimate one in England was the 'Big One': versus Bromley, the amateur team of the moment, holders of the biggest prize in their section of football. At half-time it looked as though another defeat loomed with the score at 1–0, even though 'Bromley were lucky to lead at the interval . . . but in the second half the cup holders were completely outplayed . . . The speed and opportunism of the visiting side were brilliant.' The 10,793 spectators witnessed more than a usual display of athleticism and quick thinking. 'The Amateur-Cup holders were unsettled by the unusual formation of Anyiam at centre-half playing as a sixth forward.' Praise for tactical awareness and flexibilty was something new. It was a measure of their 'willingness to learn' that such an improvement had brought such a swift reward – a 3–1 win.[29]

The games in London had given sports writers such as 'Hibernicus', 'Pangloss' and Arthur Salter a chance to assess the development of football in Britian's most populous African colony. Judgement extended beyond the assessment of sporting skills. In his 'review' of the Nigerians' trip, 'Pangloss' was noticeably enchanted:

> No touring side has ever been so popular with our amateur soccer public
> . . . Their zest for the game, their willingness to learn, the thoroughly
> sporting way they accepted the referees' decisions, and the gentlemanly
> manner in which they fetched the ball when they conceded a corner kick
> deservedly earned the plaudits of our crowds.[30]

Verdict: the Nigerians were not simply footballers, they were also gentlemen. It was their adherence to a sports code, not the results, which was the primary influence upon the minds of these football critics and therefore upon the complexion and tone of their evaluation. In a letter to the editor of *WA*, 24 September, 'Hibernicus' asserted that the tour had not only been 'successful' but provided for many Britons a cathartic cultural experience:

> The conduct of the African on the sportsfield has contributed
> considerably to the abolition of the old idea existing among so many of
> the British public that the Africans are just a woollyheaded nebulous sort
> of people.

The tourists had proved, through action, that the remaking of the colonised

African was continuing to plan. But the very success of the Nigerian footballers, added 'Hibernicus', should also be a warning about potential hazards. 'Football has attained such a remarkable place in Nigeria's social and industrial life, that there is a danger that it may even become entangled with politics and professionalism. It would be a great pity if that were to happen.' He warned against the spiritual decline that would inevitably occur should the players be openly paid for their labour:

> Those in Africa and many in the UK who have contributed so generously and disinterestedly to finance the recent visit will undoubtedly do so again, but only because they admire the spirit and enthusiasm of the amateur. It is right that the players should fully realise this, and also that they are considered sportsmen in the real sense of the word, uninfluenced by politics, racial bias or political gain.

'Hibernicus' and many other British-based sports writers understandably had a limited awareness of the machinations going on in Lagos. They – and 'Hibernicus' in particular – fell hook, line and sinker for the agenda set by the sporting barons of Lagos. 'Hibernicus' failed to recognise that the players were 'sportsmen' *despite* the activities of the administrators. Of course, within the administration of sport in Nigeria there were differences in style and approach. In fact, Holley was praised in the *WAP*, 12 October 1949, for 'brilliantly piloting the team to and from the UK'. And his wife, to her credit, coached ZAC swimmers. Thus, while all expatriates involved in organising the tour would want to put on a good show 'back home', the methods used by individuals in the colony to ensure success may have differed. Welch and Urion were criticised in Zik's press for their manner in settling industrial disputes on the Railways, the inefficiency of the system itself, their unprincipled poaching of players and their influence upon rule-making to obstruct the success of African-managed teams. And there was a clear inference that the same methods applied to both work and play: for these two it was not the playing of the game but the winning of it that mattered. While such a manipulation – politicisation – of football creates an uneven surface, it can also lead to greater satisfaction when those playing the whole game pushing up the hill and against the wind are victorious. A defeat of Railways by ZAC on the football field would have had implications on the engine footplate, amongst the station porters, even amongst the relatively privileged clerks.

From the perspective of the colonial régime and FA in Nigeria, the tour had achieved its objectives even if it did bring friendly warnings about the future direction of the game in West Africa. The economy of Britain's most prized African possession – with its immense mineral resources – was dominated by the United Africa Company. Closer cultural links such as those acted out by the tour would, it was hoped, smooth and enhance the de-colonisation process. This would help steady the nerves of European capital about their ability to continue to export goods and profits from Nigeria once the protection of the colonial state had gone.

For the players it brought mixed blessings. It had certainly raised the status of Nigerian players: many of them had shown they were equal, at least, to many of their opponents. Titus Okere was the star of the show and is reported to have signed for Swindon in the early '50s, although there is no record of him having played for the first team. Henshaw, who stayed on in Britain, had 'been the subject of several enquiries by Football League clubs'. He eventually signed for Cardiff Corinthians, an amateur club, while studying marine engineering at Cardiff Technical College. The player to achieve the greatest success as a returnee to Britain was Tesilimi 'Thunder' Balogun, whose career will be discussed later. For a few, such as Ottun, a draughtsman from the Marine department, the trip to Britain bequeathed a fatal legacy. He committed suicide soon after his return because 'he could not find a job commensurate with his skills'. Ironically he was nicknamed the 'Rock of Gibraltar' because of his sturdy defending. Another defender, Dankaro, 'disappeared'.[32]

The 1949 tour gained respect for West African football and footballers in Britain. Balogun was not the first from that region to play in the English League, but he certainly helped pave the way for others to follow. And this could only be good according to a conceited, patronising but not atypical *Times* editorial, 29 September, that heralded the departure of the squad:

> There is a special place in Africa for sport. The disappearance of tribal warfare and other inconvenient forms of self-expression has left a gap there. Too often, while exempt from terror and famine, the African peoples are nowadays powerfully afflicted with boredom. They need new interests, cultural and sporting. Given a chance, the African is a voracious reader and avid sportsman. The Nigerian visit has a sociological significance.

The success of the tour, both in football and political terms, led to further experiments in sports politics through football.

THE GOLD COAST TOUR 1951

Competitive football has been played in Ghana since at least 1881. It was from the then Gold Coast that Arthur Wharton originated, the first professional footballer of African descent. Unlike Nigeria, Africans in the Gold Coast were in control of their regional and state Fooball Associations. Nevertheless, the competition for a limited number of places on the tour party led to argument and dispute similar to that which had occurred in Nigeria. The important Kumasi-based Asante FA, in particular, felt that the officials of the national body, the United Gold Coast FA based in (Fante) Accra, had picked too many bureaucrats. The row also reflected tribal tensions between the vast interior kingdom of Asante, historically the most powerful grouping in the region, and the smaller, less numerous, longer-colonised Fante people of the coastal belt, over who should go.

Fund-raising too was beset by argument. Arrangements for financing the tour followed a pattern set by the Nigerians. There was a government grant and loan, and fund-raising activities involving popular and well-known political figures. Kwame Nkrumah, leader of government business in the Legislative Council and later to become the president of an independent Ghana in 1957, kicked off a match between two top clubs, Hearts of Oak and Standfast, to raise funds. The *Ashanti Times*, mouthpiece of Asante, criticised what it saw as the abuse of public money. It protested over the number of officials and the selection of players scheduled to tour, citing concern expressed by the collective voice of Asante football, The Kumasi Football Clubs Union. This 'electorate body of the Asante Football Association' had passed a resolution objecting to the disproportionate number of officials – six – being paid to accompany eighteen players. Of the eighteen players, eight were from Accra, eight from Kumasi (Asante), one from Sekondi and one from Cape Coast. The critical tone of the *Ashanti Times* contrasts with the uncritical comment of the Accra-based *Daily Echo* which was supportive of the United Gold Coast Football Association. Mr Richard Ackwei, vice-chairman of the UGCFA, a graduate of Christ Church College, Oxford, and Accra schoolmaster, replied to the accusation that the size of the playing squad was small and lacking in quality. The primary mission of the visit, he argued, was not to win at all costs but to foster good diplomatic relations.

> We are going as ambassadors of Gold Coast football . . . [to] play the game for the love of it and show British sportsmen the standard we have reached . . . The winning of matches is not our objective, but the promotion of brotherly love, mutual understanding and friendly co-operation between the Gold Coast and Britain. This, we contend, is a far nobler aim than the winning of matches.[33]

The fixture opened with three matches in Ireland. In Belfast the bare-footed Gold Coasters lost 5–2 to a representative amateur XI of the Irish FA and 4–2 to top-club side Cliftonville. In the Republic they lost 4–3 to a Football Association of Ireland amateur XI. In Britain they lost 5–3 to Welsh-League side Lovells Athletic. Then it was off to London for five games, versus: Romford 2–1 (defeat); the Isthmian League 10–1 (defeat); Walthamstow Avenue 3–1 (defeat); Barnet 5–4 (victory) which was televised by the BBC; and the Athenian League 5–4 (victory). Cliftonville and Lovells Athletic were semi-professional. The other sides were high quality amateurs. The Athenian League had beaten the Nigerians 8–0. The last match was in Liverpool, the port of departure, and resulted in a 6–3 defeat by Marine.

Comparison with their West African near-neighbours, Nigeria, was inevitable.

The number of victories was equal, although they suffered three more defeats. Despite the poor record, they made an impression with their attitude, speed, accuracy and agility. In Dublin, the *Evening Mail*, 23 August, noted their 'grand play, their ball-juggling moves and their fine display of sportsmanship' so captured the affection of the crowd that many of the latter began shouting in support of the visitors. However, only E.B.H. Wallace Johnson of Argonauts FC stayed in Britain. He signed for Hendon FC while studying photo-engraving.

After their first match against an Irish FA amateur XI a civic reception was held in Belfast. In his speech to the assembled footballers and VIPs, Ackwei continued with his theme of sport as a mechanism for bringing people together. The *Belfast Telegraph*, 14 August 1951, remarked patronisingly on the teacher's 'fluent English' when summarising Ackwei's over-optimistic speech that 'it was only through sportsmanship that the brotherhood of man could be established, and their sole purpose was to play the game as it should be played'. In the Republic, as guests of the Holy Ghost Fathers in Blackrock College, Dublin, they had a meeting with the Taoiseach Éamon De Valera and the Lord Mayor of Dublin. Had Ackwei chosen to highlight his country's struggle for independence from British rule rather than trumpet his favourite theme of sportsmanship and play by the rules, his message would have reached even more sympathetic ears, given that he was in Eire, formerly Britain's oldest colony.

However, it would be a mistake to view Ackwei as a man ever ready to do his imperial masters' bidding. The Colonial Office in Britain was pressing ahead with its plans for self-government in the Gold Coast, which in fact became the first British colony in sub-Saharan Africa to win independence. A colonial administrator, Canham, called the period from 1948 'the last lap of colonial rule'.[34] Ackwei and the tourists knew they would be seen as representatives of an emerging Ghana. In this respect they felt they had to prove their trustworthiness. And prove it they did. Before beating Barnet 4–3 on the infamous sloping Underhill pitch – a feat which gained a 'great ovation' from the crowd – pleasantries were exchanged at a civic luncheon at Barnet Council Chamber. Councillor A. Booth, chairman of the Council, welcomed the visitors. He commented that it was apparent that in politics as in football these Gold Coasters showed great respect for rules and laws. After the match, they attended another reception as guests of Barnet FC. On both occasions Ackwei delivered the same message: you have nothing to fear (from us soon-to-be-empowered Africans). 'You have made us feel we are all brothers.' The backslapping was infectious. 'Pegasus', the sports reporter, wrote:

> These coal-black soccer craftsmen, who at home are civil servants, students and artisans must have promoted more goodwill in 90 minutes' inspired play than the whole of the UN Assembly in a month of Sundays.[35]

The *Ashanti Times*, 7 September 1951, in its 'editorial viewpoint' noted that 'the results of the matches played so far . . . have been one of the main topics of conversation in the country'. But, the editor argued, the results had proved 'it [had been] too early to send a team'. The poor playing record was nevertheless put down to wet and muddy pitches rather than simply being outclassed by the opposition. Next time, promised team secretary Sidney Ackun, boots would be worn. Yet despite the downbeat tone set by the results, by independence in 1957 a two-way passage of football migrants had begun moving up and down the Atlantic Ocean. British coach George Ainsley was employed by the Ghanaian government to coach Real Republicans FC, a creation of the first minister of sport, Ohene Djan. Stanley Matthews was also invited to Ghana and, dressed in Kente robes of the Asante, was crowned 'Soccerthene' (king of soccer). His former club, Blackpool, had included Ghana on their tour itinerary and were beaten 5–0 by the 'Black Stars', the national team. Travelling in the opposite direction was Black Star John Mensah – following in the boot steps of Wallace Johnson and Arthur Wharton – who played for Southern League Cambridge City in the early 1960s. The most notable recent Ghanaians to sign for British clubs are Tony Yeboah of Leeds United, who won *Match of the Day*'s 'Goal of the Season' for 1995–96, Nii Odartey Lamptey of Aston Villa and Marcel Desailly of Chelsea, thus continuing a West African presence in English professional football that began with Arthur Wharton.

EAST AFRICA: THE UGANDA TOUR 1956

The first recorded match in this former East African Protectorate of the British Empire took place in 1903:

> During a recent holiday in Busoga, I took part in a football match between Iganga and Jinja. This is, I suppose, the first real match amongst the natives. The Iganga men walked over to Jinja with Mr Skeens and Mr Owrid who played on their side, while Mr Buckley, Sergeant Moss and myself played for Jinja. But there was no resisting the Iganga team; they beat us handsomely by nine goals to one. The point of interest is that there seems to be a certain discipline at work for these men to learn to keep their places at football, and that some *esprit de corps* is engendered which is a great thing amongst naturally indigent people. Football may be a means of grace.[36]

The writer, in his description, recognised how the skills learnt in football could be used to reshape a people and their culture: a sense of place, of cameraderie, of discipline could be trained into seemingly lazy but malleable subjects. If achieved, the task of pacification and Europeanisation as 'burdened' upon the missionary, teacher, district commissioner, soldier and trader would be eased. The spread of football in Uganda was also speeded by the fact that Kabaka (King) of Baganda, Dandi Chwa, was tutored (after 1906) by Oxford graduate John Sturrock. He introduced the game to Chwa, the Kabaka of the largest ethnic group in the Protectorate. Sturrock, like the writer above, also recognised the advantage football could bring to the imperial project. If the Kabaka played – and played to the rules in the widest sense of the term – his people would follow.

> [Sturrock] had a football ground made within the Lubiri on which he taught the Baganda youth, including the Kabaka, the rules of the game . . . The boys took to football like lame ducks to water. Before long we were able to include some of them amongst the European teams.[37]

As colonialism entrenched itself in twentieth-century Uganda, those children attending missionary schools, with their ethos of Muscular Christianity, would have learned the game from a young age. By the end of the first decade of this century, many missionary schools had their own teams. The moral agenda of these institutions put personal development, according to Christian principles, ahead of academic or technical achievement. Indigenous song, dance and dress were suppressed. Africans were given British names. Anglo-Saxon culture was elevated, African traditions denigrated. Yet such was the attraction of the game to Bagandan youths that 'Mweso and wrestling and stick throwing are now no longer the national pastime of the Baganda. For some years past, football has absorbed a share in their youthful enthusiasm.'[38] Twenty-one years after the first recorded game, Uganda had its own Association, the Federation of Ugandan Football (FUFA) which was formed in 1924.

Uganda was born out of the 'scramble for Africa' during the last quarter of the nineteenth century. The document that conferred 'legality' on this colonial take-over was the 1900 Agreement. One of the clauses allowed Baganda, the most populous ethnic region within the new Protectorate of Uganda, a limited form of self-rule. It also gave the Bagandans a privileged administrative role over other Africans within the multi-ethnic Protectorate.

The collaboration of the Bagandan élite began to lose its usefulness for the British colonial government after 1945. In 1949 a general strike and nationwide uprising broke out. A number of issues – Bagandan collaboration with the colonial régime, political reform and wages and conditions – had fuelled discontent amongst workers and peasants to burning point. Subsequently the Bagandan monarchy fell out with Governor Andrew Cohen over their diminished role in a reformed political system with Kabaka Mutessa II being exiled by Cohen in 1953. This political turbulence led to the appointment of a Royal Commission. Unsurprisingly it recommended a free-market route for economic development. In its socio-psychological analysis of African nationalist leaders, it put their 'embitterment' down to failure in business! 'Frustrated and dissatisfied . . . these are the new leaders of the African.' The duty of governments, said the report's authors, is the creation 'of a responsible African middle-class who can meet members of other races on equal terms'. This could not be done solely through 'associations which provide artificial links between the different elements in the population by promoting leisure activities' such as sport and leisure clubs. Rather, 'the stability of a community depends on the awareness of a genuine identity of [economic] interests among its members'.[39] In other words, encouraging middle-class Africans to see that they have a common (economic) interest with middle-class Whites. The off-pitch agenda of the football tour in this new political era therefore had a specific purpose: to foster a Ugandan identity amongst an emergent, multi-ethnic African middle-class that would be pro-western and capitalist.

FUFA included both Africans and Europeans. Those officials chosen to tour were Malcolm Harris, a sports officer representing the Northern Province; J.W. Kiwanuka, vice-president of the Baganda FA and member of the Lukiko, the Bagandan parliament; P.K. Kakoza, representing the Western Province FA, and Peter Murphy, secretary of FUFA. Harris would be in charge of training the squad whose occupations included two district sports officers, a captain in the Uganda police, an Oxford student, Okot p'Bitek – who was later to become a world-renowned poet – and a European assistant district commissioner, Peagram. The last, said Harris in the *Uganda Argus* (*UA*), 5 October 1956, '[was] the only white man in the territory good enough to make the grade'.

The organisers estimated that £9,550 would be needed to cover the expenses for the first of the touring teams to travel by air. The Ugandan government offered £2,000 if a similar amount was raised from the public. Grants from the Bagandan government and provincial governments left a £6,000 shortfall. Novel ways of meeting the target were suggested by Canon J.B. Sturdy, education general secretary of the Church Missionary Society and honorary treasurer of FUFA, and by other interested individuals and groups. It was even suggested that there be a progressive tax upon ethnic groups: Africans one shilling, Asians two shillings and Europeans five shillings! Despite organising a fund-raising double-header with the main event a match between European notables and Baganda chiefs, Sturdy failed to reach the target. The government intervened with a questionable constitutional practice. It gave the tourists £1,000 and then asked for approval from the Legislative Council:

> Some might consider the government generous in the way it dealt with sports and sportsmen, but the total value of a tour of this kind far exceeded the value to any individual in the party . . . Such experience as members of the party gained would be passed on to hundreds of young Africans.[40]

This statement, by the deputy financial secretary of the government, makes clear that those [Africans] going would benefit culturally from their stay in Britain. And that, on return, they would repay politically that outlaid economically. The benefit would outweigh the cost.

Like Nigeria and the Gold Coast, the Ugandans preferred to play in bare feet which brought the usual and predictable problems when the pitch was wet and muddy. Against Peterborough United, one of three professional teams they played, they were forced to wear boots. 'It was a great pity that the heroic Uganda touring team had once again to play with their boots . . . accepting the fact that it hinders their speed and spoils their accuracy in shooting, the result might have been vastly different.'[41] The tourists won three of their 11 fixtures. If victories were weighted according to the quality and status of the opposition, the last against the British Olympic XI surely made up for the seven defeats. The British footballers, bound for the 1956 Melbourne Olympic Games, had two players signed with professional clubs, while others like forward Bob Hardisty of Bishop Auckland were players of great experience at the highest level of amateur football. The pitch was dry which allowed the visitors to 'play faster . . . more direct and intelligent football than the Olympic XI'.[42] A noted feature of the Ugandans' play was the high-leg kicking instead of heading. This balletic attribute had been recognised in the previous African tourists.

No players were signed by British clubs or later returned to play professionally. However 25-year-old Okot p'Bitek remained in the UK to study education, law and later anthropology. During the 1960s, he emerged as an internationally acclaimed poet. On the team's return to Entebbe, they were met by acting Governor Hartwell along with other African and European dignitaries. The fire brigade had to be sent to the airport in an effort to stop the anticipated large crowd swamping the tarmac. Commenting on their experience, Seruwagi, a forward and captain in the Uganda police, thought the spectators wonderful. Sittuma, a back and vice-captain felt 'our two opponents were the superior tactics of the English teams and the wet and slippery grounds'. Harris too revealed his uppermost thoughts. There is 'no better place for the different races of Africa to get together than on the field of sport'.[43] Unfortunately he didn't explain the absence of ethnic Asian players. (Asians comprised the second-largest group of ethnic peoples in Uganda, behind Africans.) Harris also envisaged sending teams to tour Rhodesia and participate in the Rome Olympics of 1960.

In 1968, the Ugandan national side, the Cranes, reached the African Cup of Nations final in Ghana and lost 2–0 to the hosts. The Cranes are the most successful national team within their regional confederation having won the Confederation of East and Central African Football Associations (CECAFA) Senior Challenge Cup eight times. However, success at an Africa-wide level since 1968 has been as elusive as Unilever and other European multi-nationals' expressions of guilt over their role in the imperialist rape of Africa. The frequent political in-fighting within FUFA and its strained relationship with the government doesn't help. Throughout 1994, the continent's governing body, the Confederation of African Football (CAF), banned all Ugandan teams from their competitions because of unpaid bills. Responsibility as to who should have paid was disputed by both FUFA and the government. Indeed, the wider administration of football in East Africa leaves a lot to be desired. In December 1998, CAF agreed to lift its three-month ban on members of the CECAFA competing in CAF tournaments.

The Trinidad Amateur Football Association (TAFA) was formed in 1908. The
president of the TAFA in 1953 was a European – Lieutenant Commander
Hayward. Trinidadian Eric James, the brother of Trotskyist C.L.R., was
honorary secretary and his compatriot Sonny Vincent Brown was vice-
president. James, who was the driving force behind the visit – and that of the
Caribbean tourists in 1959 – had in fact been in England in 1949, the year of
the Nigerians' visit, on a British Council football course. The Nigerians' exploits
may well have inpired him. Inter-colony matches began with British Guiana in
the mid-1920s. While the West Indies had sent cricket teams from as early as
1900, the 1953 visit was the first football excursion to Europe. Yet as has already
been dicussed in chapter two, a Trinidadian, Alfred Charles, had played professionally in Britain some 20 years earlier. The names of clubs in Trinidad
mimicked those of the English League, and each half of the game was usually
30 minutes long.

Both tours took place against a background of social, political and economic
unrest, symbolised by the Cuban revolution of 1959, a Caribbean event that had
a global consequence and repercussion. This revolution was part of an anti-
imperialist Caribbean tradition that stretched back to the successful slave
uprising led by Toussaint-Louverture in Haiti in 1796, the first Black democratic
republic of the modern era. The Caribbean region is sometimes euphemistically
labelled as being part of the New World. For those, such as myself, who were
taught a very selective view of Britain's past, it came as a shock to discover that
there has been a consistent British presence in the Caribbean since 1605.
Barbados had been a colony of the UK almost as long as Ireland.

It wasn't until 1944 in Jamaica and 1946 in Trinidad that most adults were
allowed to vote. Until this time, those of European descent dominated political
and economic life. The extension of the vote followed a series of revolutionary
uprisings across the British Caribbean during the years 1935–38, including a
general strike in Trinidad and revolts and strikes on the sugar plantations and
docks in Jamaica. After the uprisings the colonial administrators attempted to
neutralise anti-British nationalism by providing basic reforms such as democratic
elections. However if this (partial) democratisation threatened to seriously
interfere with the relations of power between the colonisers and the colonised
naked force, a reminder of the methods used in the slave era was used: the choice
of the people of British Guiana (BG) was put to one side in 1953 when the
Colonial Office decided it didn't like the political complexion of the newly
elected Jagan government, 'the only Communist colony of the Commonwealth'.
It sent 'naval and military forces'[44] to Georgetown, BG to restore the *status quo
ante.*

After the First World War, successive British governments had acknowledged
the rise of nationalism and internationalism within the new found trade union

and political organisation of West Indian workers. The policy challenge, for the colonisers, was to accommodate the rising tide of Black consciousness within a non-Communist resolution of their grievances. The solution offered by the Foreign and Commonwealth Office after the Second World War, when the momentum for independence became unstoppable, was a nominally independent West Indies Federation within the Commonwealth. This was established in 1958 but collapsed in 1962 when Jamaica declared full independence. Post-war relations between Britain and its Caribbean colonies and ex-colonies influenced the nature of the tours, why they were organised, and the way they were perceived and received, in the Caribbean and Britain, respectively.

THE TRINIDADIAN TOUR 1953

On the eve of departure, A.G. Alkins, football correspondent of the (Trinidad) *Evening News*, 6 August, wrote, 'With high hopes in their hearts . . . these pioneers of British West Indies football [travel] to the mother country, comprising the 20 best players in our colony . . . [and] will contest 13 matches in two and a half months'. The Trinidadian government provided a £5,000 loan to ensure the challenge took place.

In England the team had its day-to-day needs looked after by the West India Committee (WIC), an organisation originally established by British sugar planters and slave owners in the Caribbean. Colonel C.F. Linnitt, president of the Dorset FA, acted as liaison officer between the WIC and the FA and relevant County FA's with whom the tourists had arranged matches. All but two games would be in Western Britain – the West Country and Wales – 'where the FA at the moment is spending big sums of money encouraging soccer'.[45] Arriving at Southampton dock, the players were greeted by Sir Stanley Rous, secretary of the FA and the secretaries of County Associations. West India Committee chairman, Alan Walter, however, couldn't attend and sent a telegram. By absenting himself he missed the début rendition of the calypso 'Fire Brigade Water the Road, Trinidad is Coming Down', sung by the team to greet their welcomers.

The tourists, along with Harold Hobbis their British co-trainer, made a few friends in the West Country with the quality of their football. The Trinidadians' results were the most successful yet of any of the touring teams. Of 14 matches, they won 5 and lost 6. Their most notable victory was a 4–0 thrashing of Division Three (South) professionals Torquay United. The *Western Morning News* credited them with 'playing fast and intelligent football . . . with amazing speed and agility'. Their last game – a draw – against an FA representative XI contained Jamaican Gerry Alexander, captain of Cambridge University FC, cricket Blue and Cambridge City amateur. After this match, at a dinner in the evening, Linnitt argued that:

... sport will help international understanding. We have learnt a lot from the Trinidad visitors. We have discovered that their hearts beat just like ours and that they also enjoy a good game of football just like we do. If they carry back to their home country impressions like those we have gathered from them, then international understanding will be much nearer as a result of the visit.[46]

This military officer commanding the Dorset division of the Football Association – patron, Her Majesty the Queen – was well aware of the wider political significance carried by this football affair. However, his speech carries an inferred question that begs an answer: why, at the Empire's core, had some of its people not yet understood fully the culture and lifestyle of the colonised Trinidadians? The island had been seized from the Spanish in 1797 for the British Crown. Yet 156 years on, Colonel Linnitt felt the need to emphasise 'their hearts beat just like ours' and play up the shared characteristics of all those on the tour. And as an old soldier he'd been around the block a few times! For the visitors, Sonny Vincent-Brown, confirmed by way of reply that the Trinidadians knew more about the British than the other way round. He assured the old guardians of the Empire that the new inheritors would do their best to uphold past customs and traditions:

We may be far away from you in England but there is little difference between us. We appreciate you and are proud of the position Trinidad holds as a member of the British Commonwealth of Nations. We pray that the British Empire will continue to maintain its place in the leadership of the world.[47]

The sporting and diplomatic success of the 1953 'ambassadors' led to speculation in the Trinidad *Evening News*, 14 September, of a tour to the West Indies by an FA team 'next year'. This didn't occur. Instead, the British Caribbean FA sent a team in 1959.

THE CARIBBEAN TOUR 1959

The 1959 tour took place within a changed social and political environment, both in the UK and West Indies. In Britain, those on the right opposed to further Black settlement were engaged in a two-pronged assault on people of colour, by word and deed. On the same day that Paul Robeson sang in St. Paul's Cathedral to raise money for defendants in the South Africa Treason Trial, the Conservative Home Secretary R.A.B. Butler, sent a message to non-Whites. He roused the Tory Party Conference with the information that 'the government would very likely seek the power to deport out of Britain "undesirable residents"' from the Commonwealth.[48] In July 1959, one of Butler's Black 'undesirables' was shot in the hand by White youths. A year earlier there had been frequent and mob-handed violent beatings of Black people in Nottingham and Notting Hill. The racists, too, took a few hammerings.

In the Caribbean, the Cuban Revolution of 1959 provided inspiration to those people and groups determined to win independence from colonial rule. Meanwhile the British government had achieved their goal of a West Indies Federation. However, Jamaican premier Norman Manley, at odds with his island partners in the federation, still wanted independence for his country. Why remain part of a stitch-up by a governing party – the British Conservatives – that rubbishes Jamaicans at every opportunity? His government replied to the 'numbers game' played in the UK by people like R.A.B. Butler over Black settlement. An economic survey of Jamaica prepared by the Central Planning Unit in 1958 showed 2,371 British immigrants into the country out of a total of 2,600 immigrants. This represented British immigration to Jamaica as being 14 per 10,000 Jamaicans. In contrast, Jamaican immigrants to the UK represented four per 10,000 UK residents in the peak years of 1956–7.

Dominated by Trinidadians, the manager, trainer and captain of the Caribbean tourists were all veterans of '53. Eric James, who was now secretary of the British Caribbean FA, was again tour manager. Fellow Trinidadian and coach Noel Pouchet once more teamed up in Britain with trainer Harold Hobbis of Wolverhampton Wanderers, who had assisted the 1953 side. The Trinidadian bias was reflected in the composition of players, with nearly half – ten – coming from Trinidad, six from Jamaica, four from British Guiana and one from Barbados. The tourists returned to the West Country, but this time added East Anglia to their itinerary where in fact they played the majority of their games. While in the region they lodged at Corpus Christi College Cambridge, using it as a base for matches against Ely City (won 2–1) and Newmarket Town (won 3–1). The *Cambridge Daily News*, 26 September, noted that Newmarket were not unaccustomed to Black footballers at their ground. Two African–Caribbeans, 'Choc' Grannum and 'Bowen' played for 'The Jockeys' just after the war. The other games in the region were against Kings Lynn (lost 3–1) and Wisbech (lost 5–4). At Portman Road, the home of Ipswich Town, they also played England Amateurs – losing 7–2 – travelling from their new base in London, where opposition included two professional clubs, Crystal Palace (lost 11–1) and Millwall (lost 5–1). The tourist played over two games a week, winning four and losing eleven. They scored in all but two games, but were weak defensively and conceded 52 goals.

Back in the Caribbean, the tour attracted greater interest in Trinidad than the other islands. Not surprising, given the composition of the squad. In terms of column inches, the Trinidad papers, the *Guardian* and *Port of Spain Gazette*, gave more coverage to the visit than the Kingston-based *Jamaican Times* and *Daily Gleaner*.

Although one of the 1959 tourists, Anthony Hill, trained with Fulham, none of the players from '53 or '59 signed for British professional clubs.

However, during the 1950s Jamaicans Lindy Delapenha and Gil Heron were turning out for Middlesbrough and Celtic respectively. Now, in the 1990s, footballers of African–Caribbean origin and descent are a common feature of the game in Britain, where Black players form around 15 per cent of full-time professionals.

FOUR

Nurses, Tubeworkers and Footballers

Travelling to Work 1945–70

After 1945, for the first time in the history of professional football in Britain, the insularity, arrogance and short-sightedness of the game's administrators was tempered by a shifting balance of power between employers and employees. Workers were more confident, bosses less so. This shift had been influenced by a generalised labour shortage occurring in the wider economy, encouraging workers to demand better pay and working conditions. Trade union membership grew and union officials, shop stewards and members had a greater influence in the workplace. In 1946, 2,158,000 working days were lost through strike action. In 1970 this had risen to 10,980,000. During this period, and because of these actions, working people retained an increasing share of the wealth they produced.

Some sectors, most notably the National Health Service, transport and football were unable to recruit enough labour from the pool available in Britain. They looked to, among other places, the Caribbean. And in the case of football, some clubs even chanced their arm in Africa – to cast their eye over White players! In the process, however, scouts and their local agents – players, coaches and managers – increasingly noticed the wealth of Black talent on offer. And, more importantly, actively sought them out as potential employees.

Between April 1948 (when Portsmouth signed Jamaican Lindbergh 'Lindy' Delapenha as a full-time professional from Arsenal where he had played as an amateur) and 1968 (when West Ham signed fellow West Indian Clyde Best from Somerset FC, Bermuda) nine key migrant footballers, and a number of lesser ones, have been identified. Best was the only one 'discovered' in the Caribbean.

Why did football clubs not look to the English speaking West Indies, in common with recruiters in health and transport? Some kind of answer emerges if we compare the histories of the development of modern – 'British' – sports in Africa and the Caribbean. In the former, especially in the west and south of the continent which provided the majority of football migrants, soccer was the most popular sport of urban Blacks. However in the West Indies, longer colonised and with a more finely graded racial hierarchy, cricket was the premier sport. Only in Trinidad did football climb to the shoulders of cricket's towering popularity.

Those in charge of football attempted to ensure that Black, White and Coloured didn't mix. The administration of sport should conform to the principle of apartheid: 'separate development'. The Nationalist Party under Dr Malan stood on this platform – the separate development of the 'races' of South Africa – in the 1948 elections and won. The vast majority of South Africans did not vote. However there were alternative unofficial organisations that attempted to organise sport without reference to colour. Our discussion of football in South Africa needs to be aware of its intensely political context.

Three players were recruited from South Africa between 1956 and 1961: Stephen Mokone, Gerry Francis and Albert Johanneson. Mokone was the first Black South African footballer to be allowed a passport to play abroad. From the 1920s numerous White South Africans had been signed by British clubs. G. Hodgson of Liverpool, in the decades before the Second World War, set a scoring record and played for England. The Anfield teams of this period contained at least two other White South Africans: goalkeeper Riley and outside-right Berry Nieuwenhuys. The side that won the First Division Championship on its resumption in 1946–47 included another compatriot, Robert Priday. However it was Charlton Athletic, managed by Jimmy Seed, who employed the greatest number: Dudley Forbes, Stuart Leary, Ronald Oosthuizen, Sydney O'Linn – and Eddie Firmani who became a household name in Britain and Italy through his much publicised transfers. There also seems to have been a willingness by the British FAs to select South Africans for their representative XIs. The English were particularly keen. As well as G. Hodgson, also chosen were F. Osborne (1924–6), R. Osborne (1927–8) and W. Perry (1955–6). J. Hewie played for Scotland (1955–60) and P. Kelly for Ireland (1949–50).

The apparent eagerness of British clubs to scout, trial and sign White South Africans was down to a number of factors: the early development of competitive football in South Africa; the superior facilities enjoyed by White South African footballers; familial and fraternal contacts between members of clubs in Britain and South Africa; and racial prejudice. The primary factor however, more important even than the last named – but linked – is cultural prejudice: British club managers thought White South Africans would fit in to the dressing-room/training-ground environment and settle comfortably in Britain. This is discussed in more detail later.

Southern Africa played a pioneering role in the development of football on the continent. Football clubs began forming in the 1870s, though regular national competition did not begin until the 1890s. This 20-year interval between club formation and nationwide contest was characterised by an uneven pace of growth of the game in the various provinces and states: Natal appears to have been at the vanguard of development, with several clubs in Maritzburg and Natal itself. By 1899, as discussed in the previous chapter, a Black African team from Basutoland called the 'Kaffirs' toured Britain under the auspices of the Orange Free State FA.

Even before the election of the unashamedly racist Malan government in 1948 there had been segregationist pressures in sport. Thabe describes how Black footballers became more concerned with establishing their own administrative bodies after the First World War, the military conflict galvanising Black grass-roots political movements. He cites Soloman 'Snowy' Senaone as the founding father of the Johannesburg Bantu FA (JBFA), whose goal was to 'place football amongst the natives on a sound footing'.[1] The JBFA wanted control of all football grounds allocated to Africans in the Johannesburg area. From the JBFA grew the regionwide Transvaal Bantu FA and then the nationwide South African Bantu FA (SABFA). However, rival organisations were also forming such as the Johannesburg African FA (JAFA). Thabe thinks it was ethnic, geographical and social differences that lay behind this fracture. Yet it was through co-operation between JBFA, JAFA and SABFA that inter-ethnic matches were organised under the composite Transvaal Inter-Race Soccer Board.

During the inter-war years, a number of succesful Black clubs were formed including the Orlando Pirates (1937) who were South African champions in 1997. In addition, the first international between Black representative teams in Southern Africa took place in 1934 when a JBFA XI played a Bechuanaland XI.

From 1948, with apartheid now official government policy, football was under even greater pressure to divide ethnically into White, Coloured and African leagues. What in fact occurred was indeed a three-sided division, but structured White, non-White and non-Racial. During the 1950s the struggle for control of football became intense. The (White) Football Association of South Africa (FASA) was the official governing body, recognised by FIFA under the presidency of Englishman Sir Stanley Rous. (Indeed it was his inability to challenge effectively the racialised nature of football in South Africa that eventually lost him his job.) Affiliated to FASA was the National Football League (NFL) which represented all the White professional clubs and some non-White professional teams. Opposed to this body was the South African Soccer Federation (SASF), not recognised by FIFA but seeking to oust the FASA as the official representative body. Affiliated to SASF was the non-racial South African Soccer League. SASL claimed that most non-White professional clubs were members and importantly, in Natal, it claimed to have several White club members. I'm sorry if I've overloaded you with organisations and their acronyms! The point I'm trying to get across is that South African football was highly politicised. As has been said many times about apartheid South Africa, 'You cannot have normal sport in an abnormal society.'

These competing institutions within South African football mirrored the political division of society into, fundamentally, those who opposed apartheid and refused to work with it and those willing to work with, and/or maintain, the system. The umbilical relationship football had with politics is exemplified by Albert Luthuli, president of both SASF and the African National Congress, and by Dr James Moroka, elected president-general of the African National Congress in 1949 and founder of Moroka Swallows FC. With R.G. Baloyi, he donated the Baloyi–Maroka Cup to be contested by Black teams.

It is no coincidence that both the non-White footballers and non-White peoples of South Africa simultaneously stepped up their campaigns of defiance to apartheid in the 1950s. Wider political developments couldn't help but shape football and its role in popular culture. While anti-apartheid activists were putting their lives at risk for a non-racial state, in 1955 SASF publicly announced their claim to be the official administrative body of football in South Africa and called for the expulsion of FASA from FIFA. (Steve Mokone, the first Black South African to play professionally in Europe, claims to have lobbied Sir Stanley Rous at the Dorchester Hotel in London while playing for Coventy City.) FIFA responded by initiating the Lotsy Commission to investigate the administration of football in SA and determine whether it conformed to the agreed rules and requirements applicable to all (FIFA) affiliated members. FASA was forced to act. It immediately struck out the colour-bar clause from its constitution.

Ultimately, despite making certain suggestions, nothing concrete came the findings of the commission although it did force the issue of apartheid in football firmly on to FIFA's agenda. In 1958 FIFA did indeed concede that FASA was racist but declined to recognise SASF. In fact, despite its condemnation of FASA, it continued to treat that body leniently. Two years later FIFA gave FASA 12 months to de-racialise football under its control. It failed, and in September 1961 was suspended by FIFA. Digging in, FASA reiterated their intention to ensure ethnic separation in football. To this end, in November 1961, it created the Transvaal Professional League specifically for African Footballers.

FASA, however, found itself squeezed between two powerful forces: the government which continued to advocate and implement apartheid; and SASF who wanted rainbow football. Matches that were inter-ethnic and teams that were ethnically mixed were messed about and messed up by the government and police: SC Lourenco Marques from Mozambique were told that their match with Durban City, scheduled for February 1962, had been cancelled because the ethnic mix of their team violated South African government policy; the Coastals FC of Durban, with White, African and Asian players, found special branch detectives warning off their White contingent. To their credit, the Coastals ignored the police threats.

FASA reluctantly acknowledged that their stance of separate development and fucking-up the opposition would not allow FIFA to lift their ban. Consequently, in April 1962, representatives of segregated and non-segregated football met in Durban. Though no practical solutions were agreed, the meeting was a preliminary exploration into the possibility of accommodating non-Whites within the administrative executive of South African football. Yet eight months later FASA declared, 'We will have no more negotiations with [SASF]', and re-dedicated themselves to separate development.[2]

FIFA returned to South Africa in 1963 with a heavyweight investigative team: none other than president Sir Stanley Rous, accompanied by James McGuire of the USA FA. From the outset, Rous was not seen as impartial by SASF officials because of his publicly stated anxiety over FASA's suspension by FIFA. In their meetings with the Englishman, SASF found him partisan and dictatorial.[3] To the latter's anger, Rous and McGuire recommended to the FIFA executive the lifting of FASA's suspension, which was duly carried by eleven votes to six. It was a decision that African football administrators and their allies in other parts of the world were not to forgive or forget. When elections for the presidency of FIFA were held ten years later, African countries backed Brazilian Joao Havelange, who promised a greater influence for Africa in FIFA affairs, against Rous. If only . . .

Rous did not feel that the non-White SASF were able, suitable or responsible enough to replace the White FASA. While he may have sincerely held his opinion, he was not seen to be fair by the vast majority of South Africans who saw in his apparent prejudice the mindset of a patronising colonial, a mentality characteristic of the English FA which for years had sent touring teams to South Africa – to play only White teams. The inaugural visit was in 1910, followed by three more during the inter-war period. In fact it was British league clubs rather than an FA representative team that first played Black opposition in Africa.

Stephen 'Kalamazoo' Mokone was the first Black South African allowed to play abroad. He is also one of the few to have co-written an autobiography, *Kalamazoo: Life and Times of a Soccer Player* – from his prison cell.

Mokone has been described as 'easily the greatest soccerite South Africa has ever produced'.[4] Born on 23 March 1932, at Doornfontein, a suburb of Johannesburg, he was soon noticed. According to his autobiography – which relies greatly on uncorroborated memory for obvious reasons – he was at 16 selected for a Black National XI, although it was while playing for Bush Bucks FC that he was invited to England for a trial by Stanley Cullis, manager of Wolverhampton Wanderers. Mokone's father said no, both to Cullis and a further approach by Newcastle United. In relation to the Magpie's offer, Mokone said he was not too disappointed because he found the accent of the visiting Newcastle official very difficult to understand. And there were no 'Learn Geordie' books knocking about locally that he could use to translate! However, these overtures did light up Mokone's imagination. He applied for his passport in 1952 and in March 1955, after investigation by the police into his political activities, it was issued.

In the summer of 1956 Mokone, a qualified teacher working as a clerk in the Pretoria Native Affairs Department, joined Coventry City. He was met in London by ex-professional Charles Buchan, editor and founder of *Football Monthly*, who'd helped to raise £100 towards the cost of allowing the 24 year old to travel to Britain. Mokone had to leave a £100 surety with the SA authorities against returning destitute! While on trial Coventry provided work in the club offices at £5 per week. The low wage which amounted to little more than players would have received before the First World War and the overlong appraisal period was not what the young South African had expected. He felt he was being treated unfairly and confronted the manager. 'That's the trouble with you people,' he responded, 'you're never satisfied.'[5] Mokone signed a contract the following day.

Despite this unpromising start he got on well with the two other most important characters at the club, his coach George Raynor, with whom he shared a mutual respect, and his captain, who also encouraged him. However, he considered himself to be on the periphery of the dressing-room camaraderie – or worse 'ignored' – and was never invited to the house of a playing colleague. 'I could not get close to the players.'[6] Mokone played just four first-team games for the Division Three South club, and scored one goal. He made his début against Queens Park Rangers who had recently signed Nigerian international Tesilimi Balogun (whom he met for a photo shoot at the London offices of Charles Buchan's *Football Monthly*). Brought up to play in a different style, Mokone did not like the kick and rush, robust and, as he saw it, unmethodical approach of Coventry. He was similarly disenchanted with the training routine which he lamented, in large measure consisted of 'running around a track'. The technique of his colleagues did not overawe him. 'English players seem to have little finesse. They concentrate on fitness rather than ball control.'[7] He felt the climatic conditions under which football was played in Britain contributed to the game being 'stuck in the past'. Refined techniques could not be developed while playing in the snow! In contrast, surfaces in South Africa were invariably hard and uneven which necessitated learning the skill of immediate control or 'first touch', so important in the fast-paced professional game.

Though he felt isolated at Coventry City, and 'very lonely',[8] the White family with which he lodged were active in the anti-apartheid movement.

The following season he joined Heracles FC of the Dutch Second Division. Mokone writes that they enticed him to sign with $10,000. He scored twice on his floodlit début against Swedish club Goteborg. One of his team-mates argued he should have managed more because 'the opposition couldn't see you because you're Black'.[9] This hurt Mokone more than any kick from a defending donkey. Yet it was on the mainland of Europe that the outside-right was most content, both professionally and emotionally. He lists Marseilles and Torino as the other clubs he played for. It was in Turin that he was at his most comfortable, playing five seasons between 1961–66 for the number-one club of the motor city. A British team-mate was Gerry Hitchens.

Mokone's spell on the mainland was interrupted by a season, 1959–60, at Cardiff City of the Second Division. Again he scored on his début against Liverpool. He played for the following two games and was then dropped from the first team, never to regain his place. (At this time Leeds United had Gerry Francis, another Black South African winger and friend of Mokone's.) Cardiff finished runners-up and were promoted to Division One but 'Kala' did not share in the team's success.

Mokone found Europe a 'culture shock'. Blacks were, legally, equal to Whites. He could use the same toilets, talk to White women and move around without having to ask permission. This deepened his political conviction that apartheid must be destroyed in South Africa. While coaching and playing in Rhodesia in the early 1960s, he joined the Zimbabwe African Peoples Union (ZAPU), dedicated to overthrowing Ian Smith's White-might dictatorship. Mokone's determination had been steeled by a trip back to South Africa in July 1958. He was met by a crowd at the airport, which included White reporters, and their real presence confirmed the *symbolic* political significance of his achievements. 'My success could not be viewed independently of the South African struggle.'[10] Another visit nearly 20 years later to present the Sportsman of the Year award in Johannesburg was the occasion of even greater adulation. Guest of honour at an Orlando Pirates *v.* Kaiser Chiefs match, he was given a rousing welcome by a crowd of over 40,000.

At the dusk of his career, Mokone took a coaching job in Australia. Within six months he was back in Canada, his home after he left Torino in 1966. It could be argued that his experiences as a Black man in North America – particularly in the USA – were as politically formative as his South African upbringing. He took a degree at the University of Rochester in upstate New York and by the early '70s had a Ph.D. 'University campuses [during this time] were vibrant.'[11] To be a Black man in urban North America was to witness, and in Kalamazoo's case be active in, movements that forced issues of racism, civil rights and the Vietnam War on to the streets. Swept willingly along in this surging momentum of collective political struggle, Mokone, who believed he was under surveillance by the CIA and FBI, eventually found himself marooned behind the locked iron doors of the jailhouse – another number in a system that channels a greater number of African–American adults into prison than education.

By the end of the 1970s he had been convicted of seriously assaulting his wife by throwing acid in her face and was sentenced to 8–12 years. At another court on a later date, he was also found guilty of plotting a similar acid attack on his wife's lawyer and sentenced to a further, concurrent, prison term. He has always denied these charges, arguing that he was arrested in the first instance on a 'fabricated charge of credit-card fraud'. His autobiography tells of beatings, torture, threats and obstruction and denial of his constitutional rights by the police. Despite the court verdicts, given the racialised environment of the USA judicial system – 'being Black in America means being in jail' was Malcolm X's verdict on the courts – it is impossible to determine conclusively Mokone's guilt or innocence. There were influential figures from the anti-apartheid struggle who did believe Mokone's version of events. 'Bishop D. Tutu and professors Edwin Powell and Jeff Blum of the Buffalo University Law School, with students, fought for my release, organising picketing and student marches.'[12]

Banged up with a pen, writing during these bleak years he may have felt that he had swapped a South African nightmare for an American hell. Yet the demolition of apartheid in South Africa provided the opportunity for a similarly liberated Dr Mokone to start his life again. At the time of writing, 1999, he is South Africa Tourism's Goodwill Ambassador based in New York. He has also established the Kalamazoo South Africa Foundation for Education through Sport. In the autumn of 1997, this institution facilitated the transfer of 19-year-old Benedict McCarthy, seen as the rising star of South African football, to Ajax

Amsterdam. And a film script about Mokone, written by Dutch journalist Tom Egbers, has been optioned by Sigma Productions of Holland.

Football is the most popular sport in South Africa. British scouts had been active in the country since the 1920s. So why had no Black player been invited for trial before Mokone in 1956? Obviously, the restrictions on Black and Coloured movement after 1948, in the form of the Pass Laws, constrained the Black footballer. More influential, though, were the cultural values of agents and officials of British clubs. As has already been discussed, Jimmy Seed, manager of Charlton Athletic in the 1940s and '50s, introduced by far the greatest number of South Africans into the Football League – all White. These included Sydney O'Linn, Dudley Forbes, Stuart Leary and Eddie Firmani who went to play for Italy. Explaining in 1954 the reasons for his South African preference, Seed argued that the yield of footballers out of the pit villages of his native northeast England had 'apparently dried up, and we were forced to look elsewhere'. One scouting trip to South Africa in 1949 harvested four players: John Hewie, Norman Neilson, Stuart Leary and Eddie Firmani. In reply to the charge that he was overlooking indigenous Black African talent, the Charlton manager argued that he would sign players from anywhere 'irrespective of what country he comes from, provided . . . the player's character satisfied me that he is of the good club type.'[13]

Seed's partiality for White South Africans developed after he visited the country in 1929 as captain of an England XI. While there he made friends with George Brunton. It was Brunton who later suggested candidates to Seed, who in turn used Frank Bonniwell as his agent. Another contact was a Mr Priday whose son Robert was a professional in England. Indeed, by 1954, so many South Africans were playing in Britain that an Anglo-South African XI played the visiting (White) 'Springbok' football team. (Charlton FC toured South Africa the same year.) In 1955–6 the Scottish FA asked Seed to manage a British–South African XI to play Scotland in order to raise money to send competitors to the Melbourne Olympics in Australia. In front of 50,000, the Scots won 2–1.

Seed liked South Africa and White South Africans. His time there in 1929 made a lasting impression. He and Charlton chairman Albert Gliksten even contemplated selling The Valley stadium in London and relocating the club to Johannesburg. 'I was all for the scheme as I knew South Africa well and I liked the country and its climate.' Additionally, 'South African footballers are unspoilt by money', and he appreciated their commitment, obedience, loyalty and sportsmanship. For all his talk of 'looking anywhere', Seed did not recruit from the South African equivalent of his beloved northeast pit villages, the townships and mining compounds. He signed over thirteen White South Africans because he felt they could be trusted to fit into the changing-room culture at Charlton. White South Africans were 'one of us' while their Black countrymen were not. Ironically it was in 1956–7 that the first two Black South Africans, Mokone and Francis, came to Britain to play professionally just at the time Seed stated in his autobiography, *The Jimmy Seed Story*, that he was becoming frustrated with his South African searches.

The post-war boom in crowds in British football peaked in the late '40s-early '50s. Clubs at this time demanded more and better players. The *News Chronicle* of September 1949 carried a series of articles with leading figures from the football industry, including Charles Buchan and Tom Whittaker the Arsenal manager. Both complained of the scarcity of talent in Britain. In fact Seed had predicted this in 1942. 'As soon as peace is declared there will be an abnormal demand for football talent, and the men who can supply demands will be in clover.'[14] Consequently, such was the haemorrhage of good White South African footballers that Freddie Fell, the president of FASA, issued new rules regulating the work of agents of British clubs. With the increased activities of scouts in South Africa – 'big-game hunting'[15] – it is not surprising that Black players too would be noticed.

Soon after Mokone, Gerry Francis became the second Black South African to be signed by a British club. Born in Johannesburg on 6 December 1933 of African and Asian parents, Gerry Francis was signed by First-Division Leeds United from City and Suburban FC in the summer of 1957. He played fifty games – usually on the wing – over four seasons, scoring nine goals. In 1961 he was transferred to York City of the Fourth Division, where he played sixteen games and scored four goals.

It was not until 10 October 1959 that Francis made his début for Leeds against Everton, becoming the first Black South African to play in the First Division and the first man of colour to play for the Elland Road club. However, United were relegated at the end of the season. Described as a 'shoe repairer',[16] the diminutive Francis did not show a clean set of heels to his opposing full-back enough to earn himself a regular first-team place. He laboured through four undistinguished seasons at a depressed club which felt sorry for itself, with few personal highlights to lift his confidence. In October 1961 he signed for York City and then, in the close season of 1962, joined Southern League Tonbridge. On retirement from football, Francis initially became a postman, eventually emigrating to Canada where he still lives. In the summer of 1997, along with Steve Mokone, he returned to Britain for a celebratory evening dedicated to the Pioneers of Black British Football, held in Birmingham. Also present were many of the players featured in this book along with others of more recent fame.

Despite his uneventful interval in Leeds, Francis managed to raise the status of Black South African players in the minds of the club officials for the club to sign another compatriot and winger, Albert Johanneson, whom he had recommended to the Leeds management.

Since finishing his career in the early 1970s, Albert Johanneson has become a Black icon. During the research of this book, his name was mentioned more than any other Black footballer, remembered because of his skills and the fact that they were showcased along the Shaftesbury Avenue of football, the First Division.

Within days of signing for Leeds from Germiston Colliers at the age of 21, Albert 'Hurry, Hurry' Johanneson was making his Division Two début (unlike his compatriot Francis who served a longer apprenticeship in the reserves) and immediately made an impact:

Johanneson was 'making good' after arriving at Elland Road from Johannesburg in 1961 with his modest belongings packed in a suitcase. He was given a trial with United on the recommendation of a South African schoolmaster who had spent hour upon hour teaching him the skills of the game until he could control a tennis ball with his bare feet almost as easily as he could walk . . . [He] impressed United sufficiently to be taken on as a full-time professional after making a fine début against Swansea Town in April 1961 when he made his mark almost immediately, measuring a centre perfectly for Jack Charlton to ram home a header.[17]

His superior skills on the training ground 'demoralised' the other players who were consistently 'run into the ground' by the South African.[18]

During the 1963–64 season when Leeds won promotion to the First Division, Albert was top scorer with 15 goals in 41 games, at that time a post-war club record for a winger. Over the next two seasons in the First Division he continued to score freely: 12 in 36 games in '64–65; and 12 in 28 in '65–66. Team-mate Johnny Giles felt Albert could have become 'one of the game's outstanding personalities', on a par, even, with another contemporary winger who was capturing the imagination and gaze of many, George Best of Manchester United. Giles argues that the South African scored one of the best goals he had ever seen. It was Easter Monday 1964, and:

Albert was surrounded by three Newcastle defenders as he brought down a long pass through the middle and it looked certain that he would be forced away from goal. Yet in the space of five yards he side-stepped them all, one after the other, and nonchalantly slipped the ball past the goalkeeper as he came off his line.[19]

Albert was the first Black South African to play in an FA Cup final, against Liverpool in May 1965. In fact it was the first time Leeds had reached the ultimate round of this competition. He also featured in Leeds' first European competition, the Fairs Cup, the following season.

The seasons 1962–65 were Albert's most successful at Elland Road. He won a Division Two winner's medal, and played in the FA Cup final and the Inter-City Fairs Cup. He made a resurgence in the 1966–7 season with 28 first-team appearances but never recaptured his earlier, mesmerising form. And competition for places was hotting up at Revie's revitalised United with another young winger and future Scottish international Eddie Gray along with Mike O'Grady vying for the outside-left position.

When Albert joined Leeds in 1961 they were going through a difficult time. Recently relegated, discipline among the players was lax. Eric Smith, signed from Celtic during 1960–61, was amazed at the cheating in training sessions:

You wouldn't believe this, but I can remember some of the players taking their money with them on cross-country runs so they could stop off for a quick drink and then finish the course by bus . . . Pre-season training was a shambles.[20]

Albert and other recent arrivals such as Bobby Collins, together with new manager Don Revie, helped revive and build Leeds into a successful First-Division side. However, while Johanneson's abilities were unquestioned, his ability to apply his skills consistently and when it mattered, was. 'Albert . . . is a nervous type of person . . . when he got into Division One he seemed to be affected by the big crowds and the tension of playing for major prizes.' He froze in the FA Cup final.

Johanneson was chosen for the final in the hope that his speed and ball control along the wing would enable us to get behind Liverpool's tightly knit defensive system. But the gamble failed because, if the truth be told, Johanneson was completely overawed by the occasion.[21]

In these accounts, Albert's colleagues argue that he felt the pressures of playing at the highest level and being in the public eye. However, only Johanneson himself mentions racism as being one of these pressures. He once complained to Revie that the opposing full-back was calling him a 'Black bastard'. 'Well,' said the thoughtful, methodical manager, 'call him a White bastard.'[22] Fellow players recognised that Albert came in for special treatment. Even Jack Charlton, a prize graduate of the hit-'em-'ard-and-knock-'em-high school of defending, remembers Albert being assaulted. '[He] . . . was fouled with a tackle which would have enraged anyone.'[23] A friend of Albert's, Guy McKenzie, reflected in 1995 on how his late friend became a target for the 'hard men' in opposition defences; and how Jack Charlton and Billy Bremner took it upon themselves to become Johanneson's on-field minders. The roughing-up of creative players by defensive 'destroyers' was a common practice in the '60s, when the bruisers were allowed to play with a level of violence that Charlton Heston and (United States) National Rifle Association would have been proud of. Then, the two-footed lunge from behind was a legitimate weapon in a defender's armoury. With Albert usually the only Black man on the field, and with a manager totally insensitive to the issue of racist abuse, such battles were often faced and felt alone. Back over the other side of the white line – in the changing-room, front-room or high street – there were little or no support structures available to galvanise a battered confidence. To play well steels the soul against such abuse; to play badly weakens that protection. Albert eventually turned to drink and dope – cannabis, marijuana – to escape the pressures. He had a lot to lose: a wife, two daughters and a comparatively well-paid career. But his method of escape was one familiar to many Black South African youths of the townships ring-fenced by institutional racism and grinding poverty. The older Albert never did return to

SA after being released by his last club York City (having once again followed the boot-steps of Gerry Francis); instead he returned to relative anonymity and eventual poverty in Headingly, Leeds where he died alone in September 1995.

The failure of Johanneson to fulfil his potential at Leeds – he peaked for just three seasons – has been explained differently by different people. Giles and Bremner believed he did not have the temperament for the physical side of First-Division football. And there is little doubt that Johanneson found earning a relatively large wage, being Black, ostensibly equal and constantly in the public eye, a cultural and emotional shock. After the Cup final in May 1965, he played only 42 times over the next five seasons, with Mike O'Grady most often filling the left-wing position. McKenzie cites an unresolved and debilitating achilles-heel injury, sustained during the 1965 final, as a niggling brake upon Albert's form. It was during this second half of the '60s that the winger began to drink more and puff longer. His last two seasons in professional football, at Fourth Division York City in the early '70s, saw Albert play just 26 games – scoring three goals – but helping York to promotion.

The circumstances of his final – non-football playing – years and the nature of his death at 53, however, were a fatal consolidation of decline. Journalist Luke Alfred visiting a yellowing, decrepit and deprived Johanneson in 1992, was alarmed to find a man who still believed better times were ahead. He even had an agent, David Robinson, who promised to carve and fashion that bright future. Unfortunately agent Robinson's greatest ability seemed to be in convincing Albert that what came out of his – Robinson's – mouth was not bullshit but realisable hope. Attempts were made to help Albert, most notably by former colleague Peter Lorimer, but it was too late. Robinson's promise of a brighter dawn never broke. But Albert's spirit did. Out for good, he lay alone for days. Since his death in that Headingly tower block, Leeds teacher Paul Eubank has compiled an exhibition detailing Albert's career and has also helped ensure a headstone has been laid at his grave, paid for by Leeds United with an inscription chosen by his two daughters, one of whom, Alicia, is writing his biography.

Guardian journalist Richard Williams feels that Albert may have been responsible, unwittingly, for the stereotype of the fast Black winger without 'bottle' on the pitch but firmly grasping one off it. And this stereotype has taken years to demolish. Without an exhaustive and conclusive study there can be no definitive answer to William's supposition. However what can be said is that wingers and ball players – footballing artists – do seem to attract this type of reputation as wayward, vulnerable characters: George Best, Alan Hudson, Robin Friday, Charlie Nicholas and Stan Bowles are names from that genre which spring to mind. And when it comes to Black players, comment's like, 'Can he make it through the winter?' (said about Tewfik Abdallah) and 'lacked resource when challenged' (about Gil Heron of Celtic, a former Golden Gloves Boxing Championship semi-finalist) are usually thrown around before the player has had a chance to prove himself one way or another. In Albert's case, as the one Black player in the team, he faced such obstacles alone. And while racist chanting in the 1960s may not have been so universal and vociferous as it was in the '70s and early '80s, institutional racism – the systematic exclusion of people of colour from unhindered access to the privileges and benefits accorded to Whites – was firmly ingrained in Britain. On Johanneson's death, many former players and associates said Albert had become a hermit, rarely appearing at United matches.

Despite the circumstances of his death, Albert is remembered by many as a footballer of unique talent, 'as close as [you] get to seeing Garrincha or Gento in the flesh. He was our first glimpse of that kind of silky soccer player.'[24]

> When I think of Albert Johanneson I think of an exciting and intelligent player in an era of famous cloggers. I think of Leed's early and great European nights against the likes of Valencia and Real Zaragoza with Albert darting in from the wing, leaving a defender gasping for air.[25]

As the obituaries testify, the chasing full-back would not have been the only one gasping.

WEST AFRICA

From Nigeria came three players who signed for professional clubs during the mid-1950s and early '60s: Tesilimi 'Thunder' Balogun, Elkanah Onyeali and Francis Feyami. Though none played at the top level, their presence testified to the thaw in the historic unwillingness of British clubs to consider African players.

Tesilimi 'Thunder' Balogun, a tall centre-forward, first came to notice as a member of the Nigerian FA touring team of September 1949. While playing in England during that autumn, the Nigerians' technique and competent yet expressive performances against the country's top amateur teams attracted scouts from Football League clubs. 'It is inevitable that West Africans will be asked to join English professional sides in time, just as South Africans are being asked now.'[26] In fact it was six years later and only Balogun who played for a Football League club. Thunder's heading, speed and strength of shot – thus his nickname – were his footballing qualities. Did Malcolm MacDonald ever watch him!

The 6ft 2in, 27-year-old bandy-legged Yoruba signed for Midlands League Peterborough United on a month's trial at the end of August 1955. The intermediary in the deal was Darby Allen, secretary of the Nigerian FA. 'Nigeria's best player'[27] made his début almost immediately for the reserves against Holbeach in the Eastern Counties League, impressing manager George Swindin. 'I think he's a good prospect. He'll take time to get used to the speed [of the British game] but he showed he has the football ability and the football brain.'[28]

Like those first and second generation African footballers, Balogun hadn't come to Britain merely to pocket a few quid kicking a ball around. He wanted real work as well as the footy. He attached a 'gis a job' clause to his period of trial: to commit himself to the club they would have to find him employment in a trade he could practice on return to Nigeria, preferably something in the printing industry. I'd like to have heard the comments of the full-timers at the London Road ground on that one! This issue soon became a public affair. Throughout September the sports pages of the local rags ran with periodic updates of the job hunt. And, as the trial deadline edged closer, so did the intensity of the speculation over the success of the search. The club even accused a print union, The Typographical Society (TS), of putting obstacles in the way of finding 'Tesi' suitable work. The local TS official, J.T. Garfield, refuted the allegation countering that he had spent 'a whole day' trying to find an opening for the Nigerian. A few days later Swindin confirmed that he was 'anxious to keep [Balogun] and has been doing his utmost this week to find a niche for this likeable Nigerian'.[29]

Just before the midnight hour, a number of offers materialised. Eventually Darby Allen announced that his protégé would be getting a leg-up at the Patent Safety Ladder Company of Bridge Street. Meanwhile another position in printing had been offered at the same time, Garfield reporting that he had arranged for Tesi to work for the printing firm Casters. Company director E.J. Hurd assured Posh fans that '"Thunder" will get every opportunity to learn the trade thoroughly and will get time off to play in all games – at home or away'.[30]

Sorted with a day job and overalls, the Nigerian international could concentrate on his football, soon becoming one of the most popular players at London Road. Yet he was never picked for the first team, who at this time were beginning a run of five consecutive Midland Counties League championships between 1955 and 1960. Even so, the reserves did win the Eastern Counties League in 1955–6, not losing a game until their 30th fixture in March with crowds regularly reaching five to seven thousand. When Swindin announced his list of retained players the *Peterborough Citizen and Advertiser*, 11 May 1956, commented at the end of the season:

> What may please [supporters] is the name of 'Thunder' Balogun on the
> retained list. This cheerful Nigerian has won the hearts of the London
> Road crowd and from a playing and financial point of view, he was one
> of Swindin's best signings of the past season.

Yet he signed for Queen's Park Rangers of the Football League Division Three South at the beginning of the following season – after a brief stopover at Skegness Town – with little ceremony, his rapid departure in stark contrast to his prolonged introduction. George Shepperson, a historian of Africa who watched Balogun as a youngster in his home town, tells of rumours about drugs that did the rounds following Tesi's exit. Whatever the circumstances – which weren't publicly explained – the transfer didn't go down well with 'Posh' fans.

At home to Watford, Balogun made his QPR and Football League début, scoring once in a 3–1 defeat of the Hertfordshire side. (In fact there were two Black players on the score sheet that day. Among the opposition was Black Briton

Roy Brown – whose father was also Nigerian – who put the ball into his own net.) 'Thunder' played a total of 15 games for QPR, 13 of these in the League, scoring three times, the remainder in the FA Cup where he averaged a goal a game.

Yet he couldn't settle in West London, the flat fenland and boastful skyscape of East Anglia calling him back, this time to Holbeach FC in Lincolnshire in the Eastern Counties League, with whom he played in the 1957–58 season. Against Peterborough United Reserves he scored all four Holbeach goals with none conceded. If ever there was a message from a man who felt unjustly treated by his former employees, this was it, delivered in style: direct and damaging.

I doubt if the 'will he – won't he stay' drama that overshadowed Tesi's arrival at Peterborough will ever be repeated with another player. He was genuinely loved by the majority of 'Posh' fans. Yet he was also unique in that through his nickname 'Thunder', he managed to retain some control over his public identity. Nearly all Black footballers who'd played in Britain, up until the 1960s, had 'Darkie' prefixed to their surname, automatically distinguishing them from their White colleagues. This didn't happen with Balogun. Naming players according to their most obvious characteristic was and is still common among African supporters. One West African player, Cyril Asoluka, had the honour of being called 'Local Stanley Matthews'! That Tesilimi, as a Black player, was defined by his skills rather than his colour was progressive and unusual.

By 1958–9, 'Thunder' had returned to Nigeria to be employed by the Western States Sports Council (WSSC) as football coach. He never did need those printing skills and overalls. In 1964 he came back to Britain for an FA coaching course. On completion he was promoted to chief coach of the WSSC. He died in his sleep, in his early forties, in 1973.

> His name [had] become synonymous with all that was considered best in his country's soccer. He could dribble, feint, sell a dummy, head the ball and above all kick the ball with the strength of a mule in either leg. Tall and gangly, he was a bit bow-legged and walked like a sailor on shore leave.[31]

Though Nigerian football lost one of its folk heroes in 1973, that year also saw the fruition of a legacy established by Thunder and his 1949 team-mates: the Green Eagles, the national team, won their first international competition, a gold medal at the 2nd All-African games, held in Lagos. In 1994 and 1998 they reached the World Cup finals.

Like Balogun, Elkanah Onyeali's primary objective in coming to England was to acquire cultural capital – a trade – that could then be translated into economic capital – money/wages – on return to Nigeria. Football was the means by which this could be achieved. The 21-year-old Nigerian international, on enrolling as a student in electrical engineering at Birkenhead Technical College in the autumn of 1960, wrote for trials with Liverpool, Everton and Tranmere Rovers. Only the last invited him along for a try-out. Impressed by what they saw, Rovers signed the centre-forward as a part-time professional. Although the smallest of the three Merseyside clubs, at least Rovers was in Birkenhead where he was studying, no ferrying across the Mersey to the land of . . . how does that song go? After just three games with the reserves in the Cheshire League he made his Division Three début at home to Bournemouth. Scoring twice in a 4–3 victory and generally playing well, Onyeali soon became 'the new idol of Prenton Park'.[32] Despite the adulation, the thrill, the high and all the other ego-bursting baggage that playing well and scoring on your home turf brings, the *Liverpool Echo*, 29 September 1960, delivered an unequivocal message from 'Onyeali [who] makes it clear – study comes first'. In the article, the Nigerian stressed that finishing the course in electrical engineering was his main goal. And, even though he'd signed as a part-time professional, his academic timetable included evening classes which would prevent him from playing in mid-week games, especially those away from home. For example, he would not be available for the coming Monday-evening fixture with Torquay. 'I am sorry I cannot play. I must be at Technical College that night. My father at home in Nigeria would be very angry with me if he found out I was playing football rather than studying.'

On another occasion at the beginning of November, 'Al' returned to Nigeria for two weeks 'and even modern communications could not track him down'.[33] (Once these natives are back in the jungle, la, there's no fuckin' chance of finding them.) On return to civilisation he was fined but immediately selected for the forthcoming game against Crewe, necessity being far too important to stand in the way of principle.

These two episodes – Elkanah's public pronouncement and his 'disappearance' – highlight a common-purpose characteristic of many of the migrant Black African footballers: that they came primarily to learn a trade or profession, rather than to earn a living from playing football. This gang of economic migrants – enemy aliens according to present-day politicians – ranges from Arthur Wharton, Hassan Hegazi, Tewfik Abdallah, Mohammed Latif through to Ghanaian John Mensah who signed for Cambridge City in 1964, and beyond. It reflects both the value that is placed upon education among certain sections of the urban African population – particularly in North and West Africa – and the privileged environment of competitive league football in colonial and immediately post-colonial Africa. In English-speaking West Africa before the Second World War it was the urbanised, educated, middle-class Africans that were able to acquire the necessary skills to play the game at an organised, competitive level because they had continued with their schooling beyond elementary level.

The cultural importance of education over football in the value-system of these migrants created a humorous and paradoxical relationship between these middle-class Africans and their British, working-class club colleagues. The attitude to football of the former would have been heavily influenced by the amateur, Corinthian ethos of the colonials running the game back home. On the other hand, to the British players – White and Black – it was a job of work, albeit glamorous and out of the ordinary, where winning was the overriding objective. Mokone noted this difference in *Football Monthly*, January 1957: 'I have realised that in League football in [Britain], points and goals count for everything.'

Onyeali made 13 appearances and scored eight goals, a commendable average of over one goal every two games. He finished the season as the club's second-highest scorer despite the scarcity of his first-team outings. John King, who joined Rovers in February 1961 – later becoming their manager – recalls that the Nigerian international was '. . . quick. Great skills. Couldn't play in the winter. He used to shiver before he went out . . . A different character, different breeding. Centre-forward. Good mover. Score you a few goals. At that time a novelty, having a Black man, and a quality player.'[34] (Since Onyeali, Tranmere – with King as manager for most of that period – have recruited fewer Black players than nearly all other Football League teams, contrary to employment trends at clubs generally.)[35]

Walter Galbraith, who took over as manager midway through the 1960–1 season, released 50 per cent of his professional staff at the end of the season including both his top scorers. Even though Rovers had finished 21st in Division Three and were relegated, it was viewed by some supporters as a barmy decision. Peter Bishop, programme editor at Tranmere, felt the new manager 'obviously didn't fancy [the Nigerian]'. Leaving aside the financial pressures weighing upon any relegated club, the decision to release the most influential players will always be controversial. Onyeali signed for Holyhead Town before moving to Chicago – from where, on one occasion, he was flown back to Nigeria for an international match with Ghana – to continue his studies.

Francis Dejo Feyami signed for 'struggling, unhappy'[36] Cambridge City, a full-time professional Southern League club, in October 1961, becoming the third Nigerian international to sign professional forms for a British club. However, unlike Balogun and Onyeali, he did not play in the Football League. He came to the notice of Cambridge City manager Oscar Hold playing for Ibadan, while Hold was coaching in West Africa.

His arrival in the UK from Lagos had the ingredients of a farce and wasn't too different from Barbadian Clyde Best's entry to Britain on his way to West Ham (see below). Feyami had caught an earlier plane than originally agreed without telling anyone, so there was nobody to meet him at Heathrow. On explaining his predicament to a policeman, a car was organised to drive Feyami to Hold's house in Cambridge. Meanwhile the manager was travelling to the airport. When the two finally met, a pyjamaed Feyami opened the front door of Hold's house, invited his new boss in, and got back into his bed! (No, Hold's wife wasn't in it.)

Like his fellow Green Eagles who'd played professionally in Britain, Feyami was tall – 6ft 2in – agile and skilful. While in Cambridge he wanted to learn carpentry and football coaching. Unfortunately he did neither.

The 22-year-old had appeared ten times for Nigeria, including once against Egypt, the most successful African national team. Feyami had also faced British club sides touring West Africa, most notably Sheffield Wednesday and Blackpool. Indeed had he stayed in Nigeria for a further week before travelling to Britain he would have faced Barcelona – reputedly playing for a fee of £20,000 – 'in the finest stadium in West Africa'.[37]

Yet Francis played only five games for City. He made his senior début on 10 October against Corby in the Southern League Cup. Prior to this match, Hold had recognised a problem. 'Feyami is a good player but there is one snag. He has difficulty in keeping his feet warm! It will be up to us to devise some means whereby he can keep warm.'[38] (The report also describes Feyami as an amateur, contradicting an earlier statement in the same newspaper of 7 October.) He did not excite the crowd of 5,518 but 'despite his awkwardness, revealed an ability to cross accurately and move sensibly'. A week later he received 'a great ovation as he scored his first [and last] goal [for the first team] with a flashing drive'. Despite an appreciation of his skills – 'superb ball control' – he was not considered 'strong enough for [the] rugged style of [City's] play'.[39]

Though Feyami's career in Britain was brief, we once again find those stereotypes about the Black player as fast and fancy, but lacking in 'bottle' and unable to perform in the cold. Such views became common in the '60s, with Johanneson as the most obvious example, persisting until the '90s with the infamous statement by Ron Noades, chairman of Crystal Palace – made to camera for a television programme on the growing presence and influence of Black players in British professional football – that skilful Black players needed physical, robust White players to help them through the mud-heavy winter. Noades must really have been in Offensive Dick-Head Chairman mode when he mouthed this rubbish because Crystal Palace employed more Black professionals than nearly any other and has a catchment area of support in South London that includes a large Black population.

Before the Second World War it wasn't the case that Black players were universally labelled as being of particular type. Though Black people in general were caricatured, footballers were not seen – in the minds of White managers, players and supporters – as having particular strengths and weaknesses; as particular *types* of players *because* of their colour. Though this is not to argue that some writers, as we have seen, did try to construct them as 'different'. After 1945, with the greater number of migrant Black footballers, playing against the backdrop of an increasingly racialised political environment, certain myths emerged as to this 'new' generic type. While there may have been substance to the view that Feyami did not like playing in cold weather – he was certainly not used to playing on frosty or snow covered pitches – this difficulty could be said to affect many players performing in climates substantially different from that to which they are accustomed: in October 1997, Chelsea played a UEFA Cup-tie against Tromso of Norway, a town inside the Arctic Circle. The match took place in a snowstorm at sub-zero temperature and Chelsea lost 3–2 to the part-time professionals. Ruud Gullit blamed the weather for the defeat. His team wasn't used to performing in extreme cold. During the 1994 World Cup finals in the USA, Republic of Ireland manager Jack Charlton complained that midday kick-offs in temperatures of 90° Fahrenheit plus were unfair to his players who were just not used to playing in such heat. In November 1991, Cameroon's 'Indomitable Lions' played, froze and were defeated at a bleak Wembley.

Some players and some teams are affected by the climatic conditions in which they play. Indeed the style and speed of performance in different cultures is greatly influenced by the weather. To draw universal conclusions about ethnic groups – White players hate playing in heat; Black footballers in cold – is simplistic nonsense. Yet this is what occurred in post-war Britain. The influx of Black migrants to meet the industrial demand for labour generated further and refined myths 'explaining' the character and culture of these 'Others'. Consequently third-generation Black footballers, whether British, African, African-Caribbean or Asian were ascribed behavioural characteristics because of their colour. This emergent stereotype of the Black Footballer was applied across the board, without a distinction being made between British and foreign-born Black players. And it had practical consequences with the popularisation of the idea that Black players were most effective in wide positions. Thus, while Black footballers before 1945 were generally not seen as suitable or unsuitable for a particular role – and had in fact played in all positions from goalkeeper to left-wing – those of the third generation were infected with a stereotype that stacked them out wide.

By Christmas 1961, Francis Feyami was back in Nigeria. 'His inability to become fully acclimatised to our winter is the deciding factor in his departure. He is expected to go into training with other players for the Nigerian national side.'[40]

Sierra Leonian Eddie Dillsworth also played in the Southern League in the 1960s but perhaps his most noticeable achievement was turning out at Wembley in 1966 to play for Wealdstone in the Amateur Cup final. Some days before, another Black player, Mike Trebilcock, had scored two goals for Everton in the FA Cup final. Indeed the previous season Albert Johanneson had turned out for Leeds United in their FA Cup final defeat to Liverpool. Thus, in the space of just over a year, three Black footballers had appeared in Wembley finals. In fact Dillsworth was not the first Black player in an Amateur Cup final. In 1909, W.D. Tull wore the stripes of Clapton in their 6–0 thrashing of Eston United.

Midfielder Dillsworth, though much travelled, played only twice in the Football League – for Fourth Division Lincoln City in April 1967. Apparently he had not told Wealdstone he was playing for 'The Imps'. Consequently, the Londoners suspended him, Lincoln decided to get shot because he'd kept his mouth shut and he was reduced to beginning the following season with Barking (for whom Jack Leslie had played just after the First World War). Within a few months, Eddie moved further east to Chelmsford City of the Southern League, his fourth club in six months. The West African also played (as an amateur) for Fulham, Brentwood, Kettering Town, Ilford, Hemel Hempstead and Woodford Town.

THE CARIBBEAN

Across the English-speaking West Indies archipelago, cricket used to be king, with notable exceptions – baseball in Cuba, for example. However one of the largest islands, Jamaica, produced two pioneers of the third generation: Lloyd Lindbergh Delapenha and Gil Heron. Yet interestingly, it was in Trinidad that football captured popular emotions as much as cricket. We have discussed already the Trinidadian FA tourists of 1953, the first West Indies football team to visit Britain, and noted also that the first West-Indian-born professional was Trinidadian Alfred Charles.

Lloyd Lindbergh 'Lindy' Delapenha, born in Jamaica on 25 May 1927, was the first Caribbean footballer to play at the highest level in Britain. His talent was spotted while playing in the Middle East during the Second World War. Peace resuming, he signed for Arsenal as an amateur. Unable to win a professional contract at Highbury, he joined Portsmouth in April 1948 just before his 21st birthday, who did offer to pay him. The South Coast club were then established members of the First Division, having had a consistent presence since 1927. The young Jamaican, though never managing to secure a regular first-team place, spent two unique seasons at Fratton Park as his club won and retained the First Division title. He made seven appearances – and therefore did not receive a championship medal – before being transferred to Middlesbrough, also of the First Division, in April 1950.

It was at Ayresome Park that this stocky, 5ft 7in forward achieved his greatest success. He made 260 appearances for the first team, scoring 90 goals. For three seasons – '52–3, '53–4 and '55–6 – he was the club's leading scorer. It was his friend Brian Clough who eventually dislodged Lindy as marksman-in-chief. If Clyde Best later came to personify the popular image of the Black forward in the early 1970s, Lindy was the 1950s prototype. Despite his robust style, Middlesbrough trainer Harold Shepperson – who later assisted Alf Ramsey in steering England to their World Cup triumph in 1966 – remembered that:

> Lindy hated the cold weather; he had to be pushed in training whenever there was any snow or ice around. But when he got going he was really exciting. He possessed a lethal right foot [shot] in keeping with his very fine athletic physique. He played for us at outside-right and was very popular with the other lads. I can still remember his style of play with fierce shots from 25 to 30 yards outside the box, which would crash into the back of the net. Lindy was also an accomplished cricketer, playing for the local team.[41]

In his pioneering book *Black Pearls of Soccer* (1982), Al Hamilton mistakenly argues that Delapenha was 'generally regarded as the first Black migrant to play within the English Football League', apparently unaware of the contributions of first- and second-generation players. However, what could be more accurately said of Delapenha is that he was the first Black footballer to play in a First Division championship-winning team.

Near the end of his Footbal League career he arrived at Mansfield Town, joining while they were in the Third Division North and leaving them in the Fourth. He played 115 games, scoring 27 goals between 1958 and 1961. Lindy was signed by Charlie Mitten, the forward-thinking player–manager of the 'Stags'. (Mitten, a stylish left-winger with Manchester United, had achieved notoriety by migrating *out* of Britain in 1950 to join Santa Fé of Bogotá, Colombia, to escape the feudal restrictions on pay and conditions that trapped British players.) At impoverished Mansfield he was trying to build a team of attack-minded players who were at ease with the ball:

> Because I hadn't any money to buy players, I had to keep my eye open for
> footballers who couldn't get in their first team and who might be available
> on a free transfer – like Lindy Delapenha. A brilliant outside-right . . . He
> was in his thirties and Middlesbrough thought he was past it.[42]

Unfortunately, Mitten left to manage Newcastle immediately after Delapenha had signed, his departure beginning a decline in Mansfield's fortunes. Lindy ended his playing career in the Southern League with Burton Albion in 1961–2. With his Middlesbrough-born wife he later returned to Jamaica to pursue a career in sports journalism with the Jamaican Broadcasting Corporation.

A contemporary and compatriot of Lindy's was Gilbert 'Gil' Heron, father of the red and hot and universally acclaimed jazz musician Gil Scott Heron: 'The revolution will not be televised.' For an ex-professional footballer to be overshadowed as a celebrity by his son is unusual, especially when the father played for one of the most prestigious clubs in Britain.

Born in Kingston, Jamaica, on 9 April 1922, at his athletic prime he stood at 5ft 11in and weighed 12 st 7 lb, an ideal physique for a centre-forward. It was while playing for Detroit Corinthians that he was spotted by Celtic who, in the summer of 1951, were touring North America. Jimmy McGrory, the club's manager, invited the professional cameraman to take shots in Glasgow at trials in August. Heron arrived, scored twice and signed on the line.

He made his début in the Scottish League Cup against Morton, scoring one goal with another disallowed. The 'Black Flash' – as he became known – was quickly popular. According to the *New York Times*, 19 August 1951:

> Heron succeeded in scoring what proved to be the key goal a few minutes
> before half-time. He took a pass and ran through, then sent a drive from

16 yards range at Morton goalie Jimmy Cowan. Cowan partially blocked the drive, but not sufficiently to prevent the ball rolling into the net.

The day before, the same newspaper ran the headline 'Negro becomes the first US soccer player to win place on famous Glasgow squad', claiming the Jamaican as an African–American despite Heron having played for the Jamaican national XI.

The Kingston Bhoy played only five games for the Celtic first team, scoring two goals. Midway through the season he flew back to the Caribbean to play for Jamaica against Trinidad and the Caribbean. In May 1952 he was released, and signed for First Division Third Lanark – now defunct – yet the clubs could have been on different planets. The Detroit Jamaican found a poor team which eventually finished last, five points adrift of the club above, and relegated. Gil then decided to try his luck in England by joining Kidderminster Harriers of the Southern League. But the legacy of having played for one of the biggest clubs in Britain devalued the thrill of kitting up elsewhere. After just one season in the Midlands, Heron returned to Detroit and the Corinthians. In 1956 he became a referee.

As well as being a professional footballer and photographer, Gil excelled in many other sports. He once played ice hockey, reached the semi-finals of the United States Amateur Boxing Federation's Golden Gloves contest; and in athletics he had competed against sometime 400 metres and 440 yards world-record holder Herb McKenlay. While in Scotland he played cricket for Pollock and Ferguslie.

Quite why his time at Parkhead wasn't a success isn't clear. The simple answer would be that he was just not good enough. Heron joined Celtic the same season as an undistinguished centre-half, Glaswegian Jock Stein, who'd been playing for Llanelli in Wales and was coming to the end of his career. Ironically, Heron was expected by many contemporary observers to make a bigger impact than the big man who later, as manager, led 'The Bhoys' to Britain's first success in the European Cup in 1967.

> After [Heron] joined the Parkhead club as a forward, those optimistic supporters who feel that every addition to the playing staff must be the solution to some problem or other were hailing him with enthusiasm, and . . . christened him the 'Black Flash', but he lacked ball control and resource when challenged.[43]

Yet Eugene McBride, another chronicler of Celtic FC history, quotes others as remarking that Heron '[had] ball control and [could] trap like a veteran'.

As to the charge of lacking resource – 'bottle' – only a complete prat would mouth this accusation at a Golden Gloves semi-finalist. Heron enjoyed himself at Celtic – 'my days at Parkhead have been wonderful'[44] – about which he has written two poems: *Bonnie Scotland* and *The Great Ones*.[45] Yet he felt that some referees were prejudiced against the club:

> There have been some very raw decisions against Celtic . . . [that] had
> tremendous bearing on the outcome of the game. To me, there should be
> no mistakes made, those in charge should be capable of handling the
> game in a manner justifiable to both sides, then there would be no doubt
> in the minds of the players and spectators that there was no prejudice on
> the referee's part.[46]

Although Heron makes no direct statement about the problem of racism in
Scottish football, Paul Elliot, the third Black professional at Parkhead, felt that
'the racial abuse I've suffered in Scotland is far worse than anything I've had to
put up with in England or Italy'.[47] Heron's comments may also have been sparked
by a sending-off and subsequent seven-day suspension on 2 January 1952 against
Stirling Albion reserves.

While Gil has fond memories of Parkhead, the pay, or rather the lack of it,
probably made him cast an envious eye back across the Atlantic to the relative
affluence of professional sportsmen in the USA. Charlie Mitten reflects that it
was while he was in New York with Manchester United that the glaring injustice
of having their wages capped was made plain (along with the potential to do
something about it):

> It was an exciting new adventure . . . And [we] got a taste for the high
> life . . . They looked after us well, and we often drove around in huge
> cars . . . What the hell are we doing here! We'd toured the United States,
> beaten their best teams, yet we'd nowt in the bank to show for it. We all
> felt this way.[48]

Yet in the USA, Mitten couldn't have helped but notice it was the reaction to (the
darkness of) skin colour which acted as the brake upon potential earnings (and
many other life chances).

Of the Caribbean-born players among the first three pioneering generations of
Black footballers, the most remembered, revered and loved, by pros and fans
alike, is Clyde Best. A Bermudan international at 16 years of age, he was
recommended to West Ham United by Graham Adams, the English manager of
the Bermudan national team. The East London club invited the 17-year-old for
a trial, sending him a single air ticket (so confident were they he'd make it?).
Arriving at Heathrow on a rainy August Sunday in 1968, there was no one from
the club to meet him. Taking the unfamiliar Underground, Best made his way on
the District Line to 'West Ham' only to be told after exiting that the nearest
station to the stadium was Upton Park. To add to the cock-up, when he
eventually arrived at the ground he found the gates chain-locked. Wandering the
streets and anxious, he was eventually accompanied by a concerned passer-by to
the home of the Charles's brothers, John and Clive, two of West Ham's Black
professionals. Cor blimey, would you Adam and Eve it?

However, the sodden Sunday of cock-up and coincidence was not a dooming augury for the future. Best spent seven relatively successful seasons in East London. He became a totem, a representation, of Black footballers in Britain; an inspiration to other Black youngsters. The downside was his name became synonymous with the stereotype of the technically skilled, exciting but unpredictable and unphysical Black footballer.

Best, 6ft 1in and 13 stone, had immaculate timing and balance, unusual traits in such a big man.

> They were doing simple movement, first time volleys at goal. A ball came to him that just wasn't playable first time and it needed a bodily adjustment and I was sure he was going to miss. He sensed what was needed and without pausing he caught the ball on his knee and in the same movement whacked it into the net. A lesser player could never have done that.[49]

His style of play was similar, in some ways, to John Charles of Leeds and Juventus, also considered a 'gentle giant' and icon of the '50s and '60s in both Britain and Italy. Yet while the technique and sophistication of the Welshman's play was admired, his lack of raw aggression did not draw criticism, unlike Best. 'Ron Greenwood [the West Ham manager] teased [Clyde] for being a "big softie". The feeling was that Best was . . . too well mannered on the pitch and his opponents were taking advantage.' Ironically it was during West Ham's tour of Bermuda in 1971 that Best utilised his dormant physical powers – after being called 'whitey' by the locals! Greenwood's assistant John Lyall noticed that, after being dissed by his homeboys, '[Best] started to push his weight about and immediately looked twice the player. It was the turning point for him.'[50]

What was simply a cultural difference – West Indian footballers were more concerned with technique, while the British game demanded a robust, physical style – was translated as a weakness in the young Bermudan. Cyrille Regis, a centre-forward at West Bromwich Albion in the late 1970s and early '80s, born in French Guyana, also complained that club coaches were demanding he be more physical in his style, a pressure he did not feel comfortable with. While more migrant footballers were entering the British game, the attitude to them by coaches, managers and those in the boardroom was similar to the message being trumpeted by most politicians, especially those on the right – assimilate and integrate or leave. The acceptance and celebration of difference as a positive addition to football, and British cultural life in general, did not seem to be on the football industry or political agenda. Now, in the late '90s, with numerous internationals from all continents playing in Britain, respect for what they've added to the game is duly given.

Best's career at West Ham coincided with an increase in racist abuse on and off the pitch. 'Nigger, nigger' was the chant of the Stretford End at Old Trafford during West Ham's visit in 1971–2. The acceptance that it was just part of football was often implied in the tone of the newspaper reports. 'The racialist chanting . . . must have been sweet music to Clyde Best because there was more than a hint of jealousy behind the apparent prejudice.' Even West Ham supporters would scapegoat their Black players for bad team performances. In response to Hereford chants of 'we want two' during a 1–1 draw in the third round of the FA Cup, some Hammers' fans replied, 'Take any two. Take Clyde Best and [Nigerian] Ade Coker for a start.'[51]

Though Best was the third West Indian centre-forward to play in top-class British football after 1945, following Gil Heron and Lindy Delapenha, his team-mates at West Ham thought 'that he could become English football's first Black hero'.[52] I'd like to have heard the comments of Jack Leslie, then a member of the club's backroom staff, to that sentiment.

Many young Black Britons were inspired by Best to try for a career in football. Ron Greenwood felt the Bermudan had kicked open wider the changing-room door, making it a little less hard for young, gifted and Black aspirants to realise their dreams. 'I believe that many immigrants will soon start to make the breakthrough at League level. There's no reason why we should not see four or five coloured players in League sides in ten years' time.'[53] Clive Charles, Best's close friend and fellow Black professional also thought Clyde 'broke some ground', pulling along those Black youngsters following in his wake.[54]

Though Best came to be seen as the embodiment of those myths created about the Black player – lazy, inconsistent, unreliable etc – myths that were excuses for racist thinking and practice, one stereotype – that such footballers did not like the physical aggression of the British game – contrasts absurdly with the violent and threatening image of the Black youngster at street level. This construction of inner-city Black youth as 'big, broad, massive and hard' contradicted the football stereotype of the sensitive, unpredictable, artistic ball player. Yet both were devised to constrain movement: into professional football and on the streets. Each creation, at one and the same time, merged with and contradicted the other. These images of 'The Black' bore little resemblance to real, lived experience of Black (and White). Where was, for example, the real image of the Black trade unionist? Black workers have a higher rate of union membership than their White colleagues; the Black churchgoer? African–Caribbeans attend religious services in greater proportion than their White neighbours; the educated African? Of ethnic minorities in higher edcuation in Britain, Africa-born students comprise a disproportionately high percentage.

Clyde Best's career in Britain peaked in 1971–2 with 17 goals in 42 games. In 1976 he left Britain to continue his winter football in Holland with Feyenoord, spending the summers in the North American Soccer League in the USA. West Ham colleague and England midfielder, Trevor Brooking, felt the Bermudan had never fulfilled his potential, a failing he put down to Best's lack of aggression, undeveloped left foot, slowing pace and periodic lack of confidence. Yet Best spent seven seasons at the club, making over 188 appearances and scoring 47 goals. Despite Brooking's assessment, this is not an undistinguished achievement.

Indeed, at the Tribute to the Pioneers of Black British Football dinner in Birmingham in May 1998, Clyde was addressed simply as 'The Legend' by other pioneers and Black players. Since May 1997 he has coached the Bermudan national team.

AUSTRALIA

Charles Perkins, an Australian Aborigine of the Eastern Arrente people, was born on a table-top in a disused telegaph station near Alice Springs some time around 1936. He lived his early childhood at the Bungalow Mission, an institution for 'half-castes' where his mother Hetti looked after the girls' living quarters and, in so doing, was able to have daily contact with her son, a 'privilege' denied many Aboriginal mothers. Charlie's father Martin Connelly, of the Kalkadoon people from the Mount Isa region had an Irish father, Joseph. Ann Whip, Charlie's grandmother, was also a Kalkadoon. In 1945, as part of the government's bleaching campaign, nine-year-old Charlie, along with five other boys, was removed from the Bungalow Mission, itself a removal camp of Stolen Generation (Aboriginal) children, to a 'family-group home in Adelaide', St Francis House.[55] He left behind his close friend Wally MacArthur, later known as the Borroloola Flash. At 14, Wally was reckoned by some who knew his times to be the fastest runner in the world. For 30 years, Charlie never returned to the place of his birth for a period longer than six weeks. Charlie and the Borroloola Flash teamed up again in Britain in the '50s when Wally was playing Rugby League for Rochdale Hornets.

At St Francis House Perkins developed into one of the best footballers in Australia. His break came in 1951 when the South Australia state Under-18 squad held its training camp next door to St Francis House. Needing opposition for an unscheduled practice match, they took on the hostel boys for a confidence-boosting thrashing. Funny old game. Trudging off at the end, the state's starlets found their boots on the wrong feet. They had just been turned over by a bunch of younger, fitter and better Abos. Charlie and another lad, John Moriarty, were subsequently invited to join the squad. Perkins's approach to the game was simple: 'Every person I tackled, they'd know I tackled them . . . I'm going for the ball and nothing's going to get in my way.'[56]

After starring for Adelaide club International United, a multicultural team of ethnic allsorts, unusual in Australia soccer, Budapest and Fiorentina in 1957, Charlie was invited to Everton for a trial – if he paid half the fare. Arriving in Liverpool in the winter of 1957–8 the 'Kangaroo Kid', as he was nicknamed by his Goodison team-mates, soon found that, compared to them, he was not fit enough for the muddied-cold athleticism of the English game. Also, in trial matches, he felt the other players deliberately made it hard for him to impress by playing difficult balls. Or not playing him in at all. Edged out, he offered to fight other team-mates and the coach. Yet, 'at least . . . the Everton players were professional footballers, not racists'.[57]

While it was not a haven of tolerance and respect, coming to England helped Perkins confirm to himself that, back in Oz, it was the (rich, élite, powerful) Whites who had the problem, despite the enormous disadvantages all Aborigines were burdened with. 'For the first time he could see himself not only as an Aborigine but as a human being in an equal relationship with others.'[58] While Charlie was a contender, waiting for the Toffees to chew things over, he worked at the docks where, no doubt, the fact that he was a footballer with the city's top club automatically drew respect. Yet he could see that the racial hierarchy he'd been used to in Oz was replaced by one of class in England. And that the anger he felt towards Whites in his homeland didn't travel. In fact the Black Australian and British worker had much in common. 'There never has been justice for British working men and women.'[59]

Everton offered a part-time contract which he didn't fancy. After playing locally in Wigan and in the north east for top amateurs Bishop Auckland, he was offered a trial with Manchester United by Sir Matt Busby. The deal offered was the same as Everton, the answer given the same. 'I was homesick . . . I just wanted to play in Australia.'[60]

Returning to Oz as player/coach of Adelaide Croatia, he didn't just play. He became active in politics and a pain in the arse of the Establishment. 'A bastard', to use his own phrase. The rights of the Aboriginal people put football in its place. Charlie enrolled at Sydney University in 1963 and graduated three years later, only the second Aborigine to do so. He took a seat on the Freedom Ride buses of the '60s, stopping at sports and leisure venues demanding an end to the colour bar. Getting back on, he'd be wet with adrenalin-induced sweat . . . and spit. Maybe even cut and bruised from a police truncheoning. But how could Charlie concentrate on his football when to be a First Australian meant you didn't have the rights you were born with? The Australian Human Rights Commission, reporting in *Bringing Them Home* on the Stolen Generation of Aboriginal children, decided that 'what was done meets the international definition of genocide . . . which is the attempt to destroy a people, a culture'.[61] They weren't treated like shit, that gets cleaned away. They were helped and encouraged to self-destruct. Even today Aboriginal people suffer diseases, like rheumatic fever, that occur only in the most poor, deprived and neglected parts of the world. Diabetes disables 25 per cent of adults. Suicide, the other escape for many, is an exit used more frequently than the swing doors of a Reserve saloon bar.

Though fucking up the *status quo* became the goal of Charlie's post-university life, much of what he'd learnt on the football pitch came in handy: digging-in, being single-minded, giving and taking knocks. On the premise that they would rather have him inside pissin' out, than outside pissin' in through the door – he'd called Australia 'a rotten, stinkin' hole'[62] – the government invited him to join the Office of Aboriginal affairs in Canberra. After nearly twenty years fighting and publicising the cause of his people, pressurising successive governments not to continue remaking First Australians last, he was sacked. During that time he'd also annoyed, angered and embittered some of his own people who felt he did more harm than good.

During the 1980s Craig Johnston made a name for himself at Liverpool while fellow Australian Tony Dorigo did the same at Leeds United. Presently Harry Kewell is entertaining the Elland Roaders with his skills first learnt down under, while the dodgy Mark Bosnich is fighting for his life at Old Trafford. But no more Black Australians have followed Baines and Perkins to Britain.

There were other migrant players of colour in the British game between 1945–70 such as Chi Doy Cheung from Hong Kong at Blackpool; Ghanaian John Mensah at Cambridge City; Zambians Frederick Mwila and Emment Kapengwe at Aston Villa; and Bermudan Calvin Symonds at Rochdale, though none of these made a lasting impression.

Most migrant footballers came to Britain to fill the labour shortage in the football industry and further careers that had been stunted by the underfunded and underdeveloped nature of football in their home countries. The passage to Britain, a trickle rather than a flow, slowed appreciably with the introduction and gradual enforcement of the 1962 Immigration Act. Until then, Africa provided the largest number relative to any other continent. This particular route, Africa to Britain, has taken generations to recover. Only now, in the 1990s, have British clubs once more begun to recruit African players in any number, although they usually look to other European, rather than African clubs – France in particular – for talent.

The following chapter examines the contribution of Black British footballers between 1945 and 1970.

FIVE

'66, '68, Football in Black and White

Black British Footballers 1945–70

For many with lions in their hearts it was a red-shirted, red-blooded England that won the Jules Rimet trophy at Wembley Stadium, north west London on 30 July 1966, the third birthday of my younger brother Neil. Two other more significant brothers, Bobby and Jack Charlton, played in the Wembley sun and rain alongside two small, gritty midfielders, Alan Ball and Nobby Styles. The latter, with his socks down and his front tooth missing, did a memorable jig of triumph after the match, a dance that expressed the mood of millions. It was a working-class victory in an era of working-class triumph. It exemplified the confidence of ordinary England (and Britain). In the new 'Modern Britain' of the new millennium, recapturing the texture and feel of that collective sense of self-worth of over thirty years ago is difficult. Up until the mid '70s, working-class people of post-war Britain, through institutions such as the trades unions and, yes, the Labour Party, fought confidently to improve the quality of every minute of every day: over wages and holidays; tea breaks and wash-up time; free school milk and dinners; home helps and invalid cars. And we often won.

In the football industry two important victories had been won by the players through their union – the PFA – in the early 1960s that upset the balance of power between footballers and their employers. The maximum wage of £20 per week had been abolished, as had the feudal contract which effectively tied players to one club for life or until the club decided to get rid of them. Footballers, in common with workers in other industries, were again flexing their muscles off the pitch as well as on it. However, with the revision of the rules over the contract came another decree that players with non-British passports would have to reside in Britain for two years before they could sign professional forms.

Three of the players in the England team that won the Jules Rimet trophy were from West Ham United, a club deep in the heart of east London: Bobby Moore, blond, handsome and England's captain; hat-trick hero Geoff Hurst, the only person to score three goals in a World Cup final; and Martin Peters, who scored the other goal in the 4–2 defeat of West Germany. The fact that they weren't from clubs with Establishment pretensions, such as Arsenal or Blackburn Rovers, merely affirmed the identification of the event as the property of the People. The team was managed by Alf Ramsey, a dour Londoner whose attempts to 'talk proper' made him sound like a cheap social climber – his working-class upbringing was betrayed by the involuntary dropping of the 'g' in 'ing'. The World Cup final was then, not surprisingly, a peculiarly 'English' affair made all the more parochial by the site of the victory, that symbol of national sporting pride, Wembley Stadium. This image of a 'national' sporting triumph is one that Little England romanticists wholly identified with: honest, workman-like toilers led by an East End boy from a family club – which had won a European trophy the season before – overcoming the superior tactical and technical skills of their opposition. The script could not have been acted out better.

Ten years old, I watched the final alone. My Greek–Cypriot father Varnavas – anglicised to 'Billy' – and younger sister Anna were not football fans; my kid brother was too young to notice. My commitment to the cause had been pledged at the beginning of the campaign with the creation of the Peverel Road branch – unofficial – of the World Cup Willie Club, along with the only members, the Mansfield brothers, Gary and Graham. So not-bothered was my dad that he asked a mate round to help him tile the kitchen while Bobby and the Boys were getting our own back on the Chippy Bombers (well, that's how it seemed at the time). So, while in one ear Uncle Kenneth Wolstenholme was describing the action, the other was full of, 'More matchsticks Billy, yes, lovely . . . next one please!' When West Germany scored first I couldn't take anymore. The *Daily Mirror* article pinned to our club noticeboard naming Beckenbauer, Haller, Held and the rest of the white-shirted Teutons as the dark horses of the tournament, flashed through my mind. The horror of an England defeat loomed. That cold, sweaty feeling you get when you're about to start rucking at school with 'fight, fight, fight . . .' being chanted on all sides enveloped me. I went to the cinema. I don't remember the film. The large, dark theatre was just a sanctuary from the horror of Wembley. Towards the end of the screening, the news that England had won the World Cup flashed on to the screen. Everybody stood up and started clapping. Except me. Fuck it! *I've missed English football's greatest day.*

At primary school the following year, those who wanted to go, and had paid their half-crowns, were taken by bus to watch *Goal*, a filmed documentary of the tournament. An image from *Goal* that has stuck, along with a ball-bag full of other confused and contradictory symbols, is of a Black teenager sitting at the side of the Wembley pitch during the final. He was, I think, a member of St John's Ambulance. It was as if he'd gate-crashed the party. On this day of all days, as racists have drivelled, there should not have been any black tarnishing the Union Jack. England's victory was a purely Anglo-Saxon affair and, unwittingly, young blond Bobby embodied that lily-white construction. West Germany *v.* England was an All-European affair. And the play, its stage and its actors projected an image of Europe and its football that was monochrome. This representation could have been different had France reached the World Cup final. Black players had been a feature of their national team since the 1930s. Nevertheless Eusebio, the Mozambican playing for Portugal, just like that Black St John's ambulance man, did tarnish this ethnically pristine

SAMMY CHUNG
Watford 1958.

KEVIN KEELAN
Aston Villa 1959.

Tommy 'Bull' Best on his début, Cardiff City 1948.

STEVE STACEY
Bristol City 1961.

STAN HORNE
Aston Villa 1963.

Albert Johanneson, York City 1971.

MIKE TREBILCOCK
Everton 1966.

FRANK PETERSON
Millwall 1968.

Dennis Walker, Manchester United Youth team, 1961.
Dennis is seated front row, extreme left.

ABOVE: Tony Whelan,
Manchester United 1971.
Tony is front row, extreme right.

RIGHT: Tony Whelan as
Manchester United Football
Academy coach, in his office
at the Cliff, Salford.

Laurie Cunningham: the best winger of his generation.

Viv Anderson, the first player of African-Caribbean parentage to play for England, is chased by Ryan Giggs whose father's descendents originated from Sierra Leone.

The 'All Black' star cast for Len Cantello's testimonial in 1977.

Cyrille Regis, charcoal drawing by
Colin Yates.

The legend: Clyde Best
'hammering' a magpie.

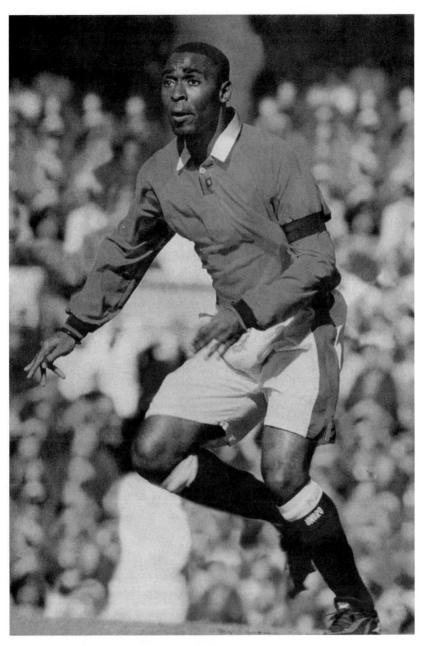

Andy Cole: the best striker that England do not use.

production by finishing as the tournament's top scorer with nine goals.

Yet the reality of football in Britain tells a different story. Non-British and migrant players have been a feature of the game since its inception, as has been illustrated above, with Britain's colonies or ex-colonies providing the greatest number. The right of commonwealth and colonial subjects of the United Kingdom to live and work in the UK was legally confirmed in the British Nationality Act of 1948. This formalised the right of players such as Yoruba Tesi Balogun, Jamaicans Gil Heron and Lindy Delapenha and South Africans Steve Mokone, Gerry Francis and Albert Johanneson to play in Britain. However the Commonwealth Immigrants Act of 1962 changed this right of access. This legislation was introduced to greatly reduce the number of Black workers and their families, who were commonwealth citizens, from entering and settling in the UK. The law demanded that immigration officials filter out and, if possible, exclude from Britain people of colour, despite the fact that White emigrants into the British Isles from Europe, the Americas, Australia, Canada, New Zealand and other countries was much greater in number than from Africa, the Caribbean and South Asia. It wasn't migrants *per se* that were were a 'problem' for the government but migrants of colour. However it would be wrong to suggest that all Whites have been treated equally. The Irish, for instance, have always had hassle, made worse by the introduction of the Prevention of Terrorism Act in 1974. And two incidents from my father's life remain fixed in my memory: his arrest one evening because he could not find his (British) passport; and the headline 'Cypriot on a Harbouring Charge' on an inside page in the *Cambridge News*, 20 September 1962, after he was tried for sheltering my mum Pamela's best friend, Gwen, who was on the run. The report of the court case opened, 'A Greek–Cypriot was committed for trial yesterday . . .' The origin of the defendant was as important as the nature of the charge. The farce that led to the charge was an Ealing comedy:

A knock at the front door. Varnavas answers to find the police.
'Mr Varanavas Vasili?'
'Yes.'
'We believe Gwen Roberts is at this address.'
''Scuse me?'
'Is there a Gwen Roberts staying here?'
''Scuse me pleese?'
'Are there any women in your house?'
'My wife she no here.'
'Listen, we believe you are harbouring Mrs Gwen Roberts who is wanted for questioning by the Metropolitan Police . . .'
'Who is a want?'
' . . . we have been watching your house . . .'
'You been looking outside?'
'Look if you don't . . .'
[Gwen, offstage] 'Oh fuck it Billy, let them in!'

The '62 Act was not the first piece of legislation that century aimed at restricting access of Black workers to jobs in the UK. There had been the Aliens Acts and Orders passed in 1905, 1914, 1919, 1920 and 1925, all designed – in part or in full – to restrict the free movement of Black labour – usually seamen – in Britain. And in many intances these laws were applied by the police to those Black Britons who were not subject to them. During the Second World War, the British government introduced the United States of America Visiting Forces Act in 1942. The effect was to legalise the racism and segregation of the US Army while it was stationed in Britain, putting its apartheid structure above UK law. White British women would not be allowed to marry African–American soldiers. Public places could now be designated 'Whites'/Coloureds' only. Yet it had even more sinister repercussions. Of 19 GIs hanged in Shepton Mallet prison, 12 were Black. Yet African–Americans formed only 10 per cent of the US Army. Under the '42 Act, rape committed by a GI in Britain was a capital offence and at least one Black soldier was hanged for this. Under British law it had not been a hanging crime since the ninteenth century. Such was the legal framework regulating the actions of those African–Americans who'd come to fight the racism of the Nazis. The contradiction of waging a war on behalf of those who were themselves racist was not lost on these soldiers. Their experience in wartime Europe galvanised the struggle in peacetime America for civil rights. And in turn, as we shall discuss below, their marches and uprisings of the '50s and '60s fed back into the culture of resistance and fightback in Britain.

The 1962 Act, which introduced a three-grade voucher system of entry to the UK for commonwealth citizens, institutionalised racism making it a public instrument of government policy. It's message to all Blacks was: don't call us, we'll call you (when we need you to fight our wars, or do jobs nobody else wants). Such a political stance, masked, of course, by full-on bullshit which talked up issues such as 'overcrowding' through 'unrestricted immigration', was a green light to side-of-the-mouth racists who could now give full voice in the knowledge that their views had an official stamp of approval. The equation was a simple one. Immigrants were a problem. All Blacks were immigrants. Therefore all Blacks were a problem. Fortunately not everyone in Britain was so gullible.

The overt racialisation of British political culture was exemplified by Enoch Powell's 'Rivers of Blood' speech given in Birmingham two weeks after the murder of Martin Luther King in April 1968. The gist of his argument was that Black and White could not live together in Britain. And the fact that they were living, working and playing together in the same land would eventually result in bloodshed. On a number of occasions in his speech Powell made reference to 'American Negroes'. His intention was to recall for his audience scenes of devastation from inner cities in the USA, such as Watts and Harlem, following uprisings by working-class Blacks. He used these mental visual aides and annotated them with anecdotes and statistics that conjured an apocalyptic scenario for Anglo-Saxon Britons. Powell's solution was repatriation and, in suggesting this, he became the racists' icon. Shortly afterwards, London dockers marched in support of both his speech and the 1968 Immigration Act, aimed specifically at stopping the entry into the UK of East Africans and Asians with British passports.

For migrant Black footballers, the message was the same as for other Black workers. Legally it affected African players particularly hard because they tended not to have relations already living in Britain whom they could join and thereby prove they had 'close ties' – a provision demanded by the '68 Act. After the implementation of the Act, very few African footballers were invited to, or in fact could, play in Britain.

Prior to the period under discussion, men of colour had played in every position. Arthur Wharton stood between the posts at a time when only the stupid, or the incredibly brave, or those both fearless and a bit behind with the rent, did so. The Anglo-Asian Cother brothers of Watford played at full-back and half-back. Both were tough tacklers who weren't shy. Walter Tull was noted for his 'robust' style (as well as his skilled footwork). Jack Leslie and Eddie Parris of the inter-war period played in central positions. Charlie Williams was centre-half for Doncaster Rovers in the '50s. Lindy Delapenha was a free-scoring centre-forward for Middlesbrough in the early '50s. The list could continue. Until British political culture became overtly and consciously racialist during the late '50s, Black players were not seen as being good or bad, suitable or unsuitable in any particular position. This form of universal stereotyping occurred when Blacks in Britain *per se* were labelled as 'Immigrants' and 'Others'.

On the field, players of colour can only respond to this kind of re-construction of themselves by being themselves, by playing. Actively refuting stereotypes through practice has always been the unspoken agenda presented to Black sports men and women. And in some respects it has pushed them faster, harder, higher and longer. Resistance was on the field, the track and in the ring and sports hall. And paradoxically, while any athlete would prefer to be judged by their actions as athletes, their activities take place within an arena that is politicised because of the symbolic value sport has within any society. By being sports men and women they are unwittingly politicising themselves. The same actions by different people convey different meanings to a spectating audience. The draping of the Union Jack over the shoulders of Linford Christie at a sporting event feels, looks and reads differently than when the same flag is paraded by a Nazi on his way to an England match. (Yet the subjective reason for using the flag may be similar – patriotism.) During the early '80s, a few players began wearing white tights under their shorts in cold weather to reduce the risk of pulling muscles. Despite the piss-taking that followed, it was never suggested that the players were wearing them because they couldn't handle the British winter. Yet when Nigerians Francis Feyami at Cambridge City and Elkanah Onyeali at Tranmere wore gloves, this was precisely the reason given by supporters and colleagues who remember these players. And they may have been correct. But they wore gloves because they were from a tropical climate, Nigeria. Not because they were Black. Roy Brown did not wear gloves, nor did Walter

Tull. But racial stereotyping does not make such fine distinctions. Britain's wartime Foreign Secretary Anthony Eden complained that African–American soldiers – from northern cities such as New York, Detroit and Chicago – should not be stationed in Britain because they wouldn't like the cold British winters!

By redrawing players of colour to a shape and style that suited the dominant ideological trends of the era, they were effectively de-skilled. In other words, they did not receive the appropriate rewards for their skills and abilities. They tended to be undervalued, playing in the lower divisions and prone to being on the wrong end of an arbitrary decision by a manager, especially if that manager did not initially sign the player. Tony Whelan's career at Manchester United and City appears to bare this out. Valued by chief scout Joe Armstrong and managers Matt Busby and Wilf McGuinness, he was shown the door as soon as Tommy Docherty arrived. (Whelan's career is discussed further below.)

Racist abuse and chants from the terraces reflected the tone of disrespect by Britain's rulers to people of colour, becoming louder, more cutting and more common as Black footballers became a more common sight. Racism within the stadium occurred because it was sanctioned outside. It did not increase simply because there was a growing presence of Black footballers. However, while third-generation Black footballers had to contend with it, and continued to play despite such crude reconstructions of themselves, Black workers and communities were responding by fighting back in the workplace and on the streets.

Organising in response to racism has a long history in Britain. Despite the historical presence of people of colour in the British labour movement of the nineteenth century such as Chartist leader William Cuffey, political activist Robert Wedderburn and revolutionary William Davidson, there was still a battle to be fought within the trade union movement in the twentieth century for equality between Black and White workers. After the Second World War, with more Black workers in more workplaces including football stadia, resistance to de-skilling – the industrial repercussion of racist employment practices – within the Black working classes became better organised. In 1951 African–Caribbean workers on Merseyside formed the West Indian Association out of secret meetings they were forced to hold in workplace toilets and washrooms. In 1953 the Indian Workers Association was created in Coventry.

Collectively, Black workers were doing it for themselves; individually as well. Fed up with being dissed by passengers, one Jamaican bus driver in the 1950s jumped down from his cab and walked away, leaving the abusers stranded. While Black workers in Britain were organising themselves, it was in the USA that the fire inside exploded outwards, into the workplace and on to the streets. The Vietnam War, in which Black conscripts were disproportionately called up, the assassination of Malcolm X in 1965 and Martin Luther King in 1968, inflamed a generation of African–Americans. Black car workers in Detroit, for instance, formed the Detroit Revolutionary Union Movement – DRUM. Indeed the visit of Malcolm X to Britain in 1965 led to the formation of the revolutionary Racial Action Adjustment Society. This radicalisation of the Black working class in the

USA bolstered the confidence of Black workers in Britain. In May 1965 the Asian workforce of Courtauld's Red Scar Mill in Preston went on strike; in April '67 and October '68, Asians employed at the Coneygre Foundry in Tipton, Staffordshire, struck. This was the wider cultural climate in which players of colour, after 1945, were performing.

BLACK BRITISH PLAYERS 1945–70

Two players that have become representative icons for this period are Clyde Best and Albert Johanneson. Very few of those I interviewed in the course of this research mentioned Black British players such as Tommy Best, Tony Whelan, Dennis Walker or the (other) Charles brothers. It is as if the unwritten, oral version of the history of players of colour has remembered the presence of a number of 'exotic' migrants but forgotten the contribution of many Black Britons. This has much to do with why the past is remembered. If all Black Britons are perceived as migrants, their experiences, for people who think like Bernard Manning, become less essential, less worthy.

Below are the biographies of all the full-time professional players of colour born and/or brought up in Britain. I don't doubt that there are others, but I haven't come across them. They are presented in chronological order.

Hubert 'Bull' Best, or Tommy – as he prefers to be known – was a stocky, aggressive inside/centre-forward who, at his footballing peak in 1949, stood 5ft 9in and weighed 15 st 10 lb. While at the summit he felt he deserved to wear the red shirt with a dragon motif, yet he never did become the second Black man to play for Wales, despite public amplification of his inner feelings by football correspondents of the *South Wales Echo*. Born 23 December 1920 at Milford Haven, Pembrokeshire, his Jamaican father was a fireman on fishing trawlers and his mother Welsh. The former died when Tommy was 12 years of age after entering a sanatorium because of deteriorating mental health. This left his mother to raise seven children. To say 'life wasn't easy' in this pre-welfare state era would be mouthing the obvious. However, for Tommy at least, football provided both a focus and an escape: he could concentrate on something he knew he was good at; and it would keep him out of an overcrowded house – in fact in the field opposite. He was encouraged at Milford Haven Central School by a teacher, Mr Vivian Lewis who, noticing something extra, proposed him for a Wales schoolboy cap. Tommy played in the trial game and thought he had done enough to be given a second chance. It never came.

He made his Football League début at the relatively late age of 27 with Chester City who had signed him from home-town club Milford United in October 1948. Tommy scored 14 goals in 40 games for the Division Three North club, attracting the attention of Cardiff manager Cyril Spiers. The Bluebirds, playing one division higher, fancied the tough and tenacious Tommy enough to fork out £7,000 with a £150 signing-on fee (Tommy was originally offered a much smaller sum). The transfer fee was a substantial amount for a player who had been a full professional for just 16 months. (A year earlier Tommy Lawton, considered one of the best centre-forwards, if not the best, in the British game was sold by Chelsea to Notts County for £20,000.) Apparently Blackpool, Sunderland and Leeds United were also interested in him. Best's wages at Cardiff were £12 per week during the season, £10 in the summer – a rise of 50 per cent from that paid by Chester. Having chosen Cardiff because it was near his home town of Milford Haven, he felt he was at the height of his powers while playing for Wales's premier club. In his first season they achieved a creditable fourth place in the league, with the 1–0 defeat of Tottenham at Ninian Park remembered as the high point (the Londoners had to settle for fifth spot). The low point was a fixed game at Leicester City at the end of the season. The Cardiff team was approached by a Leicester player who offered £10 a man to draw the game 0–0. A point each would ensure the home-team's survival in Division Two and qualify the Cardiff players for the club's 'talent money' bonus, paid for reaching an agreed league position and/or accumulating a certain number of points. In fact it ended 1–1 with Cardiff scoring an unscripted freak goal and Leicester allowed to put the game back on an even keel with a shot that barely trickled beyond the goal line. Leicester stayed up, the Cardiff players got their 'talent money' bonus and their little, untraceable extra of £10 a man. As Tommy and others have confirmed, such end-of-season scams when a lot is at stake, were nothing new or unusual.

Within a month of the following season kicking off, Best had become the regular centre-forward. '[Cardiff City] manager Cyril Spiers had one slight worry when the season opened – his centre-forward position. It's gone now. Tommy Best is playing grandly and leading the line in true championship style.'[1] He scored five goals in the first nine matches, including the winner in the local derby against Swansea before a crowd of 57,510 – then a record for a League game at Ninian Park. Yet he was never called up for Wales. Trevor Ford of Aston Villa was the first-choice centre-forward of Welsh selectors. (Interestingly, given the bribed match with Leicester, Ford in his autobiography writes about drugs such as pheno-barbitone and dexadrine that were on offer to players in the '50s. The good old days, eh!) The aggressive, fearless Ford may simply have been the better player. It could be argued that he was more versatile than Best, though the *Sporting Mirror* describes the 'Bull' as having '[a] deceptive lumbering run, magnificent flicks and [a] footballing brain and intelligence . . . Tommy is acknowledged as one of the speediest leaders in the country.'[2] Indeed, during the war Best played a number of representative games, most notably for the Combined Services against an Ireland XI at Belfast in May 1943 when he scored three in a 5–2 victory. He was the only Navy footballer to be selected. If a forces game was coming up, Tommy joked he would be left ashore for safe-keeping when his ship sailed for hazardous duties like minesweeping! Playing for the RAF against Shropshire Sportman's XI on 13 May 1944, Tommy played with another

Black player, Roy Brown. While serving in the Navy Tommy turned out for Belfast Celtic as a loan player. Despite the sectarian divide in Ulster football, he enjoyed his time in Belfast and felt untroubled by racial prejudice. From Ireland he was posted to Australia where he played for Thistle FC in Queensland. He didn't like Oz, especially the openly racist treatment of the Aborigines. Once his time had finished on that continent he was off.

Best believes his 'Bull'ish but thoughtful forward play endeared him to Cardiff fans and helped them overcome any prejudice they may have held towards his colour. (If anything, racial abuse from players would spur him on to do better.) 'The crowd used to love me.' Nearly double the normal attendance, 18,000 turned out to see his début in the Reserves. He played a total of 28 games for the club, scoring ten goals. Unfortunately he got a bad knee injury just at the time he was finding the net with the ease of a modern-day web nerd. Full-back Ron Stitfall took the number nine shirt and Tommy was unable to de-robe him. Eventually, in December 1949, unwilling to put up with reserve-team football, he signed for Queen's Park Rangers where he played just twelve games, scoring three goals. From Loftus Road he joined Southern League Hereford United and has lived in the town ever since. Over the worst of his injury, he now began to enjoy his football again. 'The old fashioned, uncompromising centre-forward . . . became a natural "target man" . . . his frame would fill a doorway and his bustling all-action style of leadership made him a firm favourite with the fans.'[3] Hereford won the Southern League Cup in 1952 for the first time. In his three seasons at the club, he made 145 appearances, scoring 67 goals – one almost every other game.

'Bull' continued playing until his forties, mostly for semi-professional clubs in the West Midlands region, such as Bromsgrove Rovers and Evesham, while whitening himself in a Hereford bakery during the day. A fit man, he has always been teetotal and non-smoking. After 50 years of marriage to his wife Eunice, whom he met while playing at Chester, he cycles to the snooker hall and back and works on his garden. He also gambles on football, the horses and boxing. He has an encyclopedic knowledge of his former profession and, in a rejection of some of his own strengths, he prefers technique to brawn and intelligence to industry, noticing the subtleties of sophisticated running off the ball, positioning and passing. And he continues to inspire, nearly forty years after he stopped playing. Interviewing this opinionated, thoughtful, open, hospitable man – and seeing him and Eunice in action – was a roar. Long after the crowds have gone, he can still put on a show.

A contemporary of Tommy's, Tony Collins possessed those attributes the Welsh centre-forward admires. Collins was a 'skilful and elegant left winger',[4] yet he is best remembered for his achievements as a manager and scout rather than a player. Born 19 March 1926 at Kensington in West London, the son of a coach trimmer signed for First Division Brentford as a 16-year-old amateur. He then played for a succession of clubs including Sheffield Wednesday, York City,

Norwich City, Torquay United, Crystal Palace, Rochdale and Watford, where he took part in over 107 games, including some alongside Anglo-Nigerian Roy Brown and Anglo-Chinese Sammy Chung.

Though Tony wasn't the first Black manager of a professional team in England – that honour goes to Arthur Wharton – he was the first Black manager to lead his team to the final of a national competition. In 1962, Rochdale of the Fourth Division played Norwich of the Second in a two-legged final of the League Cup, losing 3–0 at home and 1–0 away. They were the first and last Fourth-Division club to reach the final of any national competition open to all Football League clubs.

Tony left Rochdale's Spotland in September 1967, after seven years as manager, to become assistant manager to Alan Dicks at Second-Division Bristol City. Their greatest success was winning promotion to the First Division in 1976 after finishing runners-up to Sunderland. And, for 19 frustrating days in September 1980, following City's relegation from the First Division, he was caretaker manager. In reality his primary duty at City was chief scout, a role he also fulfilled for Don Revie at Leeds United in their championship-winning days. Collin's ability in finding and managing young talent inpired Ron Atkinson to appoint the Londoner to head the scouting system at Old Trafford. According to Tony's version of events, he recommended a young, Black Watford winger called John Barnes to the club. However, Collins feels his greatest discovery was another winger, Lee Sharpe, whom he encouraged Alex Ferguson to sign from Torquay United, again a former club of the scout. It is noticeable that the two players Collins felt most excited about were both, like himself, wide players.

Alex Ferguson, however, believes that the scouting system at United waned under the influence of Collins. He disputes the latter's assertion that he first alerted the club to Lee Sharpe. 'The credit . . . was not down to a scout . . . The initial tip came from a retired journalist, Len Noade.' Ferguson also criticises Collins for not pressing the club to move quickly for John Barnes.

> A manager needs a chief scout who is prepared to commit himself with a firm decision for or against . . . I'm afraid Tony [Collins], maybe too much of the old school, was too cautious for me. Perhaps experience had made him wary, but the result for me was that we lost John Barnes to Liverpool and we have paid for it more than once.[5]

As an ex-winger Collins had an acute eye for those with skills that matched or bettered his own. He, like Tommy Best, is an advocate of technique over muscled athleticism. Interviewed at Watford's centenary dinner in 1993, he complained about the decline in wide play and in the general level of skill of senior professionals. He put this down to the increased speed of the game and managers' fear of losing:

> They talk about wingers, but how many of the modern-day or more recent wingers were in the mould of an Eddie Gray, a Matthews or a

Finney? How many can go past their full-back? Some can hit good, accurate crosses but they can't go past their full-backs. In the past, wingers used to pick out a player with his cross. Now the winger hits the ball generally into the area and you just get numbers in there to contest it. It is a lottery. The game has speeded up but although they flash the ball about at great speed like lightning, so many passes are given away because you cannot play faster than you can think.[6]

Collins's perception of the past is a condition of age that afflicts all of us. The older we get, the better it was: the past a golden era that the not-so-young were privileged to experience. The ex-Watford man mentions players from his era that were, by any standards, brilliant. But he fails to mention the wing play of Ryan Giggs, Mark Walters, Mark Chamberlain (and others), all skinning their full-backs in the period he gave the interview.

Despite Alex Ferguson's reservations, Tony Collins was a sought-after scout. On leaving Manchester United, he joined Jim Smith at QPR, then followed him to Newcastle. When Smith resigned from St James's Park in 1991, Collins worked as a part-time scout at Millwall. He is one of the few Black professionals to have spent his working life in the game.

While centre-half Charlie Williams did not have the privilege of a lifetime's employment in football as enjoyed by Collins he is, like Tony, best remembered for his achievements after lacing his hard-toed boots for the last time. As a comedian, Charlie became a household name. Gigging the northern Working Men's Club circuit during the 1960s, Charlie's big break in show business came with his success in *The Comedians* TV showcase of the early '70s. It was broadcast at prime-time, early Saturday evening and soared to the top of the ratings. For the first time in his life, the up-and-at-'em ex-centre-half of Doncaster Rovers was top of the table. However, Charlie's self-deprecating style of humour was not to everybody's liking. Young Black viewers in particular felt the comedian's light-hearted treatment of racism and issues of colour played to popular prejudice, rather than confront it. Charlie's experience of growing up in a White mining community and working down the pit, and of being the lone Black man in an all-White team as a footballer in the late '40s and '50s, had conditioned this response. Indeed, he was known as the dressing-room comedian at Rovers, graduating to the supporters club once his off-field talents became known.

Interviewed for the Radio 5 documentary on Black footballers, *Across the White Line*, Williams recalled the shouts directed at him on Saturday afternoons:

It were always black this and black that which didn't really bother me a great deal. In fact it made me even more determined. I felt sorry for the centre-forward. It were nowt to do wi' 'im but he were going to get some hammer . . . I used to laugh. They'd shout 'get back to your own country', but it were only 5/6d (28p) back to Doncaster.

Though born in the pit village of Royston, near Barnsley on 23 December 1927, Williams grew up in nearby South Hiendly. Suffering from a nervous breakdown, his English mother, Doris, was hospitalised while Charlie was young, and she never returned home. His Barbadian father Charles Augustus had served in the Royal Engineers in the First World War where he became permanently injured with trench foot, which often stopped him from working. Consequently, poverty was a daily part of family life for Charlie and his sister, also called Doris. In fact his sister was sent to live with an aunt before going on to a children's home because Charles senior could not look after both children. Nevertheless, the son credits his father for instilling in him confidence and a sense of identity. His father's heroes were Black sport stars Jesse Owens, Joe Louis and Learie Constantine, while Charlie's earliest role model was Randolph Turpin. The success of this Black British boxer awakened the realisation that sport was a domain where Black Britons could literally force their presence upon an otherwise disinterested public. Charles Augustus died in 1944 when Charlie was 16. Although, legally, he could have set up house on his own, he went instead to live with his aunt Edith Bedford and his cousins at Upton, near Pontefract.

Williams had a trial period as an amateur with Leeds United during 1947–8 but failed to win a contract. However, it was while he was playing for Upton Colliery the following season that he was invited by Division Three North Doncaster Rovers to sign as a part-time professional for 1949–50. The South Yorkshire club were then drawing crowds of 20,000. For the following five years he continued to work as a miner while playing for the reserves in the Midland Counties and Central Leagues. In 1953 Rovers, now in Division Two, offered the 25-year-old a full-time contract and the prospect of first-team football. He accepted, even though this meant a drop in income. As a weekday miner and weekend footballer, Charlie had been earning around £16 per week. As a full-time player he would receive £14. Yet what compensation is there for not being able to see the light of day? Charlie felt it was worth £2 of his money.

Not noted for taking prisoners – 'the ball might've gone past me, and sometimes the player, but never both at the same time'[7] – his highlight at Doncaster was beating Aston Villa 3–1 in the fourth round of the 1954–55 FA Cup after four replays! The total playing time had been nine hours. Williams was listed for transfer in 1959 at £3,500, after 10 seasons and 158 first-team appearances. He felt this was unfair. At his age and with his service to Rovers, he should have been given a free transfer in order to entice some of the better clubs, though he was allowed two benefit matches which netted 744 compensatory pound notes. Charlie and his wife of three years, Andrea, eventually went to Skegness where he joined the town's part-time professional Midland Counties League club, lured by manager George Raynor (who coached Steve Mokone at Coventry City and had guided Sweden to the 1958 World Cup final), rent-free accommodation, £15 per week for playing and £10 for driving a confectionery wagon during the day.

Soon after Raynor moved on in 1962, Charlie was released by the club. He lost his lorry-driving job in the same week. The couple returned to South Yorkshire, where the centre-half returned to his roots as player–manager of colliery side Denaby Main. It was a labour of love, the wage a little better than nowt. Soon after this mixing of pleasure and business he received an offer of a two-year contract with a house and car from a club in Sydney, Australia via a friend and ex-player, Alick Jeffrey. Excited, Charlie went about the usual bureaucratic formalities with Australia House in London only to find the procedure wasn't a formality. Australia operated a 'Whites Only' immigration and visa policy. Once it became clear that Charlie was Black, the civil servants wielded the colour bar. Not willing to back off quietly, Charlie publicised the affair. Embarrassed and exposed, Australian prime minister Robert Menzies responded by arguing his government wasn't racist. Permission granted to live and work in Australia, Charlie decided not to go, preferring the dole queue and the odd comedy/singing turn in the Working Men's Clubs to feeling forever grateful for nothing. Then along came an offer from a TV producer with an idea to pilot a show called *The Comedians*.

Williams retired from the entertainment industry in December 1995. (The day before our interview he'd performed for pensioners in Rotherham.) 1996 would be the first year in over forty that he would not be paid to bring pleasure – and, no doubt pain – to an audience. Despite his fame he never drifted far from his working-class roots in the South Yorkshire coalfield. He still lives very close to the village in which he was born. For a time he was a director of his home-town club Barnsley and did fundraising gigs for the local miners during the Great Strike of 1984–5.

As Charlie Williams was playing out his days by the seaside, 16-year-old Stanley Horne was signing as a boot-cleaning, terrace-sweeping apprentice for Aston Villa, becoming the second player of colour, after Kevin Keelan, to join this original member of the Football League. Initially with Villa as an amateur, Horne turned professional in December 1961. He made just six appearances for the first team before moving on in September 1965 to Second Division Manchester City. At this Moss Side club, an unusual managerial duo, the avuncular Merseysider Joe Mercer (51) and the flamboyant, worldly-wise southerner Malcolm Allison (38) had just taken over. It was the beginning of the light blue and white's re-emergence as a powerful force, with the trio of Lee, Bell and Summerbee teasing and tormenting opposition. During Horne's three and a half seasons and 48 games at Maine Road, the City won the Second Division Championship in May 1966 and the First Division two years later. Mancunian writer Colin Shindler, a lifelong City supporter and United hater brave enough to 'come out', remembers Stan as a likeable 'workaday' footballer – an 'honest trier' but with limited dimensions to his game. Unfortunately for Stan, another right-half who could score goals, Mike Doyle, was emerging. Shindler also feels that the racist comments Horne received from the home crowd were mild compared to those used by other home supporters to abuse their Black players, such as Clyde Best at West Ham. A common wisecrack was, 'Where's your spear, Stan?' So, respect is due to the light blues . . . isn't it?

In the season that City reached the FA Cup final, 1968–9, Horne was sold to Second Division Fulham for £20,000. While it must have been a bind leaving one of the best sides in England – some City supporters, especially the grey-hairs, may argue it has never been bettered – for a struggling West London outfit soon to be relegated, Stan contributed fully to the Craven Cottage revitalisation that followed the drop. He played 89 first-team games over four and a half seasons, and was a member of the promotion-winning side of 1971. The final game of that season was against Preston North End, who had Anglo-Indian Ricky Heppolette in midfield. The winners on the day would secure the Third Division Championship. The match and title was settled by a diving header from Heppolette after a 22nd-minute corner. In most photographs of the goal, Stan is seen looking on helplessly in the background.

After a short spell at Chester between August and December 1973, Stan teamed up with another former Manchester City player and Black Briton, Tony Whelan, and Leo Skeete at Rochdale. Like Whelan, he also played summer football in the North American Soccer League, with Denver Dynamo.

Steve Stacey was very nearly another who joined Stan Horne and Tony Whelan in the NASL. Instead he migrated to Western Australia to play and coach. In fact he was captain of Western Australia when they beat Glasgow Rangers 2–1, their first-ever triumph over an overseas side. Steve found his experience of the antipodes quite different to Tommy Best's some 30 years earlier. The Staceys stayed in Oz. Presently Steve works for the Ministry of Education at a Residential College in Albany, the original state capital. He doesn't regret moving from the old slave port of Bristol on England's west coast, where he grew up and played for City, to this ex-penal colony of Britain on Australia's sparsely populated south-western tip.

Living in their catchment area it was Rovers, Bristol's other full-time professional team, that Steve wanted to play for as a child. However City were 'slicker and quicker' in tying up the young Fairfield Grammar schoolboy. Initially signing as an amateur while he finished his GCSE 'O' levels, he was apprenticed at 16. In practice this meant wearing your own boots in the morning, cleaning all the pros' boots at lunchtime and pushing a broom along the terraces in the afternoon.

It wasn't until Stacey's transfer to Wrexham – the city in which association football began in Wales – in February 1966 that his career took off. In three seasons he played over 101 first-team games overwhelmingly at full-back, although he was forced into goal in a match at York in April 1967 when keeper John Schofield injured his hand. (Fellow Black professional Dennis Walker was playing for York at this time.) His other most memorable match was just a few weeks later, the 1967 Welsh Cup final against Cardiff City. It produced the only senior medal he ever 'won' in British football, though he never received it.

Wrexham manager Alvan Williams was so disgusted at a tackle by Cardiff's Gareth Williams on Terry Oldfield that he threw the box of medals back at the official from the Welsh FA. Indeed, so bad was the injury that a player was literally sick at the sight of it. Oldfield never played again and had to wear a leg brace. Wrexham also lost the match 4–3 on aggregate. Steve doesn't know what happened to the medals after they hit their target.

Having built a reputation as a solid, competent full-back in September 1968, First Division Ipswich Town, under Bill McGarry and Sammy Chung, offered £22,000 for the 24-year-old. The Suffolk club had just been promoted and their managerial duo were seen as a combination going places. Stacey received 5 per cent of the transfer fee, with the PFA receiving the same. His new wage with win, appearance and other bonuses could exceed the magical figure of £100. It seemed to Steve, and his wife who was expecting their second child, that they'd finally made the big time. But football is an Alice in Wonderland world where often everything isn't just as it seems. Put straight into the first team – at home against Liverpool – the left-back played just three more first-team games.

Soon after Stacey had signed for Ipswich McGarry and Chung left for Wolves. They were replaced by Bobby Robson. 'Bob liked touch players and basically I wasn't.'[8] A hamstring tear didn't help. After a few games on loan to Chester and Charlton the following season in September 1970, he was transferred back to Bristol City for £5,000. There is a superstition held by some that it's a bad idea to try and recapture glories of the past by returning to a former club. For believers, Steve's experience at Ashton Gate was confirmation. Unable to overcome his injury, he played only nine League games, moving on the following season to St James's Park . . . Exeter, where he ended his Football League career.

Approaching thirty and injury-prone, it was time to look beyond the far terracing and entertain the prospect of real work. Offered the job of manager of a travel company in Bristol, Steve accepted, combining his day job with turning out for non-league Bath City at evenings and weekends. Then the letter with an Australian stamp arrived.

After the Cother brothers who played for Watford during the 1890s and 1900s, John and Clive Charles are the second brothers of colour to play professionally for the same club. While Dennis Walker was attempting to break into his local side, Manchester United's first team, Canning Town born John Charles was pursuing a similar struggle at his local club, West Ham United, for whom he signed in May 1962. Spotted by the club's chief scout Wally St Pier he is, as far as I've been able to find out, the first Black Briton to play for England Youth.

John captained West Ham's FA Youth Cup-winning side of 1963. As a reward for his consistency, leadership and instrumental role in that success he made his Football League and England Youth début that same season. Over the following seven football years, he appeared in 142 League and Cup matches for the Hammers, playing in the great West Ham sides of the '60s alongside Moore, Hurst, Peters, Brooking, Bonds and lodger Clyde Best. Between 2 May 1964 and

30 July 1966, Bobby Moore raised three trophies at Wembley: the FA Cup in 1964, the European Cup-Winners Cup in 1965 and the Jules Rimet trophy in July 1966. Unfortunately John didn't figure in any of these triumphs and was released by West Ham in the summer of 1971. Refusing to join Orient, he chose to sell fruit from his own market stall.

Through his association with John, St Pier became a friend of the family, also recommending younger brother Clive to the Irons. Mrs Charles recalls Wally's first visit to the Charles's council house in Ronald Avenue, West Ham E15:

> What a laugh that was. One of my daughters was in when he first came to the door asking for the boys. He said he was a chief scout and he'd call back. We all got ready, waiting for him to turn up in his shorts and woggle. We thought he said boy scout![9]

In the 1996 Radio 5 documentary *Across the White Line*, Clive praises his friend and colleague Clyde Best for inspiring young Black players. While there is no doubt the Bermudan did act as a role model, Clive modestly overlooks the very real and unsung contribution of those such as John and himself.

Seven years younger than John, Clive signed for the Hammers in August 1969. He also represented England at youth level. Yet he made only 14 appearances for the West Ham first team. He was prevented from claiming a regular place by the excellence of alternative full-backs Frank Lampard and John McDowell. However during his time at Upton Park, West Ham had the distinction of having more Black players on their books than just about any other club. In 1971 Nigerian Londoner Ade Coker and Clyde Best – together with the Charles brothers and six Black youngsters on schoolboy forms – stood as booted testament to the increasing momentum of change in the demography of British football. Eager for regular first-team football, Clive dropped a division and signed for Cardiff City in March 1974, playing 77 League games in four seasons for the Bluebirds. He could be found 20 years later coaching in Oregon, USA.

Mike Trebilcock registers among anoraks as the man who scored two goals in an FA Cup final. Born in Gunnislake, Cornwall, on 29 November 1944, he shot himself to fame in the 1966 final, playing in the blue of Everton against Sheffield Wednesday.

> A colourful final full of incident and goals saw the dramatic recovery of an Everton team that had looked well beaten. They were revived by two fine goals from an energetic little Cornishman who was a surprise replacement for the expensive and experienced Pickering. It was typical of the romance of the Cup that this one game should bring fame to a young player whose name was not even in the programme and who could never afterwards establish himself at the top level.[10]

Trebilcock joined the Merseysiders from Plymouth Argyle of the division below. He'd originally been signed by the Pilgrims' manager, a youthful Malcolm Allison, from another Devon club, Tavistock. The Black Celt made 79 appearances at Argyle's Home Park, scoring 28 goals including one on his début against Southampton. The Devonians were apparently able to bring the best out of Black centre-forwards. Another man of colour who wore the green of Plymouth 40 years earlier was Jack Leslie – he also scored for fun.

Trebilcock's 28 brought him to the notice of Everton who paid £20,000 in December 1965. Although he never established himself in the first team, he gained a place in the 1965–6 FA Cup semi-final against Manchester United after an injury to regular Fred Pickering. His next game in the final was his last for the Goodison Park club. (What a way to leave!) Having made just 11 first-team appearances in two seasons he headed back southward to Portsmouth for whom he played more games than any other club, over 100 in League and Cups (again a club which had had another Black forward, Lindy Delapenha, during the late 1940s). He ended his League career at Torquay in the county in which he had started. Mike now lives in Newcastle, Australia.

Central defender Anthony Parry began his career with his home-town club Burton Albion of the Southern League. He graduated into the Football League in November 1965 with Fourth Division Hartlepool United and, after six seasons – five in the Fourth, one in the Third Division – and 181 League appearances was signed by Brian Clough for Derby County in January 1972. Over the previous three seasons Derby had finished fourth and ninth in the First Division after winning the Second Division. For the young Midlander, such a transformation in fortune was akin to sleeping rough and then being invited to move in with Naomi Campbell. The 'Rams' won the first division the season he joined and finished seventh and third the following seasons. And, when you're riding high, everyone wants to get up alongside: competition for places was very strong. After two years and three seasons at the Baseball Ground, Tony left Clough's rampant Derby with just half a dozen first-team appearances. In January 1974 Parry metamorphosed from a 'Ram' to a 'Stag', signing for Fourth Division Mansfield Town, for whom he made just one League appearance.

Eight months before Parry moved into League football, Glasgow-born Peter Foley became the second Black Scottish winger to join an English club – after Lincoln City's John Walker in 1900 – signing from Edinburgh Preston Athletic for Workington Town in February 1965. The 20-year-old had been trialling with Leicester City and was offered a contract but chose the West Cumbrians instead. He made this unlikely decision because Keith Burkinshaw, the new, young player–manager of Third Division Town offered him part-time terms allowing him to continue his training as a bookbinder. With an injury-depleted squad of just 14 full-timers, he went straight into the first team, making his début at Reading.

'Reds' fan David Goodall remembers Foley as being 'a very popular player'. It seems that his days at small-time, impoverished Borough Park were not unhappy. He made over 70 appearances, scoring 17 goals. He also married a local woman and still lives in nearby Whitehaven. Indeed for a short time during the 1977–78 season he returned to the club as manager. His other Football League clubs were Scunthorpe United and Chesterfield. An honoured guest at the Tribute to Black Pioneers dinner in Birmingham, Peter was still active in football, scouting for Newcastle United.

Ipswich-born John Miller realised every footballer's dream of playing for their home-town club in the First Division (now Premiership) when he made his début for Ipswich Town against Coventry towards the end of the 1968–69 season. Unfortunately, like Delapenha at Portsmouth in the '40s and Tony Parry at Derby in the '70s, John was unable to secure a regular first-team place. In his first three seasons he played only eight games. (On the training ground for a while, at the side of Portman Road, was fellow Black professional Steve Stacey.) After over fifty outings, he was transferred in October 1974 for £43,000 to close rivals Norwich City of the Second Division. The 'Canaries' won promotion that season. However it was for Third Division Mansfield Town that he was to make his greatest number of appearances, over 109 in the Football League alone. As happened at Norwich, Miller's arrival had a galvanising effect. In his first season with the 'Stags' they finished as champions, winning promotion to Division Two, the Suffolk man eventually closing his League career in the Potteries at Fourth Division Port Vale.

Although Miller could point to his games in the UEFA Cup against Real Madrid and Lazio as highs, he did not fulfil the promise predicted for him. Maurice Smith, writing for the *People*, 19 December 1971, thought John would be England's first Black international. (Eighty-five years earlier, during the 1886–87 season, the football correspondent of the *Northern Echo* was calling for another player, Arthur Wharton, to be England's first Black cap!)

John later became a sports-hall manager in Sutton-in-Ashfield while continuing to play in the Northern Counties and Central Midland's Leagues.

For Millwall, a club situated in the heart of London's dockland, an area that is characterised by the coming and going of people and goods, it is surprising that Frank Peterson, who signed professional forms in February 1969 was the first Black professional footballer to play League football for the 'Lions'. However he was not the first man of colour to play for the club – that was Egyptian Hassan Hegazi in 1912. Peterson made his début in the 1969–70 season in a Division Two match against Portsmouth at Fratton Park. The boys from Bermondsey lost 3–0. In fact he made only four appearances for the first team, finishing on the losing side each time. Millwall team-mate Billy Neil 'remembers Peterson as a big, skilful forward who never quite made the transition from outstanding reserve to first-team player'.[11] After two seasons at the Den he joined Charlton but, unable to luxuriate in the oasis of first-team football, he found The Valley dry and arid.

In April 1998, as a member of the Manchester United Football Academy coaching team, Tony Whelan helped guide the club's Under-12 team to victory in the Dallas Cup XIX tournament at Richland College, Dallas, Texas. The tournament merited a double-page feature in the June 1998 edition of *World Soccer*. The 3–0 win over Academia Venezolana of Venezuela was highlighted for special attention. A European win in this most prestigious of youth tournaments is rare. Having watched Tony at his coaching sessions at The Cliff, Manchester United's training ground, and noticed his ability to encourage the best from his charges, the Dallas triumph is no surprise. Ironically Whelan was – and is, as full-time member of the club's Football Academy – providing his youngsters with the discipline and skills necessary to compete and succeed at the highest level. Ironic because, for many observers of Tony's career, 'success at the highest level' was a reward deserved but denied to this son of an English mother and Nigerian father he never met.

Like John Miller, Tony Whelan played for his hometown club – in fact he was employed by both of them. Unlike John Miller, however, Tony grew up in a city that was fortunate to contain two of the most powerful and influential clubs of the 1960s and early '70s: Manchester. If those professionals who wear the shirt of the team they supported as a boy are fulfilling a dream in playing for United and City, left-winger Whelan can be said to have realised an outrageous fantasy. He signed for Manchester United as an apprentice footballer, 27 July 1968, at £7 per week. The amount is meaningless. The Salford-born teenager, having spent his teenage years in foster and childrens' homes – thus echoing the trajectory of W.D. Tull who signed for Spurs in 1909 while resident in a children's home in Bethnal Green – was now employed by the reigning champions of Europe in a country that was the reigning World Champion: in the right place, at the right club – containing the current European Footballer of the Year, George Best – at the right time. Additionally, if these historical circumstances couldn't conspire to do the right thing by Tony, he had been signed by arguably the greatest manager of his generation, Matt Busby. The Scotsman believed in giving youth its head. He had produced the Babes and seen the first flowering deadened by the South German snow. But the Scottish socialist and ex-miner never stopped believing in his vision.

For Busby, United was a family. He liked to know and address everyone at the club by their first name. Even chief scout Joe Armstrong, who probably recommended Tony to Busby, liked his youngsters to call him 'Uncle Joe'. (Busby's legacy has continued. Amongst the coaching staff, especially within the Football Academy, there is an absence of a cold, corporate atmosphere.) Perhaps Old Trafford would provide Tony with that secure, protective environment that he'd struggled to find in his life. For a youth who'd had a troubled upbringing foisted upon him, such fortune may have been received with the feeling that here was an overdue back payment for endured suffering. In common with many of the characters in the dramas recounted on these pages the promise of youth often hardened into a lesser reality. So it was with Whelan.

After 24 years as manager, Busby abdicated in January 1969. After much speculation on the identity of his successor, the board, but most importantly the man himself, took that decision which played true to Busby's beliefs and practice. They kept 'it' in the family by offering the job to Wilf McGuinness, youth-team coach and a local boy from Collyhurst. From Tony's angle Wilf's appointment was a relief. McGuinness had guided Whelan along these last two seasons. The youth team had reached the two-legged semi-final of the FA Youth Cup, in which Tony had beaten a young David Icke in the Coventry goal to score United's consolation effort in a 3–1 first-leg defeat. They lost the second leg 1–0 at Old Trafford. (Though the youths did win the internationally renowned FC Blue Stars tournament in Switzerland in 1969.) With Wilf as boss it came as no surprise when Tony, with his cultured left-foot, athletic frame and consistently good performances for United's youngsters, was offered a full professional contract in December 1969, at a basic wage of £20 per week, £18 close-season. The boy who'd supported City would now be mixing and training with rival idols Dennis Law and Bobby Charlton. It would also give him the opportunity of learning the art of wing play from the acknowledged master, George Best. Indeed within six months – still only 17 – Wilf took him with the first team on their close season tour of Bermuda, the USA and Canada. He made his first-team début against the Bermudan national team which included Clyde Best. He started in place of George Best, who came on for Tony in the second half. Later in the tour, in San Francisco, he played against Eintracht Frankfurt.

A few months on, in October 1970, he was selected for England Youth trials at Lilleshall but wasn't one of the chosen. Tony thought he was hard done by. He had been good enough for the United first-team tour of Bermuda, the USA and Canada but not England Youth, where many of the players would not have been in their first-team squads full stop. He had experienced this kind of thing before. As an adolescent he wasn't selected for Lancashire or England Schoolboys but was signed by United on leaving school! Indeed, during the 1969–70 season, Busby, commenting on the strength in depth at the club, rated the club's generation of youngsters as the best for years. Wearing number 11, Whelan played his first game for the reserves on 10 December 1969, against Leeds United. Wearing the same number for his opponents was Albert Johanneson. For the second team, Tony played alongside footballers of international calibre such as Nobby Stiles, Ian Ure, Jimmy Rimmer, John Aston, Willie Morgan and finished top scorer over one campaign. Yet as the seasons passed without elevation to the senior team, calls for him to be given a chance became more public. In particular, *Daily Express* columnists James Lawton and Bill Fryer took it upon themselves to become the voice of Tony's inner yearning. After Busby stepped down in early 1969, and Wilf McGuinness had taken over, the shine of the golden period of the mid to late '60s was definitely losing its brilliance. Denis Law and Bobby Charlton were in their thirties and past their best, although George wasn't. He was carrying the team. Wilf did what he knew. He relied on home-grown talent: in came Don Givens, John Aston, Paul Edwards, Carlo Sartori. But results didn't go United's way and come December 1970, Wilf was sacked with Matt Busby resuming as caretaker-manager. In reality he had always been in ultimate control.

This turmoil at the top did not affect Tony. Both Wilf and Matt believed in the abilities of the young winger. He was their type of player. However, the boss was only back for a short while. At the end of the '70–'71 season, Frank O'Farrell was appointed as 'permanent'(!) manager. After stocktaking, he told Whelan, 'There is nothing down for you here', adding that Maurice Setters, manager of Fourth Division Doncaster Rovers, had made an offer and he'd be wise to accept. Tony thought he could play at a higher level.

O'Farrell's presence had not stabilised United: George Best was missing training and sometimes just missing, and Busby's shadow still covered Old Trafford. Unsurprisingly, results on the pitch reflected events off it. In December 1972 O'Farrell too was given his cards and in came flamboyant, egotistical, successful Tommy Docherty, the fourth manager at Old Trafford in four seasons. He was a man who had a way with words but was not a man of his word. Very quickly he released Tony on a free transfer after offering him a loan period at Blackpool which the player refused. It appeared he didn't rate the Black winger. (But there again, he dropped George Best, causing the Irish winger to walk away from United for the last time.) Did Docherty watch Tony and decide or did he just want rid of the Black youngster? Whatever the reason, Docherty had the balls to tell him to his face that he had no future at the club. In an unusually generous gesture, United didn't ask for a transfer fee and paid off the remaining portion of his contract, which expired later in June. Clubs would normally wait until the end of season to release players they were letting go for nothing. Yet Tony couldn't understand why United had released him without a fee – was Docherty doing it for Tony, to widen the quota of clubs who might bid for him, or because he wanted Whelan out of the door sharpish?

Whelan's talent had not gone unnoticed in Manchester. He was invited for a month's trial by Malcolm Allison at Manchester City and, despite an offer of a contract from Jimmy Armfield's resurgent Bolton Wanderers who were looking down on most others in the Third Division, he accepted. It was unusual for players to move between the reds and the blues – Denis Law excepted. In so doing, Whelan became the first Black footballer to play for both Manchester clubs. Allison, who loved to make bold, upbeat statements about his youngsters, predicted that the 20-year-old winger, back with the team he'd supported as a kid, would be ready for first-team football around the time of the derby game against United in late April. The *Manchester Evening News Football Pink*, 3 March 1973, thought he'd 'bring colour to the team'! In fact Tony tuned in and turned it on even quicker than big Fedora-hatted Malcolm had envisaged. After just two weeks, Big Mal had a permanent contract drawn up – with a better wage than he'd been paid at Old Trafford – and he gave him his League début, away against West Ham. (Another Docherty outcast, Ted MacDougall, was making his début for the Hammers who had Clyde Best up front.) Before the game Tony was given good-luck telegrams sent by a number of players at Old Trafford: Francis

Burns, Wyn Davis, Alan Gowling, David Sadler and Carlo Sartori. And 'the boy done good'. 'City's United cast-off gave an impressive display on his League début, revealing some fine skill on the ball in a game where City were rarely able to get moving.'[12] Now, not only would Tony be training alongside footballers of exceptional quality – Rodney Marsh, Colin Bell, Mike Summerbee, Francis Lee (Denis Law would join in July 1973) – he would also be playing in competitive matches with them.

Seven long days later, Tony crossed the white line in front of the Maine Road fans. The young Gallaghers may even have been there. The opposition was again from London, Arsenal. The Salford youth was encouraged to express himself by the progressive young manager. 'Whelan Gets Fans' Acclaim' ran the back-page headline of the *Manchester Evening News Football Pink*, 24 March 1973. The report noted that he had 'once [been] valued at more than £30,000 by Manchester United' but had (mysteriously) been released on a free by Tommy Docherty. Inside, on page seven, Tony's value was put at £50,000 by Malcolm Allison. 'He's got the ability to be this class of player.' The manager loved to talk-up the numbers!

Allison kept faith. In midweek Tony played against Chelsea. On Friday morning he was included in the team to face Don Revie's Leeds United the following day. However, by the day of the match, Tony's name had been crossed off the team sheet – Allison had resigned to take over at Crystal Palace. While Whelan's personal relationship with Big Mal was fine, the senior players had become increasingly disillusioned with him, as had the manager with the directors. This was reflected in the performances of the team as a whole. They hadn't won for nine games. Johnny Hart took over as caretaker–manager. Arriving at the ground for the Leeds game, Tony was told he had been dropped to make way for a 'more experienced' player. It is possible to see Hart's reasoning if we look at the achievements of the opposition over the previous eight seasons. Don Revie's team had finished as First Division champions in 1968–69 and runners-up five times. In the FA Cup they had reached the final three times and were current holders. The Fairs (now UEFA) Cup had been put in the Elland Road trophy room in 1968 alongside the League Cup, also won that season. Leeds were then at the most muscled of their strength. To get anything from the game City would need a team of battlers. Yet, in Tony's defence, the caretaker–manager was dropping an in-form, tall, strong player who was fresh and full of confidence – a decision any manager would find difficult to justify.

Hart took Tony on the end-of-season first-team tour of Greece where he played twice against Olympiakos of Athens. Whelan thought his performances justified his inclusion. Indeed, Hart must have thought the same because he included him on the 1973–74 pre-season tour of Scotland, with newly signed Denis Law spearheading the attack. Sadly, for Tony, he was the unused piece of ammunition on this foray north.

His future at City looked less gloomy with the arrival of Ron Saunders that autumn. Tony was given a pep talk by the new manager and told he featured in long-term plans including an end-of-season tour of Yugoslavia that was being organised. He was immediately promoted to the first-team squad, playing three games as substitute. However the manager's emphasis on a militaristic régime of disciplined sweat and toil, though guiding City to the League Cup final, pissed off some of the senior pros. Promptly sacked, he was replaced by one of those senior pros, Tony Book, a full-back with the club since 1966. Tony didn't fancy his younger namesake, who was unpleasantly surprised when summoned to the manager's office:

> He gave me a free transfer . . . One of the other lads couldn't believe it. He – Tony Book – said I was the 'click of [his] fingers away from being a top class player'. He felt I'd been at the club about two years and I'd be better off with a new team. They wouldn't ask for a fee because they'd got me for nothing. I still can't work out his reasoning. On the one hand I was a good player, on the other he was letting me go. I haven't spoken to him since about his decision. I felt I was good enough to play in the First Division. In some ways I felt I was a victim of circumstances.[13]

An understatement! Once more Tony was at a club which was not at ease with itself. In the late '60s–early '70s, under the joint guidance of Joe Mercer and Malcolm Allison, City had been very successful: Division One champions in 1968; FA Cup winners in 1969; League Cup and European Cup-Winners Cup winners in 1970. They had reached the final of the League Cup under Saunders but even so, after 1970, the Maine Road trophy room had been potless. Book was the fourth manager Tony had played under in a little over a year. In all, he'd seen eight come and go in his five years as a professional. And, in a career where the opinion of one powerful individual can have such a dramatic influence, Tony couldn't please all of his bosses all of the time. He had played under three managers – Busby, McGuinness and Allison – with whom there was mutual respect. These, and some of the others mentioned, had helped him become a better footballer. But he felt that, for one or two, judgements were made about him that may not have been wholly professional in their reasoning. Perhaps racial prejudice may have poisoned these managers' perception of him. One of those, in the presence of Tony, lightly informed his audience, 'I wouldn't let my daughter marry a Black man.' While it cannot be proved that those who didn't rate Whelan as a player were influenced by racist prejudice, it cannot be ignored.

What is glaringly obvious is that under more settled régimes, say if McGuinness had stayed at United or Allison at City, Tony's chances of becoming an established First-Division player would have increased. However, ifs and buts don't get your name on the teamsheet. Another worker in, and close-watcher of, the Manchester football industry, Walter Joyce, manager of Rochdale, came in for Tony instead. (Stockport County was also interested.) On meeting Walter, he impressed by what he had to say:

He was very positive about me. He had been tracking my career. Promised me first-team football. A promise he kept. He wanted to get out of the Fourth Division – they'd just been relegated from the Third. Once established in the first team I could then get picked up by a bigger club. I signed for Rochdale where we had to wash our own training kit. This meant that in pre-season we could only train in the morning! So we had really hard morning sessions of three hours. On the plus side I was in the first team and I didn't have to leave Manchester.[14]

Despite being who they were – unfashionable and lower division – Rochdale had a progressive history when it came to matters of skin colour. Already at the club were Stan Horne and Leo Skeete. Walter Joyce's signing of Tony suggests that the manager was colour blind – a man ahead of his time. Tony Collins had managed in the early '60s, steering his players to a League Cup final in 1962, where they lost to Norwich City. Collins remains one of their most successful managers and was the first to take a Fourth Division club to the final of a national competition. The 21-year-old winger was soon appreciated. In his first season Whelan was voted Player of the Year. In the second season he became, jointly with Clive Charles of Cardiff City, the first Black player to receive a PFA divisional award. Recognition and acclamation by your peers – the PFA membership vote for the best 11 players in their division – is a great honour in any walk of life. (Though this didn't stop the on-field abuse from opposition players and fans!) Yet he would have willingly traded it for another form of recognition of his consistently good form – a step up to a higher division. Joyce thought Whelan had been brilliant on some occasions, especially in the three epic FA Cup third-round matches against Norwich City, who included Kevin Keelan, Martin Peters, Phil Boyer and Ted MacDougall, and it seemed only a matter of time before a bigger club would make an offer. Another fellow Rochdale player, Alan Taylor, had been sold to West Ham the previous season and had scored both goals in the Hammers FA Cup final defeat of Fulham in 1975. Joyce believed Tony could play at higher level and, privately, wanted him to. That would have been the most personally satisfying end to his season.

The PFA recognition of his excellence put Tony in the shop window. One of those lookers offered him the opportunity to play summer football for Los Angeles Skyhawks in the American Soccer League (ASL). Playing in the West Coast sun again – he'd played for United against Eintracht Frankfurt in San Francisco – his career appeared to be blossoming after the changing and changeable climate of the early years. The Skyhawks won the ASL and Tony was on a roll. Returning to Rochdale for the 1976–77 season, he found Brian Green had replaced Walter Joyce as manager. Buoyed up by his experience in the USA, and disheartened by seeing another managerial change with all the career-damaging ramifications this might bring, he decided his future lay in the USA where, it seemed, football was about to take off. And, compared to winters in Rochdale, the life was exciting, the weather warm and the wages better. Why settle for a 7.30 kick-off away at freezing Hartlepool in February? No competition. Even an offer from Ron Atkinson to play for Cambridge United could not dispel Tony's disillusionment with day-to-day routine in the paupers section of the Football League. He was intent on returning to the West Coast sunshine. (Had he signed for United he would have finished the season with a Division Four champions medal. As a CUFC supporter I think this was the biggest mistake of his career!)

Green didn't make it easy for him to leave. From the manager's side he was going to lose one of his best players for nowt, so why not fight to keep him? From Tony's angle he had fulfilled his contract at Rochdale and was under no obligation to re-sign, especially since he'd arrived at the club on a free transfer. In his three seasons he'd missed only a handful of games and felt he'd deserved this chance to do something for himself and his wife Trish. But the club insisted on retaining his registration, in effect preventing him from playing in the States. The dispute was settled by a Football League Tribunal at a London hotel. One of the members was Matt Busby. After putting his case forward, Whelan was asked to wait outside. While passing time in the foyer with Trish, the genial ex-boss appeared. 'You're too good a player for that division. Go away and enjoy yourself.' So they did. Initially to Fort Lauderdale, then to the Atlanta Chiefs. During his six summers in the larger and reorganised North American Soccer League (NASL), he played alongside Gerd Muller, George Best, Brian Kidd, Gordon Banks and Peru's Teofilo Cubillas, a star of the 1970 World Cup. He thought the South American one of the best players he'd ever seen or played with. For the winters of '81 and '82 Tony played for Philadelphia Fever – with ex-Liverpool winger Steve Heighway – in the professional six-a-side Major Indoor Soccer League. Perhaps one of the most memorable highlights of his time in the USA was the invitation to guest for Pelé's New York Cosmos against an all-star team that included Johan Cruyff – though he didn't subsequently play.

The Whelans returned to Britain in 1983 with their America-born son Mark. In fact both their children were conceived in the USA as Trish was now pregnant with daughter Nadine. (In the summers of '96 and '98, Mark returned to the USA to coach football at a camp run by Denis Vaninger, a former colleague of Tony's at FLS.) While playing for the England semi-professional representative team against British Universities, Whelan broke his leg which ended his career. Yet as the changing-room doors shut, the world outside opened up. He put his past as a child and youth who'd experienced institutional care to positive use as an educational social worker, and in February 1987 began studying for an Open University Humanities degree. He also upgraded his coaching qualifications first acquired as a 19 year old in 1972. Tony now holds a UEFA 'A' coaching licence. In 1990 he was invited by Brian Kidd to become one of the part-time coaching staff at United's School of Excellence. In 1998 he was promoted to the full-time post of deputy assistant director of the Football Academy Under 9–16. The assistant director is Wilf McGuinness's son, Paul! Not one to chill, in the autumn of 1999, he handed in his dissertation on United's youth policy in the 1950s to Manchester Metropolitan University for an MA degree.

Ex-Rochdale manager Walter Joyce, as local recruitment officer overseeing scouting and regional coaching centres, was also part of the Manchester United Football Academy boot-room. Being at Europe's top club meant a lot to him, not in egotistical terms but because there would be the resources at United to do the job properly. Though he had managed in the bargain basement of football, Walter had played at the highest level. At the Cliff, the ex-manager and his winger teamed up again. Whelan readily acknowledges the great influence Joyce had on his career –he instilled confidence in his play and belief that he could and should go higher.

At United in the '90s they had a great time together developing the club's youngsters. Seeing talent – sometimes raw, sometimes mature – fulfil its potential was Walter's life work. Even as manager of Rochdale, he was happiest on the training ground passing on his experience and knowledge. Suddenly, on 29 September 1999, Walter died after a brief and unexpected illness. To say he was popular at the club would be an understatement. He was the father figure of the Academy. His knowledge, kindness and ability to get the best of people – his sensitivity to others – were attributes that are hard to find and replace, especially in an environment like football that can be very harsh and unforgiving.

I met Walter in 1996 when I interviewed Tony at the Cliff. 'Go upstairs and have a chat with Walter about Rochdale.' So I did. He had a laid-back manner with a cheeky, schoolboy glint in his eyes. Finishing up, he offered me two tickets for that evening's match. (Generosity is a family trait. His son Warren, as manager of Hull City, left me two tickets for the game in 1998–9 with Cambridge United at the Abbey – in the away end!) Walter also allowed my son Alex's Under-11 team, Fulbourn Falcons, to take part in an Academy training session and practice match in 1998. He, along with Paul, Tony and the other coaches gave the children an experience they will remember for the rest of their lives. Walter was buried at Rainford Parish Church in St Helen's on 7 October 1999. There to pay their last respects were Sir Alex Ferguson and his assistant manager Jimmy Ryan; all the senior coaching staff at Old Trafford; the Lion of Vienna Nat Lofthouse; ex-Bolton manager Ian Greaves; players from Walter's Burnley team of 1961–62 that reached the FA Cup final; David Cross; Kevin Ratcliffe; representatives from the north west's professional clubs including Rochdale and Blackburn – for whom Walter had also played – and the PFA, amongst numerous others. Tony and Paul McGuinness helped bear the coffin along with Warren and Wayne Joyce, Walter's brother and his son-in-law. Warren, who followed his father's profession and is therefore a living, breathing testament to his influence, read the epitaph.

While Whelan played all his League football on the west side of the Pennines, a contemporary, Ces Podd, was doing the business at full-back over the eastern side of the hills. Born in St Kitts in August 1952, Podd came to Britain as a nine year old. His parents, with six children to care for, decided to chance their luck in the 'mother country'. Like thousands of other West Indians, especially the men, the jobs they were allowed in Britain often didn't match up to their skills, so although a clerk on the small Caribbean island of a little over 35,000 people, in Britain his father worked on the buses.

While growing up in St Kitts, Ces did not play any competitive football other than street and backyard kick-arounds. It wasn't until he started at Matthew Murray School, near Leeds United FC, that organised sport became part of his life. Initially it was rugby. He didn't play colts league football until he was around 12 or 13. On leaving Matthew Murray, Ces enrolled at Bradford College of Art hoping for a career in commercial design. Football was just an enjoyable weekend hobby. All weekend in fact – for three teams: Beeston YMCA on Saturday afternoons; the 'Travellers Rest', Farsely on Sunday mornings and St Peter's Church, Leeds, in the afternoon, usually on the right wing. While playing for St Peter's he was approached by a Wolves' scout and invited for a trial. At the try-out two teams were chosen with Ces in neither. He was told to come back at a later date. But he had more pride and self-respect.

Soon after, a friend wrote to Bradford City asking for a trial on Ces's behalf. Watched by City manager Jimmy Wheeler, despite Podd's pleas to play in his normal position of right-wing, the Bradford boss put him at full-back. And that's where he stayed, playing over 502 League games plus numerous other first-team appearances during 14 seasons at Valley Parade – five in the Third Division and nine in the Fourth.

Ces was an artisan; he was skilled at his trade and dependable. His attributes were his speed and commitment. He never played higher than the third, his other Football-League clubs being Halifax and Scarborough. Interviewed for the Radio 5 series *Across the White Line*, Podd cites the Brazil team that won the World Cup in 1970 as a great inspiration because not only were they brilliant players, they were mostly Black. For his testimonial game against Bradford City on 30 March 1981, Podd put together his own team of Black All-Stars. The line-up was Derek Richardson, Sheffield United; Ces Podd, Bradford City; George Berry, Wolves; Bob Hazel, QPR; Brendan Batson, WBA; Terry Connor, Leeds United; Remi Moses, WBA; Vince Hilaire, Crystal Palace; Joe Cooke, Oxford United; Justin Fashanu, Norwich City; Cyril Regis, WBA; Tony Cunningham, Lincoln City; Luther Blissett, Watford; Trevor Quow, Peterborough United; Trevor Lee, Colchester United; Ricky Hill, Luton Town; Colin Stein, Luton Town. Aside from the box office attraction of such talent, the turnout testified to the standing Ces had among fellow Black professionals.

The match inspired tributes from Podd's various managers at City. Jimmy Wheeler, who initially signed Ces, noted his emotional durability:

> It must be realised that as a young black player Ces could have come up against many problems in his chosen profession, but his strength of character and ability to handle any situation has always served him well.

As far as I am concerned he has always been a credit to football, himself and his family . . .

His manager at the time of the testimonial, George Mulhall, thought him a great wing-back and impersonator:

> Cyril Podd . . . a very popular player . . . It is not difficult to realise why he is so well liked. He is a very hard-working professional both in training and in matches and he often delights the crowd with his overlapping runs down the flank. He is also very popular with the players and he is never short of doing an impersonation of the manager giving a team talk.[15]

As well as football and impersonating, Ces worked with youngsters in his neighbourhood, the Chapeltown area of Leeds. What started as coaching soon developed into counselling. As an adult the respected young people would discuss their personal anxieties with him. In this role Podd believes his Christian faith has helped him. 'Becoming a Christian has helped me a lot. A Christian knows where he is going and what he should be doing. I feel more relaxed in the whole of my life.'[16]

During the early to mid '90s, Ces worked for Leeds United on their Football in the Community programme. At the 1998 World Cup in France he met up with Peter Jenkins of the St Kitts and Nevis FA who asked Podd to return home and stir up football in the eastern Caribbean. So he did. Installed as director of football in St. Kitts and Nevis in the summer of 1999, Ces invited his former club Bradford – just promoted to the Premiership – to take part in the second annual St Kitts and Nevis Football Festival. Things seemed to be working out even though the West Yorkshiremen whacked a local side 4–1 in the final. At the time of writing, the 'Sugar Boyz' – the national team of St Kitts and Nevis – have to play the Reggae Boyz of Jamaica to make it into the next qualifying round for the 2002 World Cup. Already a Sugar Boy, 26-year-old striker Keith Gumbs is playing professionally abroad for Greek First-Division side Panionios.

Chapter six discusses the contribution of players of Asian birth or antecedence to the game in Britain between 1919 and 1970.

Too Small, Too Smelly, Too Clever and Not Interested

Players with Asian Antecedence 1919–70

Much has been written about the absence of Asian players in the British game. And when people write on the subject they are usually referring to South Asians from India, Pakistan and Bangladesh. This chapter, however, includes footballers from other parts of Asia.

There is a common misconception that hardly any players of Asian origin and descent have played professionally in Britain. And, as the title of this chapter suggests, a whole heap of bizarre reasons have been thrown together to explain the myth. While it is true that there haven't been many Asian stars, it would be wrong to say there haven't been any. In previous chapters we profiled the Cother brothers of Watford and Costa of Southport Vulcan, players of colour of the first generation. And the Cothers, as we know, were Anglo-Indian professionals of the Victorian era!

There is a long history of ball games in South East Asia. Indeed it could be argued that association football ultimately derives from the ancient Chinese game of Tsu Chu. The translation of the term is 'to kick a leather ball with the feet'. There are depictions of Chinese Tsu Chu players dating from the Han dynasty of over 2,000 years ago. Essentially there were three forms of the game: one based upon individual performance of difficult tricks and two that had teams and goals. The Japanese adaptation of Tsu Chu became known as Kemari and has been practised for over thirteen centuries. This involves a group of seven individuals – men and women – who pass a ball between them without letting it touch the ground.

In South Asia, in India, there has been an association football league since 1898, based in Calcutta. A moment that has etched itself into Indian football folklore is the 2–1 defeat of the East Yorkshire Regiment by Mohan Bagan FC in the 1911 final of the Indian Shield before 60,000 spectators. It was also another Calcutta club, Mohammedan Sporting, that produced Salim Bachi Khan who played for Celtic Reserves in the mid 1930s. Yet it wasn't until 1997 that an India-wide professional league was formed. Furthermore, while Mohan Bagan can draw crowds of 80,000, football in Pakistan and Bangladesh is even more popular. It is the national game in Bangladesh.

The development of the game in Asia – and the political benefit this brought for British influence in the region – was referred to by football writer Ivan Sharpe in his survey of the game in the first half of the twentieth century:

> Before the [Second World] War a resident wrote from Singapore: 'One feels that the sight of a pair of goalposts at almost every cleared and occupied budding township is the outward and visible sign that Pax Britannica reigns supreme.'[1]

In the past in Britain most players of Asian descent have been Anglo-Indians (or Eurasians as their Victorian predecessors, such as the Cothers, were known). Anglo-Indians were the outcome of relationships between British soldiers, traders and administrators and Indian women. The East India Company, during the eighteenth century, encouraged affairs between soldiers and local women in the hope that this would create a steady supply of young men to restock and replenish the army in India. However, by the turn of the nineteenth century, European–Indian relationships were officially discouraged and eventually prohibited. But that didn't stop them. By the mid-twentieth century there were approximately 300,000 Anglo-Indians. After Indian Independence in 1947 (and the formation of Pakistan) the place of Anglo-Indians looked less secure in the sense that any residual privileges they may have 'enjoyed' under the colonial régime – such as favoured employment on Indian Railways – were under attack from the Indianisation of public services. Many Anglo-Indians decided their future lay in Britain. And some became footballers.

While I argue that Black footballers were not stereotyped in terms of their playing characteristics – as fast, skilful but lacking in 'character' etc – until after the Second World War and the period of heightened labour migration from the Caribbean, South Asia and East Africa, there is evidence of such labelling in early colonial reports on football in Asia. A feature, written two years before Mohan Bagan's defeat of the East Yorkshire Regiment, in *The Illustrated Sporting and Dramatic News*, 11 September 1909, entitled 'Sport in Burma – Football . . .' made the following observation:

> Association football as a regimental game in the native Army of India is in its infancy, and is only just beginning to find favour. The reason for this is probably that the sepoy [Indian soldier], as a rule, has not the build necessary for a first-class player . . . The recruit, when he first emerges from the jungle or village, has rather less control over his legs than a newborn camel, but in a surprisingly short time he learns how to kick and run.

In this report we find the reference to size that was later used, among other excuses, to explain the lack of Asian players in British football. Yet, in the pre-First World War Football League, outstanding players such as Fred Spikesley, Steve Bloomer and Fanny Walden were all lightweight. Nevertheless the image of the not-strong-enough Asian player has stubbornly remained.

Below are those footballers with Asian antecedence whose careers began between 1919 – when the Football League was resumed after the First World War – and 1970.

'The Victoria Ground [of Stoke City FC] was once our great delight. There we were bred to the felicity of Matthews and the ferocity of Steele, the breeding of Franklin and the orient grace of Soo.'² This description by post-war football writer and musicologist Percy Young of inside-forward Hong Y 'Frank' Soo captures the flavour of seeing life through colour that affected even the most imaginative and sensitive of post-war football writers. Though Soo was born in Buxton, Derbyshire, and had been brought up in Liverpool, his physical appearance still framed the writer's definition of his skills. Yet Young's choice to highlight Soo was not because his pigmentation rendered him exotic. He was, for many observers, one of the best inside-forwards of the immediate pre-war era. At Stoke, as Young points out, he played alongside the equally graceful England internationals Neil Franklin and Stanley Matthews and another Black footballer, Roy Brown. And during the war Hong Y played nine games for England, on occasion alongside Matthews and Franklin. However these wartime internationals were 'unofficial' – no cap was awarded – and therefore don't figure in the statistics. Soo was never selected once peace resumed. (Although this isn't strictly true. His last wartime international was against Switzerland, in Berne, 21 July 1945, after the war in Europe had ceased. The line-up included Frank Swift, Joe Mercer, Tom Finney and Tommy Lawton.) If we ignore the FA's designation of international matches as official/unofficial, he holds the honour of being the first man of colour to play for England.

The son of an English mother and Chinese father, 18-year-old 'Frank' signed for Stoke City in January 1933 for £250 from Prescot Cables, a Lancashire Combination League club, where he played while working as a clerk. He made his Football League début at Middlesbrough 11 months later. His career at the Victoria Ground almost spans that of Sir Stanley Matthews, who joined Stoke in 1932 and left for Blackpool in 1947. Such a presence couldn't have harmed Soo's development. However, like many players of his generation, the war stole his best years. In the seasons prior to the outbreak Soo played 185 League and FA Cup games. Between 1939 and 1945, while in the RAF, he continued to play for Stoke making a further 94 appearances. Regional competitions took the place of the Football League during the conflict leagues and footballers could guest for any club. Soo turned out for Chelsea, Everton, Leicester and Brentford. As well as the wartime internationals, he was chosen for the RAF representative XI. Also playing for this Football Flying Squad in Paris a month after liberation were internationals Stanley Matthews, George Hardwick, Raich Carter, Matt Busby, Joe Mercer and Frank Swift.

The Football League programme did not begin again until 1946–47. Unfortunately, before it resumed, Soo fell out with manager Bob McGrory and requested a transfer, after playing over 280 first-team games. (McGrory seems to have been in desperate need of an 'Idiots Guide to Man Management'. He irritated Stanley Matthews enough for the winger to join Blackpool. However, in McGrory's favour, his team of predominantly local players – including Matthews – did finish fourth in 1946–7, the club's highest-ever placing.) Soo eventually signed for McGrory's immediate predecessor at Stoke, Tom Mather, now manager at Leicester City, for a fee of £4,600 in September 1945. After just one season at Filbert Street, Mather left for Luton Town, also of the Second Division, with Soo soon following. The transfer payment this time was £3,000. He stayed at Kenilworth Road two seasons, eventually signing for Southern League Chelmsford City in the summer of 1948.

Once sidelined as a player, Hong continued in the game as a successful coach and manager. The immediate post-war period was a time of expansion and boom, especially abroad. Soo's first appointment at a professional club was as coach to Padova, in Italy, in April 1950. Two years later he moved north to Scandinavia, an association that spanned three decades, managing and coaching a number of Swedish, Danish and Norwegian clubs. He led Djurgaardens IF to the championship of Sweden in 1955. Soo's Scandanavian exile was broken by a return home in June 1959 to manage Scunthorpe United of the Second Division; and in the early years of the following decade he managed the Israeli national team. On 25 January 1991 he died at Cheadle, Staffordshire.

Calcuttan Salim Bachi Khan, also known as Abdul Salim and Mohamed Hashean – he seems to have had as many aliases as my mum – was an Indian winger with a reputation as a beautiful crosser of the ball. Legend has it that he ended up in Glasgow because his brother was a storekeeper at Elderslie Docks. While in the city the ex-Mohammedan Sporting Club FC forward approached Celtic manager Willie Maley for a trial. Though he only played for Celtic Reserves in 1936–7, the fact that he did so in bandaged feet has earned Salim a place in football folklore. His début for the reserves against Galton FC attracted much interest. Readers of the back page of the Glasgow *Evening Times*, 26 August 1936, found his smiling face and a close-up of his bandaged feet. One letter writer thought he was trying it on: Khan's appearance in the Alliance League game against Galston would inevitably bring a few extra voyeurs of the exotic through the turnstiles. However the indulgence of letting him perform in bandaged feet was unfair. 'No Scotsman would dare tackle a man who has no boots.' If this concession to ethnic custom was allowed – FIFA didn't prohibit barefoot play until 1950 – why 'not field a "native" of Mossend with hobnailed boots, a Lancastrian in clogs, or a Dutchman in wooden sabots'?

Khan was always going to be on a loser by playing in bandaged feet. We've discussed already how wet, muddy pitches messed-up the barefooted Nigerian and Gold Coast tourists' style of play. Though Khan was described in a contemporary football annual as an 'expert in trapping and lobbing . . . [who] fairly hypnotised the opposing defenders . . . [with] accuracy in shooting and ball control',[3] he never managed to break into the Celtic first team, playing just two Reserve games.

Cyril 'Sammy' Chung was the second Anglo-Chinese footballer to play professionally in Britain. And like Soo, the pioneer of this genre, he became a successful manager and coach. Fortunately, unlike Soo, I managed to interview Sammy. Maybe it was coincidence, maybe it wasn't, but he had a Confucian approach to his work, integrating his philosophy of life into his football. Summarised as 'respect yourself and others', he feels such an attitude engenders personal dignity, a condition essential for personal growth and development. You have to be a human being before you can be a footballer.

To illustrate, he recalled his first days at Norwich City in January 1955. He had signed for the Division Three South club from Reading, also of that division. Training was dominated by laps of the pitch at a strolling pace. Instead Sammy went for it. He lapped some of his new colleagues which, in the competitive, hierarchical environment of the football club, didn't go down well among the senior pros. To the gym he took the same attitude: why cheat myself? While it brought a few uncomfortable moments, the reward for such honesty has been a life-long career in football. The *Guardian*, 24 September 1994, labelled 62-year-old Chung as the oldest manager – of Doncaster Rovers – 'in English professional football'.

Ted Drake, ex-Arsenal and England forward, while manager of Reading signed 19-year-old Sammy from Headington – now Oxford – United in November 1951. The move, while big in career terms, was short in distance with Reading less than an hour from the family home in Abingdon, Oxfordshire. It was here that Sammy was born on 16 July 1942, the youngest of seven children: five boys and two girls. His father Henry Fong Chung came to Oxford in 1914 from Kowloon, the mainland peninsula of the British colony of Hong Kong. He married an English woman and, by the early '30s, had become a naturalised British citizen. As is usual with many migrants he took a job for which he was over-qualified, arriving as an interpreter but earning a living as a painter and decorator. 'We didn't have enough money to buy a paper.'

As a wing-half, Sammy played 22 league games (12 goals) at Elm Park before travelling east to Norwich (47 appearances, 9 goals), although it was with Watford, who paid his wages from June 1957 to July 1965, that he achieved his greatest success playing over 245 first-team games. The Hertfordshire club had then – and still has – a long history of signing players of colour beginning with the Cother brothers in the 1890s. During the early months of Chung's début season at Watford, 1957–58, he played alongside Roy Brown and Tony Collins. Thus, uniquely, the Vicarage Road club had three men of colour on their books (both Brown and Collins had moved on by the start of next season).

As a manager/coach, Chung values the input his profession can have in improving players and teams. He regrets that he didn't have the same. Had he the same, he believes he could have been a more rounded footballer. The idea that good teams can be moulded by good coaching was gaining ground in England during the '50s, despite opposition from the traditionalists and romantics. The traditionalists thought good players were born with natural talent, while the romantics held the view that system and regimentation would stifle creative urge, spontaneity and imagination. Yet the demolition of England by an organised and creative Hungary at Wembley in 1953, and in Budapest the following year, shook up the conceited self-complacency of British football. Out of the self-examination that followed emerged a fertile environment for innovative approaches, with the subsequent desire by leading managers such as England coach Walter Winterbottom, Frank Buckley of Wolves and Matt Busby of Manchester Utd to learn from progressive European clubs such as Hungary's Honved FC and respected coaches like Austria's Willy Meisel.

In 1962 Chung was appointed player/coach at Watford to assist manager Ron Burgess, and later Bill McGarry with whom he formed a manager/coach partnership that lasted ten years and three clubs. After helping McGarry guide the Vicarage Road Club to third place in Division Three in 1963–64, Chung followed his partner to Ipswich in 1965 where even greater success followed. In 1968 the Suffolk club won the Second Division Championship. The duo's record of achievement made them as sought after a double act as Morecambe and Wise. When Ronnie Allen was sacked as manager of First Division Wolverhampton Wanderers in the autumn of 1969, the Molineux chairmen and directors installed Bill and Sammy. Here the duo peaked, reaching the UEFA and League Cup finals respectively: in 1972 they lost 3–2 on aggregate to Spurs; and in 1974 they beat Manchester City 2–1. Indeed this was Sammy's highpoint. He became manager during the close season of 1976, guiding the Molineux club to the Second Division Championship the following season. There followed various managerial and coaching posts in Britain, Sweden and the United Arab Emirates before the job at Doncaster Rovers.

While Sammy's approach to football is progressive – coaches can make good players or teams great – he is alarmed at some of the so-called 'progressive' economic and social changes occurring. 'The rich [clubs] are getting richer and the poor [clubs] are getting poorer.' He has had a remarkable career in football, if for no other reason than because it has been life-long – a privilege denied to the vast majority of players. But, as we've discussed, this isn't the only reason. He has been successful. He describes himself as an optimist by nature, opposite in character to those two favourite Bulgarian internationals often ridiculed by 'Big' Ron Atkinson, Couldve and Shouldve. Sammy did. The racism he faced at school and on the park merely raised his game. However he has one regret: he was never asked to play or coach in Hong Kong.

Despite having the most English of names, Roy Smith was born in Rawalpindi, Pakistan – then part of India – on 19 March 1936, the son of a police inspector. Roy's family moved to East London in 1947, the year India and Pakistan were granted independence. The end of colonial rule on the South Asian sub-continent left those with mixed Asian and European heritage feeling politically, economically and socially vulnerable. (It is a topic to which we will return when discussing another Anglo-Asian footballer, Indian Ricky Heppolette.)

Described in a history of West Ham as 'an inside-forward of some talent' Roy was signed by the Second Division club in 1953, initially as an amateur then as a professional when he turned 19. He made his début in the 1955–56 season against Stoke City, though his parents would have preferred him to continue his career as a shipping clerk. He played only six first-team games for the Hammers before joining non-league Clacton. While residing in the resort with the 'warmest seafront in Britain' – due to the thousands of heat-giving light bulbs brightening the amusement arcades, according to hitchikers and natives of the town Baz and Tone – he was nevertheless still considering emigrating to Australia in the late '50s in the wake of his parents. Deciding to stay in Britain, he joined Southern League (and much cooler) Cambridge City in 1959. From there he moved to fellow SL club Hereford United before returning to the Football League with southcoast Portsmouth in January 1961, where he played ten League games.

The second Anglo-Indian to play for a professional club in Cambridge was Brian 'Bud' Houghton. He too was part of that generation that left India after independence. I have a vivid, fixed memory as a young Cambridge United fan of this muscled, brown-skinned, dark-haired centre-forward leading out the 'U's' at Milton Road in the local derby against Cambridge City during the 1967–68 season. I was mesmerised by the size of his thighs – I'd never seen such bulging, powerful upper-legs on my other football heroes. I think he was aware of how athletic his pegs looked – they were always well-oiled! A former team-mate at one of his other clubs, Oxford United, Sandy Brewer, remembers how Bud's physique was put to use:

> He was a strong chap. He could bustle his way through. He wasn't the most skilful player but he certainly had the physique and in those days you could probably make more use of it than you can nowadays. He was very useful. Yes, he got some good goals . . .[4]

According to Colin Harrington, another Oxford team-mate, the manager at the Manor Ground Arthur Turner thought Bud typical of good players who end up in the lower divisions because they have a major weakness in their game.

> Bud was one of those players Arthur must have dreamed about. He was everything – big, tremendous shot – but he was never able to come to terms with the game at Oxford. Arthur Turner used to say that if he applied himself he could play for his country, and we used to laugh at that because Bud was born in India.[5]

Boisterous, barging Bud was a prolific scorer. In his five-club Football League career he played over two hundred games, with an average of a goal every three games. At one of these – Southend United – the average was nearer a goal every other game. Houghton began his career at Bradford Park Avenue, signing professional forms as an 18 year old in October 1955. (Ironically, it was Cambridge United which ended the Yorkshire club's status as a Football League outfit in 1970.) The centre-forward also played for Oxford United captained by Ron Atkinson, who remembers:

> He was one of our gang. Big Bud. He'd seen something on television one day . . . di Stefano playing for Real Madrid . . . and di Stefano had this habit of going back and taking the ball off his own players' toes. We're playing this game at Brentford and Bud starts doing this to me. He did it three times. I said 'Bud, if you come back and do that once more, I shall volley you straight into the stand.' He said, 'Well, I'm just trying to do what di Stefano does.' I said, 'Well, he scores as well, so get up the other end of the field and see if you can do that.'[6]

Houghton joined Southern League Cambridge United from Chelmsford City. Manager Bill Leivers signed a number of that club's players, including Terry Eades (who was later my manager at Histon FC); Peter Leggett; Bill Cassidy; and Tony Butcher. Also at the Abbey Stadium was Bud's former Oxford United colleague Pat Quatermain. With the 'U's', Houghton finished top scorer with 28 goals in 40 games during the 1967–68 season, an excellent record. It is even more remarkable because by mid-February he'd been transferred to Wellington Town! Leivers justified his decision by criticising the centre-forward's work rate in the *Cambridge News*, 17 February 1968. 'He likes to drift about the field waiting for the chance to score one of those goals that make him so popular with football crowds.' He felt the Anglo-Indian did not put himself about enough. Yet Houghton was a poacher who liked to play in and around the goal area. His strengths were his shooting and heading. As a big man he just couldn't run up and down the pitch all match. (United eventually finished third in the league that season, scoring 12 fewer goals than each of the clubs above them. In fact even eighth-placed Margate scored more. However, over the following two seasons Leivers fashioned championship-winning sides, one of which, in 1969–70, was the Southern League's leading scorer.)

Another Anglo-Indian whose family left once Indians and Pakistanis began to rule themselves again was Kevin Keelan, who played 646 competitive first-team games for Norwich City between 1963 and 1979. Born in Calcutta but brought up, until seven years of age, in a Delhi house of 'several servants', he was the son of Ivor, a British warrant officer and Dorothy, of Indian–Portuguese descent. The Keelan family, with six children, moved to Kidderminster in 1948.

They swapped a comfortable, affluent but politically unstable environment for a migrant's hand-to-mouth existence of toil and trouble. His parents soon parted, unable to cope with the strains relocation had caused. Dorothy and the children stayed in Kidderminster, while Ivor moved to London. Despite the safety net of the Welfare State, getting by, for Dorothy and her half-dozen dependents, wasn't easy. In fact, after the ease of India, Britain was tight, hard and close to the edge. Escaping into sport rather than study, Kevin played for Worcestershire County schools representative teams and, when possible, travelled to Molineux to watch the powerful Wolves sides of the '50s managed by Frank Buckley. As soon as he was able he left school and got a job as an apprentice welder, playing meanwhile for Kidderminster Harriers youth team as a left winger (a few years after Gil Heron had played in the first-team). Then one of those life-changing random occurences: Harriers' first choice goalkeeper didn't turn up for a match, so Keelan became the man in the box. Keeping his place, he did so well he was invited to nearby Aston Villa for a trial. From the sublime to the ridiculous. He was offered a part-time contract by Eric Houghton, the Villa manager. In July 1958 this was upgraded to full-time: £13 per week; £12 close-season. He went straight into the reserves.

However the mood at the club darkened as relegation threatened, became real and throttled the life from Villa's First-Division existence. Genial Joe Mercer was installed as the new boss. He gave Keelan his league début towards the end of the '59–'60 season, in a Second-Division game at Middlesbrough. The Teesiders had Brian Clough as their free-scoring centre-forward. In front of 49,500 people, the young Anglo-Indian kept a clean sheet. Yet he was to play only four more first-team games next season. Genial Joe just didn't fancy him. In fact he blamed him – in front of the rest of the team – for a 1–3 defeat by Leicester, after which he was banished to the fourth team and told he'd be on his way and quickly.

Keelan, a good-looking, swarthy 20-year-old, his wife Bonnie and their two sons Mark and Russell moved back to Kidderminster via Stockport County where he played just three end-of-season games. He rejoined (Southern League) Harriers for the 1961–2 season, working as a lorry driver for £12 per week. However, the quartet were soon on the move again, this time to Fourth-Division Wrexham. After two seasons and 74 games at the Racecourse Ground, Ron Ashman, manager of Second-Division Norwich City, offered the Welsh club £6,500. 'I was offered £20 a week and . . . a club house . . . a move I have never regretted.'[7]

While the Carrow Road club had the reputation of being a country cousin of football, Keelan soon became an enthusiastic member – or more accurately his member became enthusiastic – of the players' Ratpack club of stop-out drinkers and shaggers. Such was the collective lack of ambition that training was seen as a chore to get through, rather than a sharpening of athleticism and skill.

> We had something of a set routine on our nights out. We would usually meet-up at the Elm Tavern . . . and have a few drinks . . . there were always plenty of unattached females around . . . Sometimes I did not even go home but would go straight into training from the house at which I had ended up the night before.[8]

Keelan was also getting a reputation as (another) goalkeeper with a prodigious punch – often applied to lippy forwards. During the 64–'65 season he KO'd

Tommy Robson of Northampton Town. A couple of years later he did the same to another Cobbler, Ray Smith. A divorce and the employment of Ron Saunders by the Carrow Road board in July 1969 forced a change in the bohemian lifestyle. 'Ironman' Saunders was from the run, sweat and die school of football and had no time for dilettantes. His approach forced Keelan to focus the aggression. It was that or fuck off. After three hard but enjoyable seasons, the Canaries had not so much sung as slugged their way into the First Division. In their first season upstairs, 1972–3, they also reached the final of the League Cup losing 1–0 to Spurs.

Of Keelan's 16 seasons at Norwich, ten were spent in Division Two, the other six in the First. The departure of Saunders in 1973 led to the introduction of a more relaxed régime under John Bond – 'I don't care what you call me as long as it's boss' – a graduate of the so-called 'West Ham Academy' of the '50s, which included Malcolm Allison and Ron Greenwood. Their approach to the game was more continental than British in that technique, game plans and practised dead-ball moves were seen as important and integral to success. Bond also created a 'happy' atmosphere at Carrow Road. While Saunders achieved, Bond allowed the players to smile in the process. Perhaps the widest ever seen on Keelan's face was when he was chosen for an England XI to play West Ham in Trevor Brooking's testimonial during the '77–8 season.

After a few seasons playing in the USA and several years working there, Keelan was, in 1998, manager of Stalybridge Celtic, 100 years after Arthur Wharton managed the first Stalybridge team, Rovers. (Other players of colour at Carrow Road during Keelan's tenure were John Miller and Justin Fashanu.)

A reason for writing this book is that however much Black players would like to be viewed as just footballers, they are not. An example of how racist stereotypes were ingrained and widely accepted in Britain can be glimpsed from an extract from Eamon Dunphy's biography of Sir Matt Busby. There was a thief amongst the staff at Old Trafford. Calling all the players to a meeting – including 19-year-old Dennis Walker, the first Black Busby Babe and with Asian antecedence – the manager referred to 'a nigger in the woodpile'.[9] And this remark, though not said with any malice, was from a socialist and manager seen as one of the more enlightened of his era.

The preceding paragraph in Dunphy's book refers to Walker's Football League début for United, away versus Nottingham Forest. It wasn't a good time to break into the first team for many reasons. Despite United reaching the FA Cup final, they had been battling against relegation for much of the season. Indeed it could be argued that Walker only played in this last game of the '62–63 campaign because Busby wanted to rest four key players in readiness for the final five days later. The ploy worked. Denis Law, Bobby Charlton – for whom Walker deputised – Maurice Setters and Bill Foulkes returned to play against Leicester, replacing Nobby Stiles, Shay Brennan, Frank Haydock (and Walker). Law also scored in their 3–1 win.

Dennis did go on United's close-season tour to Italy but did not start against Roma or Juventus, the two big-name opponents. (The Mancunians won both games.) However, this wasn't a bad start to a career for the boy from Hartford, near Northwich, Cheshire. He had been at Old Trafford since he was 12. Indeed, he was able to kick into touch any thoughts of a paper round when the club started paying him £3 a week from the age of 13 (for kit and other necessary expenses!). A number of clubs had been after him, including Everton who, on being told that he'd signed for Busby, took back the football boots and tracksuit they'd given him!

Walker joined a club still recovering from the devastation of the Munich air crash. Prior to the disaster in 1958, where eight first-team players were killed, the youth team had been the only winners of the FA Youth Cup since its inception in 1953. The first team had won the League championship in 1956 and '57 and had been losing finalists in the '57 and '58 FA Cup finals. The Cheshire youth now became part of Busby's second-generation 'Babes'. However, as Dunphy points out, the turmoil caused by the destruction at Munich was slow in easing. By 1963–64:

> Manchester United began to be respected again, but behind the scenes the gulfs remained. Many of the younger players had been infected by the poison that lingered in the air of Old Trafford for five years or so after Munich. The club's character had changed. An outbreak of thieving spread suspicion through the dressing-room. Heavy gambling in card schools and at Manchester's three-dog tracks was a plague now infecting the youngsters at the club. Contempt for Busby was not erased by the Wembley [FA Cup final] win . . . I [Dunphy] was sitting reading a newspaper somewhere between the boss and the lads at the back of the bus, feeling a little overawed at this taste of the big time, when a folded sheet of paper fell on my lap, dropped from the seat in front. When I opened it I was shocked to see a vicious caricature of Busby drawn with great skill and care in ink. The image was a perfect likeness of him in stern-faced repose. The nose was drawn as a penis, the cheeks as two testicles. The caption read 'Bollock Chops'.[10]

Clubs began to notice this son of a Limerick-born mother and Iranian–Argentinian father while he was starring for Cheshire Schoolboys' representative team (alongside Alan Oakes and Glyn Pardoe who went on to play a combined total of 864 games for Manchester City). Walker was also invited to England Schoolboy trials and says he was selected to play against West Germany in 1961, but had the offer rescinded after signing for United. After three seasons, with just the sole run-out against Forest as League experience, Walker signed for Fourth-Division York City. The Old Trafford playing staff was now awash with good left-sided wingers and midfielders – Charlton, Stiles, Giles – to name just three who became icons of their generation.

Dennis Walker soon became one of a number of ex-United players at the club. John Pearson and Eamon Dunphy joined the following season. He was the third Black player in York's history: Tony Collins had signed in July 1949 and South African Gerry Francis in October 1961, though neither stayed long. Walker's four seasons at Bootham Crescent were full of ups and downs: in his first season they finished third in Division Four and were promoted, only to be relegated the next season. The following two seasons they sunk to third and fourth from bottom respectively. The collective ambition of the team and club had gone. In the end it was to be a non-League club, Cambridge United, full of itself with a positive vision of its future, that rescued Walker's career.

Of the two professional clubs in Cambridge, United, from the working-class East Barnwell district, had traditionally been the poorer neighbour of centrally situated, better connected and more successful City. The latter had been a force in amateur football as Cambridge Town. Since turning professional in 1958, the Milton Road club had won the Southern League in 1963 (with United runners-up). Yet this was to mark the beginning of City's perennial decline and eclipse by their rivals across the river. Three months before Walker committed himself to United in July 1968, they had won the Southern League Cup and finished third in the league. When former Manchester City full-back (and 1956 FA Cup winner) Bill Leivers became manager at the beginning of that season he promised chairman Jack Wooley that United would not finish below fourth during his contract period of three years. And they didn't. The boys in black and amber did the double in '68–9 – the first side to do so for 20 years – and were champions once again in 1970. The title was clinched in incredible circumstances:

> United had to win both of their last two games to make sure of winning the Championship . . . against Worcester City on Thursday, 30 April and two days later against Margate, but the matter was complicated by a potentially lucrative friendly match arranged against Chelsea on Friday 1 May, as part of Ian Hutchinson's transfer deal to Chelsea, which meant three games would have to be played in three days.[11]

United beat Worcester 3–0 and Margate 2–0. The game against the FA Cup holders from Stamford Bridge attracted the largest ever crowd of 14,000 to the Abbey Stadium. (The attendance for Margate was 5,298. Thus, within 24 hours, nearly 20,000 people had passed through the Abbey Stadium turnstiles. A record for a southern League club?) My personal memory of the Chelsea match as a 13 year old is of their players parading the cup at half-time. On passing the Corona End – where the boot boys mobbed up – the 'Pensioners' and their pot were pelted with pennies.

The run of success achieved what all United's supporters, players and officials had been working for: Football League status. And Dennis Walker was a key figure in bringing this about. Having come on a free transfer, United couldn't really lose on the deal, though he did receive a signing-on bonus of between £300 and £500. (Manager Bill Leivers remembers the smaller figure, the player the larger. Perhaps both are valid, with Leiver's figure for public consumption and Walker's the real amount paid out?)

The Anglo-Irish (on his mother's side) Argentine–Iranian (on his father's side) Mancunian was captain of the side elected to the Fourth Division and Player of the Year that season. He, more than any other, became emblematic of the success at the Abbey Stadium. Leivers knew he had a bargain when he signed the 23 year old. 'I was especially pleased to capture Walker, whom I consider to be a very fine player, both hardworking and constructive.'[12] Almost thirty years later his view had not changed:

> Anybody that has a background starting off at Man. Utd, they've got to have something about them . . . A strong boy, willing and just one of those players that suited me. He tended to get overweight if he wasn't careful, but he was a good player. Good player full stop. Very competitive as well.

And he had no worries about making him captain. In fact quite the opposite:

> I think he needed the responsibility. To keep his eyes on what we were aiming for. I think the game came quite easy to him . . . he was a natural player, a delightful passer of the ball, particularly with his right foot. I think it did centre him on what we were trying to do . . . It never entered my head. Even talking about him now I don't think of him as coloured. It absolutely never came into it. And what's more I don't think it came into the players' heads. They just looked upon Dennis as a quality player. His colour didn't matter. In fact I don't remember anybody ever mentioning it.[13]

It would be treating the reader with contempt if the Abbey Stadium was portrayed as a haven free of bigots. As a member of the youth team at the club between 1971 and 1973, I know it wasn't. Prejudice was an issue and Walker responded to it head on, even off the field: Dennis coached part-time at St Bedes Catholic Secondary Modern School in the city. During one session, a face who'd taken a whack from Walker in a practice match and couldn't let it pass called him a 'Nigger'. Walker grabbed him by the throat and held him up against the wall: if you want to play this game instead remember there are no rules!

In his effort to ensure United not only maintained their Football-League status but continued upward and onward, Leivers began to offload the Southern League players. It was his belief that after three seasons at a club, a player, generally, will have had his best days:

> Don Revie used to say three years with any club was long enough . . .
> After three years they've seen what you can do. If you want to make

anything [money] you've got to be on your bike . . . I believe there's something in that. You can have players with you too long. I felt it was time [1973] Dennis moved, for his own good . . . I recommended him for the player/manager's job at Poole Town. I knew the chairman.[14]

(No doubt Revie himself believed wholeheartedly in this approach! He just forgot how long some of his Leeds United players had been at Elland Road: Billy Bremner 17 seasons, Jack Charlton 20 seasons, Peter Lorimer 16 seasons!) Walker left United at the end of the season in which they won promotion to Division Three (now Division Two). Dispiritingly, he had not been able to win a regular place in the first-team (although the drop in wages consequential to losing his first-team place had been cushioned by summers in the NASL with Montreal Olympic FC). He joined southcoast Poole Town on a wage £5 above his previous and a signing-on fee of £600. He also negotiated the right to run a souvenir shop, which he established with the help of Les Olive, secretary of Manchester United. Even with more money, it must have been difficult for the former captain and player of the year to accept that his very successful days at Cambridge United were numbered.

In Dennis's five seasons at the Abbey Stadium, United never finished in a lower position than the season before. They had won two promotions, two championships and one League cup. Yet his career pattern reminds us that a footballer can only usually expect seven or eight seasons as a regular first-teamer. He joined a club in 1968 that went on to make history for itself and, as Leivers points out, 'The players who were there at the time [of the Southern League Championship/Football League election years] have something to be proud of'. On the day of United's election into the Football League, a crowd gathered expectantly at the supporters club. When the news came through that we were in, there was hugs, kisses, the works! And then there was a parade around the city on an open-topped bus for fans and players, climaxing with a civic reception in the Market Square. This aspect of the celebration was, in part, payback for United being refused a civic reception by the mayor, Alderman Finbow, when they did the double the previous season. Rivals City weren't given one when they won the championship in 1963, argued the municipal worthy. Coincidentally, when not wearing his civic chain or managing his removal firm, Alderman Finbow was a City director! Such is the parochial expression of football rivalry.

Dennis was a local hero, an inspiration both for me and for many of my mates. Even now I shudder when I remember him tackling with his full weight. When interviewed in February 1997, Dennis was Operations Manager at the Arndale shopping centre in Manchester. He was responsible for clearing the complex immediately prior to the bomb explosion which destroyed the centre in 1996.

Ricky Heppolette was expected by some – *Goal*, 3 March 1969, for example – to be the first Anglo-Indian to play for England. The highest valuation of his career was £80,000. Born in Bhusuval near Bombay on 8 April 1949, Ricky moved to England with his family in 1952. Growing up in Bolton he soon attracted club scouts, with offers of trials from Preston North End, Manchester United and City, Bolton, Burnley, Everton, Southampton and Sheffield Wednesday whose manager Alan Brown, in his letter of invitation, offered to meet Ricky and his father Wilf at the ticket barrier! The much-coveted youngster was eventually signed by Preston North End in September 1964 on a three-season apprenticeship with a starting wage of £7 per week. Between August 1964 and February 1965, North End had taken over 150 trialists to Deepdale, rejecting all of them except the Bombay–Boltonian. Yet it vexed Ricky that his local club, Wanderers, had not offered him a contract. Atypically for such documents, even his school leaving report noted that Ricky had a future in football. 'He is a very likeable boy, has qualities of a high order and is maturing rapidly. He is a first-class footballer and I hope he will be successful in that line.' Indeed it was his games teacher, Mr Little, who wrote to inform those clubs that didn't already know of Ricky's talent. This belief was mirrored in a programme at his new club. The published line-up for Preston North End in a Lancashire Senior Cup game against Burnley, 17 October 1967 read: 3 (David) Bright, 4 (Alec) Spark, 5 (Richard) Heppolette!

Wilf Heppolette was a boiler chargeman on Southern Railways in India. Born in Sholopur, Madras, he can name relations from as far back as 1725 when his European great grandfather came to India to work for the East India Company. Wilf was local secretary of his union and held a similar position for the Anglo-Indian Association. Their lives were comfortable in a household of four servants. After independence in 1947, however, the social and political status of Anglo-Indians became less certain. The government introduced a policy of Indianisation of the public services, which included the railways. Wilf didn't feel able to swear absolute allegiance to the Indian government – he felt and still feels culturally more British than Indian. After 1947, many Anglo-Indians did not feel comfortable anymore in the sub-continent. The country was changing and so was their place in it. It has been estimated that about half of the Anglo-Indian population has emigrated since 1947. Arriving in Bolton, Lancashire, Ricky's father initially took a job as a cleaner on the railways. While he felt it was a demeaning position, it was nevertheless a common experience for the migrant to be undervalued in this way. Eventually he got a job as a rep for a local firm.

Another skill he had to learn quickly was that of glazier. As a schoolboy, Ricky was forever breaking windows with mis-hit balls! (I won't make any jokes connecting these childhood inaccuracies with Ricky's sparse accumulation of 30 league goals in 326 league appearances for his five clubs!) But the sound of breaking glass did betray Ricky's developing qualities as a footballer. He was more of a midfield 'grafter' in the Nobby Stiles mould – with whom he played at Preston – than a cultured, creative ball player like contemporary Colin Bell. The poignant irony here is that subsequent rationalisations of cultural prejudice by scouts and clubs towards Asian players is that they're not aggressive and physically robust enough to cope with British professional football. Yet the careers of Soo, Heppolette, the Cothers, Kevin Keelan and Bud Houghton all shout a different refrain. Perhaps Ricky's most satisfying and important goal exemplifies his tenacious spirit. Discussed earlier in the profile of Stan Horne, it was a diving header – from a corner kick – in a packed goalmouth for Preston *v.* Fulham at Craven Cottage, which decided which of the two clubs would finish as 1970–71 champions of the Third Division.

Heppolette began his full professional career on a basic £14 per week. Though bonuses could double this amount it would never have catapulted the young Indian into the showbiz category of footballers. Yet, by the age of 19, he had been labelled a 'black aristocrat' by the *Daily Mail,* 27 March 1969, the newspaper publishing a gallery of notable Blacks resident in Britain to celebrate Trinidadian Learie Constantine taking his place in the House of Lords.

> We are used to seeing them on buses and trains, in the hospitals and building sites . . . quiet, unassuming people, for the most part, whose only common denominator is that they are not white. These are the immigrants, the thousands who poured into this country from the West Indies, India, Pakistan and Africa in the post-war flood. Most do humble jobs . . . essential but unglamorous. However, almost without realising, there is a new breed of coloured people. The ones who have found their feet . . . the ones who have been here for some time . . . the ones who are taking on native-born Britons and beating them at their own game . . . the ones who are forging a new aristocracy . . . a black aristocracy based upon merit.

(How can an 'aristocracy' be meritocratic?) Under a photo of the teenage footballer was written 'His talent is worth about £60,000 say some sports writers'.

At this time the young 'aristocrat' was earning a basic £25 per week plus an extra £30 if in the first team, £3 per week travelling expenses with further bonus payments dependent upon league position. If Ricky was playing regularly in the first team and they were in the top four, his wage could reach the then magical sum – for working-class lads – of £100. This was certainly much more than his mates would have been earning in the mills and factories of Bolton, but it didn't make Ricky an equal of Little Lord Fauntleroy. As if to add a mocking footnote to the *Mail* charade, the following summer 'Mr Hepplewhite' was employed by Mr Fred 'Book Early' Pontin as a 'sports organiser' at £10 per week (supplementing Ricky's basic summer wage of £35 per week). Fred also insisted that maximum publicity be given to his employment at the Pontinental resort in Cala Mesquida, Spain, so that Preston North End fans 'can spend their holidays with one of their favourite players'.

In fact the *Mail* article is guilty of misinformation, misconception and prejudice in the tradition of its nickname the 'Daily Forger', acquired after it published a knowingly forged letter before the 1924 election purporting to come from Zinoviev, member of the Russian politbureau. The same paper also supported Hitler's purging of dissidents within his own party, the 'Night of the Long Knives'. And during the inner-city uprisings of 1981 it carried the headline 'Black Hooligans' in an attempt to criminalise all Black residents of Toxteth, Liverpool. With its patronising tone, the 'Black Aristocrat' article was guilty of spreading misinformation because the term 'immigrants' becomes interchangeable with people of colour. In fact most migrants to Britain, then and today and throughout history, are and have been White. It implied that 'native-born Britons' cannot be people of colour, despite the presence of generation upon generation of Black Britons – and other 'non-whites' – reaching back to Roman Britain, at least. It attempted to wash white the darker pigments that colour the canvas of Britain's past. The article uses contentious and value-laden descriptive words and phrases such as 'poured', 'flood', 'we are used to them', 'taking on', 'beating them'. And this feature was supposed to be sympathetic in its portrayal of this 'new breed of coloured people'!

The phrase 'new breed of coloured people' implied that wealth is merely a reflection of superior genetic stock. This thinking was classic nineteenth-century scientific racism. At the stroke of a pen it justified inequalities of wealth in society: you cannot do anything about such differences because people who make money are clever. And we know they are clever because they are rich. Similarly, those who are poor are not clever – because they are poor! Cleverness and wealth are Siamese twins. A gift from God provides intelligence and society rewards this gift in life.

By serving up the *Mail* article for dissection we glimpse the menu of language from which the myths of the '60s 'race' debates were cooked up, a subject that could not be discussed without the deployment of misleading and dishonest terms. The language used in public debate of issues of colour created an imagined nation – being overrun by dark-skinned hordes – which, in reality, never existed.

After 149 games for North End, Ricky felt he needed fresh challenges. He was 22, flush and still living at home. In December 1972 he was signed for £55,000 (reputedly – who believes public figures on transfers?) by George Petchey at Leyton Orient, also of the Second Division. While it was a new club it was also a sideways move – Orient were hardly big time, although the wage structure was less tight-fisted than at Deepdale, where he'd recently been in a pay dispute. And they did have other Black players on their books.

Two years after Orient had missed promotion to Division One by one point, Terry Venables signed Ricky for Crystal Palace. After 113 games for the East End club that had teenage prodigy Laurie Cunningham emerging as a world-class winger, Ricky was attracted by the hype and hyperbole of the Dagenham-born 'Eagle'. However the migration to south London didn't last long. Inside the dressing-room and on the training ground Heppolette was racially abused by one of the senior pros. He didn't need it and didn't put up with it. Four months later he'd moved to fellow Third-Division club Chesterfield. Only once had Ricky responded violently to such insults, in an away match against Nottingham Forest where, according to Petchey, Heppolette 'put up with the most appalling provocation throughout the match'. The evening culminated in a punch-up with Northern Ireland international Tommy Jackson which led to both being sent off. While Ricky felt he did not hear a great deal of racist abuse directed at him, he did notice Orient team-mates Laurie Cunningham and Bobby Fisher being constantly attacked.

Heppolette is the best known and most widely remembered of those Anglo-Indians who became professional footballers. However, perhaps the most successful British–Indian, who played professionally or whose career began between 1945 and 1970, is Paul Wilson of Celtic.

Celtic–Indian Paul Wilson, born in Milngavie, north Glasgow, signed for 'The Bhoys' as a 17 year old in December 1967. Seven months earlier the club had become the first British side to win the European Cup, beating Inter Milan 2–1 in Lisbon, with a team all born within a 30-mile radius of Parkhead.

At this time there were three managers in the British game, all from mining communities, all Scottish and all socialists, who were to become legends: Matt Busby at Manchester United; Bill Shankly at Liverpool and Jock Stein at Celtic. Stein showed great faith in Wilson. After scoring four goals in two cup finals – against Airdrie and Rangers – in the space of eight days, Stein in the *Scottish Sunday Express*, 12 May 1975, commented:

> Paul has been slow in developing . . . although he was coming through in a group that established itself quickly . . . like [David] Hay, [Lou] Macari, [Kenny] Dalglish, [George] Connelly and [Danny] McGrain . . . he was running a bit behind the field and he had to be pushed a bit more. Not because the ability was not there. He is the shy type, a little bit backward in coming forward, in a way. He had to be convinced that he could be good, and he had to be developed a bit physically. But he is coming through now, and he will be better yet. Those final goals will help him on his way.

Paul was almost an ever-present in the 1974–75 season. Scotland team manager Willie Ormond recognised his brilliance with a cap – Wilson's one and only – for the European Championship qualifier against Spain in Valencia on 5 February 1975. Given the excellence of Celtic in the mid '70s, with players like Dalglish, McGrain, [Jimmy] Johnstone and [Billy] McNeil, it was virtually inevitable, if Paul shone in such illustrious company, that he would be considered for the national team. He came on as sub for Burns in the last 15 minutes of an unexpected 1–1 draw. With his 15-minute international career, Wilson became Scotland's first international of colour and the second player with Asian antecedence to play for a British national (senior) side after Hong Y 'Frank' Soo. However, the headline-grabbing story of this international was Charlie Cooke's return to the Scotland team.

While Paul played for Celtic during its most successful era, of his 11 years at Parkhead it was only during the '74–5 season that he was a first-team regular. In all, he made 214 League and Cup appearances, scoring 52 goals. He made his first-team début as a 19-year-old substitute against Finnish side Kokkola in the European Cup scoring twice in a 9–0 win in September 1970. A week later he came on as sub again and scored against Dundee in the Scottish League Cup. These two dramatic late appearances forced Stein to include him from the start against the same opposition, this time in the League, three days later. Celtic won 3–0 but the teenager didn't impress. His next and last outing for the first team that season was against Dumbarton in the League Cup in October. He had to wait patiently through another four seasons, battling against Kenny Dalglish, Lou Macari and Bobby Lennox for the number 11 shirt, before claiming it briefly as his own.

Wilson was a speedy two-footed player who was comfortable on the ball, could dribble and shoot with ferocity and accuracy. But, according to Stein and others at the club, he was a late developer and, it could be added, never reached full maturity. He left Celtic for Motherwell in September 1978 and joined Partick Thistle less than a year later. By the following season he had drifted into non-League football. If this analysis of Paul is correct – who knows how good or bad players can really be? – the question that comes to mind is what slowed his development. Was it psychological? An inability to cope with the big time at a big club? Or did the 'jeering calls from the opposition'[15] – otherwise known as racist abuse – that this brown-skinned, black-haired footballer consistently faced affect his confidence?

Another Asian–Celt, Rashid Sarwar, made 21 senior appearances for Kilmarnock in the mid '80s. Considered a good, but slow, passer of the ball, Sarwar gave up the professional game because he stopped enjoying it:

> Although I initially really enjoyed it I found at Kilmarnock it got too serious, became far too 'do or die'. I think part of the reason why I didn't go on and do anything in the game is that I didn't have that hunger, or desire, or will to win at all costs. I'm a happy loser, which makes me a bad player.[16]

We should not forget another South Asian, Nasim Bashir, who played three first-team games for Reading during 1989–90. Or Shinda Singh, an apprentice at Wolverhampton Wanderers in the mid '70s and member of the club's youth team that lost the 1976 FA Youth Cup final to West Midland rivals WBA. Southeast Asian Hung Dang from Vietnam began his apprenticeship with Tottenham in 1987. An England Schoolboy who only arrived in Britain in the late '70s, Dang was on the verge of the Spurs' first team until his knee injury stopped responding to treatment. In 1990 he joined Exeter City but couldn't break into the senior side. He eventually ended up at part-time professional Frome Town in Somerset where the less intense pressure helped him rebuild his fitness and his desire.

Working for a leather goods company in Yeovil he reflected, 'I'm happy with what I'm doing and I really enjoy my football, which is more than most people can say.'[17]

In 1996 Jas Bains and Raj Patel, concerned about the continuing colour bar operating against Asian youngsters in Britain, published a report entitled *Asians Can't Play Football* (1996). Of over sixty-two full-time professional football clubs who replied to the question, only sixteen currently or recently had an Asian player on their books.

Following this pioneering work, Bains co-authored *Corner Flags and Corner Shops: the Asian Football Experience* with Sanjiev Johal, adding weight and momentum to the campaign that highlights the lack of (South) Asian professionals in British football. And, to their credit, many clubs seem genuinely concerned to do something about it. Leeds United's Harpal Singh is on the fringe of the first team. Arsenal developed the talent of Anglo-Indian Jason Crowe who, while at Highbury, made the first team and England Under-19s. Greenock Morton had ex-Rangers youth player, full-back Jaswinda Jutla, for two seasons before he was released at the end of the 1998–99 season.

The noticeable feature about this history of Asian players in the British game is that while there have been footballers from that continent, these have tended to come from mixed backgrounds. Hong Y 'Frank' Soo was born and brought up in Britain. Players such as Keelan, Heppolette and Houghton saw themselves as 'British' – accepting that the term is open to many different interpretations – even if some of them weren't accepted as kosher by those around them. Ricky's father Wilf felt more British – Christian – than Indian. This suggests that it has not been the colour of the skin that has been the primary cause of discrimination against South Asian players, but prejudice against their cultural origins. One of the few full-time pros of South Asian descent of recent years, Chris Dolby, was brought up in an English family. There have been very few South Asian muslims, sikhs or hindus that have become professional footballers. However Sheffield United, Charlton, West Ham, Leicester, Leyton Orient, Millwall and Bradford have all introduced schemes designed to encourage and develop Asian talent. This includes: Bradford playing a UK Asian XI in 1995 and Millwall playing a select team of the Khalsa Football Federation (KFF), the body that represents Asian football in Britain, in 1998 (Millwall subsequently signed the KFF junior goalkeeper, Amritpal Sidhu, on schoolboy forms); being culturally sensitive, with flexibility over training times for those youngsters that have to attend Friday prayers or cannot eat pork; and appointing officers and coaches within the club whose job it is to work with Asian youngsters. If this enlightened attitude continues it will not be long before South Asian players – of whatever cultural background – become a fixture of the British game.

Perhaps teenage winger Harpal Singh, on a two-year professional contract at Leeds United, or Derby County trainee Amrit Sidhu will be the first South Asian player from a background rooted in the culture of the sub-continent to play in the Premiership. However, in October 1999, 22-year-old Baichung Bhutia, a centre-forward from East Bengal FC in Calcutta – crowds average 80,000 for home matches – made his first-team début for Bury FC of the Second Division (whose normal crowd is less than a tenth of East Bengal's). The Indian international from the newly formed Philips National Professional League (PNPL) also had trials with Aston Villa and West Bromwich Albion but it was the Lancashire club's manager Neil Warnock who was most impressed, offering a three-year contract. 'Baichung [is] a superb signing for us. He's very sharp and comes to life in the 18-yard box.' The forward, who has an arts degree from the University of East Bengal and is the youngest of seven of a family from Sikkim in the Himalayas, made his début soon after signing, coming on as a second-half substitute against Cardiff. And he made an immediate impact, creating his team's second goal in their 3–2 defeat of the Bluebirds. Chairman Terry Robinson saw a commercial angle to be exploited: having the Indian in the team would 'generate interest [from] Asians . . . through the turnstile'. As the leading scorer in the PNPL, and for his country, with 25 goals in 35 matches, the diminutive star of the Indian game earned around £1,800 a month. Should he do the business for Bury he could hope to be taking that amount home per week. After watching him in his first League match, Warnock commented, 'He is no world-beater but he has a Gary Lineker kind of attitude in that he can be kicked all over the place and he'll still want to get up and carry on.'[18] And, if Frank Leboeuf's observation that English football is the most violent in the world is true, that's just what Bhutia will have to do. But Frank, have you played in all the leagues in all the world?

While the lack of South Asian footballers is being tackled at the professional level, racism at amateur level still fucks up Asian players and clubs. In January 1997, South Asian Bari FC played Romside FC in a South Essex Sunday League match. Romside had come for a 'paki-bashing' Sunday-out kicking, punching and mouthing abuse. While the Bari players didn't shy away from confronting the ku-klux-klan-in-kit, they hadn't left home that morning prepared for war. Surprise, surprise – or was it? – they were the ones who found themselves charged with misconduct by Essex County FA. Despite being represented at the hearing by Piara Powar of Kick It Out, the charge was upheld. So for incensed Bari, it was bollocks to Essex and hallo London. They now play in another league under the auspices of the London FA, although this isn't without irony. Romside too are affiliated to the London FA who took no action against the racists. And, after the Romside incident, Bari were again attacked, this time by Wanstead Holly FC.

Kick It Out (KIO) now see amateur football and the administrative bodies which run it – the County FAs – as an area that needs close attention. On the day, 27 September 1999, that the ban on all racist language at football grounds came into force under the Football (Offences and Disorder) Act, Piara Powar handed in a dossier on racist violence in amateur football to the FA at Lancaster Gate. Powar argued that 'it is in the interests of professional football to do something about this, because many talented young players of the future are being forced to give up the game'. The dossier, backed by the PFA and the Commission for Racial Equality as well as KIO, details numerous incidences of racist attacks and abuse at amateur football matches. Paul Peart of Leeds Road TRA FC in Huddersfield described how his club had folded up after five years of abuse. 'The racism always seemed to start when we were winning. It was like they thought, "Let's rattle 'em. Let's give 'em some abuse."'[19] Other clubs, like the predominantly African–Caribbean Highfield Rangers in Leicester, have adopted a stance popularised by Joan Armatrading: 'The higher you build your barriers, the taller we become.'

It is only a matter of time before professional South Asian players – from the subcontinent or Britain – are not seen as unusual. And perhaps then the ghettoisation of Asian football will disintegrate. Bodies such as the KFF would not need to exist if football and society were colour-blind. During the latter part of the '90s, the number of Asian professionals playing in Europe increased: Chinese internationals Fan Zhiyi and Sun Jihai at Crystal Palace; Iranians Ali Daei at Hertha Berlin and Ali Mousavi, Mehdi Pashazadeh and Darious Yazdani at Bayer Leverkusen; and Baichung Bhutia of India at Bury are the best known. There are also several Japanese players in Serie A in Italy. Such a diffusion can only add to the positive profile of Asian footballers in the minds of club scouts and managers.

The argument of the PFA and others is that 'too many foreign players' are bad for the British game. (According to UEFA rules, Manchester United's Irishmen Roy Keane and Dennis Irwin are officially 'foreign' players.) When the rules were relaxed in the late '70s and players such as Ossie Ardiles and Ricardo Villa joined Spurs, this same debate surfaced. Chelsea's John Hollins, in a 1979 *Football Handbook* interview entitled 'Foreign "Invaders": Are they good for our game?' observed:

> We're allowed to play over there if we want to, so it's only right for them, too . . . the foreign lads already look good value for money . . . I don't go along with the arguments that foreign players deprive homegrown players of first-team places. If a lad's good enough, he'll get into the side, no matter who's there.

Fellow professional John Richards of Wolves agreed. 'All in all, I'm sure the imports have worked out well. The fans think so – and they're the ones who count.' As a trade union, shouldn't the PFA be asking for free movement of labour? Wouldn't this help all workers/footballers to earn a living without restriction, a principle for which all unions rightly argue? On the premise that ignorance breeds suspicion while knowledge fosters co-operation, free movement of labour would also break down any superficial barriers between workers, like prejudice over colour, religion and culture. Even in the PNFL in India there is a European player, Swede Ulf Johannsen. And why not? Would the PFA and others argue that British players should be prevented from playing abroad?

The following chapter discusses the 'Black Explosion' of the '70s and '80s, a period when the Black African–Caribbean presence in British football matured.

SEVEN

Exploding into Maturity

The '70s and '80s

The unprecedented growth in Black professional footballers in the 1970s to early '80s, the fifth generation, was marked by events that confirmed their presence, status and excellence in the game in Britain. Tony Whelan and Clive Charles, not household names even at the peak of their careers, were nonetheless the first Black professionals to receive a PFA Divisional Award in 1976. They were voted by their fellow professionals as the best players in their position in their division. Two years later, on 29 November 1978 against Czechoslovakia at Wembley, Viv Anderson became the first player of African–Caribbean parents to win a full England cap, while the following Spring Cyrille Regis of WBA was voted Young Player of the Year by his PFA colleagues. In 1982 a total of 13 Black players were selected for the full England and Under-21 squads. And, on 10 June 1984, 20-year-old John Barnes scored probably the greatest goal ever seen by a foreign international at the spiritual home of the Beautiful Game, the Maracana Stadium in Rio de Janeiro, Brazil. Collecting the ball around the half-way line, the Jamaican swerved, dribbled and feinted his way round and through the yellow-jerseyed defence to side-foot the ball past Roberto Costa leaving the massive crowd breathless and his England colleagues ecstatic. On the plane back to England, a group of English Nazis abused John and said his goal didn't count.

An electrician by trade, Big Cyrille Regis burst on to the First Division scene like a lightning bolt in February 1978, having signed for WBA from Isthmian League club Hayes for £5,000 the previous May. In his first full season in the Football League he shocked defences around the country with his close control, speed and powerful shot from the foot or head. Selected for England Under-21s, he eventually became their first Black captain, against Denmark at Wembley in September 1982. By then he'd already made his senior début, coming on as sub for Trevor Francis in the 4–0 defeat of Northern Ireland at Wembley in February. (As we'll discuss below, 1982 was a seminal year for Black footballers in Britain.) Despite the range of the French Guyanan's talent, England manager Ron Greenwood thought he should use his weight more aggressively! Alongside him at the Hawthorns was Brendan Batson who won a Divisional Award in 1977 while at Cambridge United, and winger Laurie Cunningham who had started his career with Leyton Orient, his local outfit. Desperately short of cash, the 'O's decided to put Laurie on offer to all other London clubs. There were no takers, so off he went up the M1 for £110,000. (It was another Black winger, Nigerian John Chiedozie, that took the vacant number 11 at Brisbane Road.) WBA manager and top-notch self-publicist Ron Atkinson nicknamed his three Black first-teamers the Three Degrees after the female soul band. Cunningham, world class on his day, won just six England caps. West Brom's ventures into Europe via the UEFA Cup – where they reached the quarter-final – awakened others to Laurie's talents including Real Madrid who, in 1979, paid over £800,000 for the enigmatic trickster. In 1983 he returned to the English game with Manchester United. Yet it was back in Spain that Laurie died tragically and young near Madrid on 15 July 1989 when a car accident prematurely ended the life of the first Black Briton to play for a major club in continental Europe. Cyrille is now – 1999 – back at the Hawthorns as coach, while the third degree, Brendan, is deputy chief executive of the PFA.

If Laurie unwittingly played out the artist's denial of mundane ordinariness through the boast 'live fast, die young', it was, in contrast, by his own hand that another star of the same era, the first £1 million Black footballer Justin Fashanu terminated his existence. Justin seemed to have all before him when he won *Match of the Day*'s Goal of the Season with his spectacular volley for Norwich against Liverpool, in February 1980. A big move to Nottingham Forest soon followed, as well as an England Under-21 call-up. Yet his sad demise may have had as much to do with his inner turmoil as an out, gay Black footballer in an all-male, macho profession, as with his upbringing by his White adoptive parents in rural Norfolk. While Gascoigne's tears in the 1990 World Cup semi-final against West Germany induced a pavlovian stretch for the Kleenex box in living-rooms all over England, sensitivity to a footballer's sexuality is rigid and unbending (sorry!) When centre-forward Justin came out, the joke doing the rounds was that he wanted to drop back into defence . . . to stiffen up the rear. There is no (hiding) place for the gay in football, while similarly in Attleborough, Norfolk, there were no other Blacks. His brother John's attempt to compensate for the inner sense of dislocation and isolation has been to surround himself with wealth and, therefore, power. Justin's response to his feelings of 'otherness' was to place his faith in God. His suicide came after an accusation of sexual harassment was made by a young American footballer whom Fashanu was coaching. The charges were never proven before Justin was found lifeless in an East End lock-up.

Born in London in 1961 to a Guyanan nurse and a Nigerian lawyer, at the age of three he and his baby brother John were placed in a children's home. Justin began his career with his local club Norwich City after starring in schoolboy football:

> The reason I became a footballer was simple: I could run faster than anybody else, that's about it. I didn't have any skill whatsoever, but I could run with the ball and hold it . . . Before I left school the papers were full of me: 'This boy will go all the way to the top'.[1]

But getting into the ring was his first love. Unable to apply for a professional boxer's licence until he was 17, he accepted the offer of a football apprenticeship by the Carrow Road club at 16 with the intention of giving it a year and then 'steamin' into boxing'. Plans, eh! By 17 he was chirping away in the Canaries first team.

The move to Nottingham was a disaster. From the off there was a personality clash with manager Brian Clough which seriously affected his form so that an average of a goal nearly every other game at Norwich was reduced to one in ten at Forest. Banned from the training ground, he once tried to take part while Clough called the police in order to protect his turf. At the beginning of the following season he was loaned out to Southampton until neighbours Notts County bought the young striker for £150,000, a fraction of the fee their rivals had paid out. In the black-and-white stripes of the oldest club in the Football League, his goal average soared to nearly one in two again. It was at this time of turmoil, frustration and confusion that Justin became a born-again Christian.

Following his three seasons at County came an unsettled meandering that took him around England, Scotland and the USA: a search for form and consistency with the hope that, on regaining these powers, some kind of stability would follow. It never happened. He even retired for a period in the mid '80s. Looking back on his formative years as a teenage footballer Justin reflected, in an interview given around 1981, that he had needed someone close to lean on in the tough times: 'Nobody could guide me, which is what I needed'. And when Justin needed that friend most, there was nobody there. Not even the God in whom he had placed so much faith.

Laurie Cunningham and Justin Fashanu were players of immense promise who died early. They are remembered not just for this reason, but also because they excelled in their chosen profession. For power, strength and aggression there were few to match the Norfolk boy. For fluid, balletic movement, artistry and beauty, Cunningham more than equalled his contemporaries.

While players such as Viv Anderson – full-back at Forest when Fashanu fell out with Clough – and Everton's Cliff Marshall – first Black Liverpudlian to play for a Merseyside club – have their niche in football folklore, we shouldn't forget those journeyman pros that played in the bread-and-butter divisions of the Football League. On the south coast, 18-year-old Chris Kamara made his début for Portsmouth in 1975. At Cambridge United, after Dennis Walker and Brendan Batson – who went on to win an England 'B' cap with WBA – in the hot, dusty and dry summer of '76, came big, broad, massive and 'ard Floyd Streete. Joining him two years later was winger Derrick Christie, signed from Northampton Town for a club record fee of £50,000 while in-between times, East Anglian rivals Luton Town captured England schoolboy star and local lad Godfrey Ingram. The youngster was expected to graduate quickly into the first-team and play alongside Ricky Hill, then being tipped to play for England. Ricky did roll on to three full internationals but Godfrey never fulfilled that great early promise. At Leyton in East London, England Youth Bobby Fisher and Nigerian international Tunji Banjo, along with teenage prodigy Laurie, were adding style and steel to George Petchey's Orient. Across the river at Millwall, the Den was home to Trevor Lee and Phil Walker. Further south, down Croydon way, Mark Lindsay and Vince Hilaire were helping the Eagles fly at Crystal Palace. In the Midlands, Pedro Richards and Tristan Benjamin were shoring up Notts County's defence, while Brendan Phillips was running with the 'Stags' at Mansfield Town. Further north, Joe Cooke was palling up with Ces Podd at Bradford and England Schoolboy Trentan Wiggan was battling his way into the first-team at Sheffield United. Between the posts at Bramall Lane, while Trentan played his 24 first-team games, was the club's second Black goalkeeper (after Arthur Wharton), Derek Richardson. Over in Moss Side, Manchester City had Alex Williams, who is now their Football in the Community Officer, making his name as their number one. By the end of the decade, well over fifty Black footballers were playing in the Football League.

At the highest level of senior international football, Wales had fielded their first Black player way back in 1930; Scotland had selected Asian–Celt Paul Wilson for the international against Spain in February 1975 and England had selected Hong Y Soo in the '40s and given Viv Anderson his cap in '79 (with the Republic of Ireland débuting Paul McGrath in February 1985).

The appointment of Bobby Robson as England manager in 1982 further enhanced the status of Black footballers. The ex-Ipswich Town and England 'B' boss had stated publicly that the colour of a player was irrelevant and, if the best 11 available were men of colour, this wouldn't make the slightest difference to his team selection. I remember going to a football forum in the late '70s comprising Robson and Ron Greenwood who was then England manager and the manager of Colchester United. In a reply to a question as to why England had failed to qualify for the 1974 and 1978 World Cups and 1976 European Championships, Robson argued it was, amongst other reasons, because of a lack of investment in the game. He had just come back from West Germany. 'Borussia Munchengladbach, great stadium; Bayern Munich, wonderful facilities; Hamburg, excellent . . . and we won the war!' Yet even if these Little Englander sentiments did ask me to question the state of his mental health, his attitude to players of colour was first class. Robson received hate mail for choosing Viv Anderson, Ricky Hill, John Barnes, Cyrille Regis, Paul Davis and Chris Whyte in the squad for the European Championship qualifying matches against Denmark and their Under-21s in September 1982. In the Under-21 game, where Cyrille Regis was captain, he himself along with Arsenal's Paul Davis and Chris Whyte and Watford's John Barnes were booed when they touched the ball. For the players this was nothing new. The manager, to his credit, chose Coventry's Danny Thomas and Gary Thompson, Stoke's Mark Chamberlain, Watford's Luther Blisset, Luton's Brian Stein, Manchester United's Remi Moses and Nottingham Forest's Justin Fashanu for the next European qualifier.

If, because of the success of the fifth generation, the mood was upbeat among young players of colour hoping to break into the professional game, this feeling was not typical throughout British football as a whole. Even though English clubs were successful in European competitions, gates were declining domestically and the international team was going nowhere. It managed to qualify for the 1980 European Championship in Italy but didn't do anything, drawing with Belgium, losing to Italy and beating Spain 2–1 before taking an early plane home. The team hit the headlines for being, well, just typically English – boisterous and boring – while the fans hit the headlines for being . . . typically English. Or, more accurately, for conforming to the stereotype in the eyes of the media and football establishment. At the game with Belgium in the Stadio Comunale, Turin, a fight between English fascists and Italian onlookers in a corner of the England end was talked up into a riot by the media to justify the overreaction of the Carabinieri, who indiscriminately fired tear gas into the end. The game was stopped for five minutes to allow the eye-stinging chemical to be wiped from Ray Clemence's eyes, the gas to clear the pitch and for the police to 'take control' of the 'riot'. Out in Italy for a jolly-up and football feast with some mates, and right in the Carabinieri's line of fire, I dived to the floor . . . into a pool of piss!

There was the usual condemnation by the British Establishment: Margaret Thatcher called the event 'a disgraceful embarrassment' while FA President Sir Harold Thompson called all of us 'moronic louts and troublemakers'. The point here is that those who were up for a bit of 'wop bashing' were the Rule Britannia/God Save The Queen boneheads draped in the Butcher's Apron; the same right-wing wankers who would later boo Black footballers playing for England and pretend that John Barnes didn't really score that goal in the Maracana. Tellingly, all the symbols the fascists used to express their patriotism would be those used by Thatcher and Thompson to express their politics. The problem was not one of substance – Thatcher is a right-wing racist who, presently, enjoys shooting the breeze with a rich South American mass murderer bang to rights in Surrey – but one of style: the Oiks were out of control again and rubbishing England's good name. The Riot in Turin, as it came to be known, encapsulated the confused state of English football and British politics. England weren't good enough at international level yet Liverpool were sweeping all before them in Europe; and Thatcher – who hates football and working-class culture – while condemning the hooligans was one of the primary influences on the mentality of the National Front recruiters travelling with the England fans. Her xenophobic rantings about being 'swamped' by [Black] aliens of a 'different culture' and Little Englander stances in Europe were nothing more than a 'swivel on it' finger extension to Johnny Foreigner. Two years after her 'embarrassment' over Turin, she and another South American dictator of similar political views decided to sacrifice young men of their country over a windswept sheep run in the South Atlantic. The enormous cost was irrelevant – wars are always affordable. Indeed her son Mark is reputed to have made a fortune offering bullets and barrels to the highest bidders. At the time of the Falklands/Malvinas War, unemployment figures in Britain were over three million, the highest they had been since the 1930s Depression, the welfare state was being slashed with education and health budgets cut to the bone. And to really take the piss without giving a fuck, she decided two years later that most miners would have to sign on because digging for coal was no longer affordable. (Although anyone with half a brain knew that the real reason was that the Board of UK plc, otherwise known as the government, had decided The Business couldn't afford strong unions.)

The problem for football was that many of its 'captains' of industry thought like the government. The hooligan was public enemy number one; the folk devil; a symptom of Britain's national decline and the cause of its internal malaise, measured weekly by the fall in people going to games. And the players weren't much better with their threats of strike action and demand of freedom of contract. Ken Bates, chairman of Chelsea, seriously argued for electric perimeter fencing at grounds. Thatcher's solution was to introduce identity cards. As for the problem of racism, we'll outlaw racist chanting in unison, said the 1991 Football Offences Act, but racist abuse shouted by one person – that's OK!

Her régime was only really interested in the image British football – in particular its English variant – presented to the wider world. She was conscious of the reach of the game into the hearts and minds of ordinary people – its influence on popular culture – but not interested in the internal health of football. The Number 10 hospitality budget would have more than matched government grants to the industry for improvements to grounds and infrastructure: if you were bustin' while standing in the Kop at Anfield, find somebody's leg. The Bradford fire of 11 May 1985, where 56 people were killed and over 200 more were burnt, was an issue of class. The stadium was old and wooden. If opera was performed at Valley Parade to the crowds the team were pulling in, it wouldn't have been old and wooden. And there wouldn't have been such a devastating fire. The Bradford inferno stood as a testament to the physical expression of inequalities in the provision of leisure. A working-class stadium for a working-class sport in a working-class city in the north of England. It was only after Bradford, and Hillsborough where nearly 100 fans were crushed to death, that concern about the condition of grounds and safety and comfort of fans within them became an issue for the government. It was in this context, after the Taylor Report into the Hillsborough disaster, that racial abuse at grounds became recognised by the government as a problem.

Yet it was in January 1981 that former Tory MP David Lane, as chairman of the Commission for Racial Equality, called for a meeting with the chairman and secretary of the FA Sir Harold Thompson and Ted Croker to discuss, as Lane saw it, the return of noisy, nasty racist abuse and chanting at football grounds. 'That used to happen three years ago when Black players first appeared at important matches but since then they've become accepted and applauded.'[2] He complained that fascist groups, such as the National Front and British Movement, were selling their papers and recruiting outside grounds and instigating, organising and encouraging racist abuse of fans and players inside stadia.

Abuse was growing but it was a little ironic that calls for action to do something about it should come from a man whose party was the governing power and who'd never hesitated in playing the 'race' card for its own advantage. In short, the Tories were part of the problem, not least their leader who had made her views on the subject quite clear with her 'swamping' speech in 1977. Very little action was taken by the football authorities as a result of Lane's plea. The FA didn't instigate a Kick Racism Out of Football campaign. At the beginning of the following season, Spurs fans in Holland for a European Cup-Winners Cup tie with Ajax fought running battles with Black youths in the Zeedijk district of Amsterdam.

Racism in society, by the police in particular, had been thrown on to the public agenda by the 1981 inner-city riots which culminated in a weekend of rebellion in July 1981. Black inner-city youth had taken the hardest licks from the recession of the early '80s and, coming on top of consistent harassment by Babylon – the police – had said whoa! I moved to Handsworth, Birmingham in September 1981. Many of the windows of the shops and offices of Lozells Road, centre of the uprising in the city, were still boarded up. The glaziers were coining it. The (mainly Black) youth of Handsworth, Toxteth, Brixton, Southall, Tottenham, St Pauls, Moss Side, Bradford and Tiger Bay together with pissed-off (White) youth in other parts of the UK, did what Catholic youth had been doing in Belfast and Derry for over a decade, they took to the streets and fought back. Fuck monetarism, fuck the free market and more specifically fuck the police. On the streets and over the white line, Black youth were demanding they be heard. In Toxteth, where the fire really did burn, a 21-year-old Southport footballer, Phil Robins, was shot by the police with CS gas shells, suffering wounds to his chest and back. Merseyside Chief Constable Kenneth Oxford pleaded, 'For a hundred years we haven't had a problem [in this city] – now they're hell bent on confrontation.' Under the *Daily Mail* (6 July 1981) banner headline 'Black War on Police' Oxford ranted that to these 'young Black hooligans . . . the police, a symbol of authority and discipline . . . is anathema'.

The riot in Brixton in April which kicked off the 'carnival of the oppressed' in the summer of '81 – a much more dramatic and serious uprising of British youth than May '68 – was in response to the Met's aptly named Operation Swamp in which the public's protectors swept the streets for offenders to law 2B: Black and in Brixton. Commander Fairbairn, newly arrived in 'L' District which included the Railton Road frontline, decided that the natives were not being good boys and that it was time to kick arse. The police in London had begun to keep an ethnic record of those *suspected* of street crimes, in particular muggings, which they published dubbed with a 'time to go for the Black mugger' soundtrack. Needless to say, the Met did not keep an ethnic breakdown of *victims* of crime where Black youngsters figured in disproportionately high numbers. Fairbairn devised a cunning plan to secretly swamp the Railton Road/Mayall Road area with 100 plain clothes officers between 6 and 11 April, with a mission to lasso those youngsters caught out on the streets and in possession of Black skin. The rope-the-dopes trick didn't work and it was he, his apprentice Detective Chief Superintendent Plowman and their street commandos, that got their arses dragged along the tarmac.

The public profile of Black – more specifically African–Caribbean – youth had never loomed larger. But it had two sides, two faces: the street-wise urban warrior that was a threat to all law-abiding citizens clashed with the creative, go-for-it athlete/musician responsible for spicing up British youth culture. Yet for the young British, Black footballer – despite the monkey chants, abuse, aggravation – even with all of these irritations, the future on the park looked bright.

If the public stereotype of Black youth was riven with contradictions, strange things were also happening within football. Falling gates, mediocre quality and rucking in and outside grounds indirectly reshaped the Black fooballer during the late '70s–early '80s. Instead of being seen as physically and emotionally unsuitable for the British game, they were reconstructed by powerful figures such as secretary of the Football League Alan Hardaker and managers Ron Greenwood, Don Howe and Bobby Robson, as potential heroes. Don Howe, while assistant to England manager Bobby Robson, argued that 'the Black influx might just be the saviour of the game in England . . . they seem to be the hungry ones'. England's failure to qualify for major international competitions in the '70s rammed home the truth that youngsters were being taught to win before they could play. Determination, aggression and courage were valued more highly than skill, technique and imagination. Yet to compete at the highest level of international football, these latter qualities were just what were needed to win; and were just what were lacking in the domestic game – except amongst Black youngsters, according to Hardaker, Greenwood, Robson, Howe and others. Alan Hardaker tempered his prediction of a bright future with a veiled warning, however:

> There is a new brand of footballer who might well revolutionise the game
> in this country, the Black footballer. It will take time for his strength and
> skill to be accepted but the Black footballer will break through and may
> even dominate English football.[3]

And, although these prominent figures were painting a picture of the young Black footballer as a particular type, there was something in their argument. Many players of colour had no problem accepting that Alan Ball was not a role model – except for his white boots. Ces Podd has told how Eusebio and Pelé and the Brazilians of 1970 were an inspiration to his generation. The message being transmitted during the second half of the '70s was if England was ever again to become world champion it needed a crew with a darker hue. But it was another Howe, African–Caribbean journalist Darcus, writing to a mood of soul searching after England had failed to qualify for the final stages of the 1976 European Championship, who had already offered this way forward in December 1975. Get more Black players 'with natural flair and skill' into the team. Over and above being dissed for their colour, he argued, Black players were more vexed over having their technique and talent undermined by the huff and puff, kick and rush character of the British game. Interviewing Millwall's Trevor Lee and Phil Walker, both of whom started their careers at Epsom and Ewell in the Athenian League, he voiced the players' concern that the most pressing crisis in football is not one of racism – though this is bad enough – but one of mediocrity. For Trevor Lee this meant not putting his money where his mouth was – he had only spectated at three or so games in Britain. 'I just can't stand to watch the kind of football served up in this country.' Despite his rejection of the values of the English game, Gordon Jago, manager at Millwall, was excited by Lee and Walker. '[They are] supreme athletes with a joy and enthusiasm for the game, sadly lacking in pro football today.'[4] Yet both players felt that what they learned on the training ground often hindered their freedom to improvise, to be unpredictable. It was this aspect to their game that they valued most, that they felt clashed and was diminished by the production line process of turning out predictable players.

Crisis point was reached once more in October 1977 after a plodding, embarrassing 2–0 win in Luxembourg, the consequence of which was that England yet again failed to qualify for the final stages of the World Cup, to be hosted the following summer in Argentina. *The Sun*, a paper never slow to wave the flag and bash any commie, wop, dago, nigger, queer, foreigner – anyone – foolish enough not to be singing Rule Britannia on command, had a centre-page spread of its Black dream team under the heading 'England's Black Magic Soccer Eleven. Presenting the Key Men in our Football Future'. After the Luxembourg humiliation the England manager Ron Greenwood commented, 'We're light years behind. The worst thing is that our managers can't see it, and the players don't want to spend time sharpening their skills. Until and unless we change our attitude we will simply go falling further and further behind.' Thus, across a couple of seasons, footballers such as Cunningham, Regis, Batson, Hilaire and Crooks were transformed from unsuitable to unstoppable; way out to way ahead. Instead of embodying values alien to the British game they were now the personification of progress, of how things should be. Respect was lavished on them by those-in-the-know. Black players were now potential saviours of the national team. It was a burden no footballer should have to shoulder. Yet to some on the pitch and terrace they were still Black bastards.

At least pros had the small compensation that they were living a half-decent life and getting paid for being abused. Amateur Black players didn't. Windsor AC of Liverpool applied to play in the city's Central Amateur League for the 1971–2 season. They were refused – as was the Afro-West Indian Association Football Club of Bradford when they ordered a round of drinks at the bar of the Union Jack Club after a match there in September 1972. Secretary of the club, Mr Fred Sutcliffe, confirmed that while they'll play niggers, they won't serve them refreshments. Highfield Rangers, after winning the Leicester Mutual Premier League six times between 1979 and 1985, decided that it was time to step up. They applied to join the Leicestershire Senior League. They were rejected. Three times. On the first occasion the reason given was that the pitch wasn't good enough. Rangers sorted out the drainage and re-applied. No change. After the third knockback they did move up a grade into the Central Midlands League outside the county. Being outcasts meant they'd also now be out of pocket with all the extra costs each away match would involve. In 1992 the bigots in the Leicestershire Senior League finally gave in.

The prevalence of 'race' as an issue in all aspects of football was highlighted by an event of the summer of 1982 that preceded the 'explosion' of Black players into the Robson's England squads: a football tour to South Africa arranged by Jimmy Hill under the pretext that it would help to repair a little of the damage done to mixed sport in a country where the majority were still being whacked daily by the fist of apartheid. Almost immediately the World Cup in Italy had ended, ex-player and PFA chairman Jimmy Hill, a man who could chin wag on football like no other, was sold a beautiful dummy by South African Breweries (SAB). He accepted their invitation to round up a 'multi-national' team to play a six-match series. John Barnwell was appointed manager. The stated aim of the tour was to encourage inter-racial contact through sport. (During the summer of 1982 the Israeli military was setting up barracks in Lebanon and touring Beirut by tank while Britain and Argentina were knocking three buckets of shite out of each other over the Falklands/Malvinas. Why not a love-and-harmony crusade to Port Stanley instead, Jimmy?) Names such as (Argentinians) Kempes and Ardiles, Smith and Alexsic (the last three named) of Spurs, Brian Greenhoff of Leeds and Calvin Plummer of Notts Forest were thrown around. Hill's Feet Blues. The tour was condemned by the FA, FIFA, South Africa's leading teams, the Kaiser Chiefs and Orlando Pirates, and blanked by most players, including Ardiles and Kempes. After three matches against no-marks, the love bus was turned around and the £5,000-per-match players told not to dwell too long in the duty-free lounge at Johannesburg's Jan Smuts airport. Hill had already sold a dummy of his own and bodyswerved back to Blighty for his daughter's wedding. SAB was reported to have spent £75,000 getting what the Azanian People's Organisation – AZAPO – labelled 'marauding mercenaries' over to the Republic. For this corporate giant, a successful tour would have presented a less harsh South Africa to the outside world, in turn acting as a pressure-release valve on the apartheid régime. Big business and apartheid were blood brothers. The former got fat operating in a state where most employees had few or no rights and were subsequently paid a weekly wage little more, if they were lucky, than the price of a crate of the brewer's finest. So for SAB – Suck the Africans' Blood (and spit it back down their throats) – apartheid kept down labour costs and upped profits. A successful tour would also have improved its own corporate 'brand' image among soccer-loving Blacks, further upping sales and market share. However, the dictatorship in South Africa was slowly being isolated internationally, while within its borders Black workers, students and political activists were building the fire. Hill, who said he was not paid, was made to look like a plonker, along with John Barnwell, Dave Watson, Stuart Pearce, Frank Carrodus, the former referee Jack Taylor and others because they were greedy and naïve. Hill was looking to enhance his reputation while the players who did participate tended to be past their best and saw the opportunity as a nice little summertime earner. All were done up like kippers by the beer makers. Asked about the Black opposition to them in SA, John Barnwell commented, 'We don't know what the Black attitude is because we were not here to find that out.'[5] Enough said. The ANC, AZAPO and virtually all those involved in the political struggle against apartheid were asking for co-operation by those beyond their borders to trap the beast. The 1977 Gleneagles Agreement between Commonwealth countries formally discouraged sporting links with South Africa. There was an international blacklist of sports people that had played in the country, produced by the UN Special Committee against Apartheid. Yet Jimmy decides to try and feed it. It was an abject lesson in political strategy. Let those involved at the heart of the struggle determine the way forward. Few Black footballers in Britain wanted anything to do with the fiasco. Those of them with the slightest nous knew that there wasn't much difference in burdening players like Laurie Cunningham and Cyrille Regis with saving the English game from mediocrity, and using footballers as pawns in an international exercise of misguided sporting diplomacy. Once players become symbols, metaphors, their individuality is lost. Players of colour knew this, having long been stereotyped as this or that, unable to be just footballers.

Vic Kasule is not a name that rings bells in most people's minds. However, as a player for Albion Rovers, Meadowbank Thistle, Hamilton Academicals, Shrewsbury and Darlington Vodka Vic, the Glaswegian winger did cause the emergency services to set their sirens wailing a few times: once when he flipped over his team-mate's car on the way to the paper shop; another time when he rucked with local lad Martin Shivers in a Shrewsbury street; or when there was a warrant out for his arrest . . . The Bad Motherfuckah of the '80s, Vic played in the English, Scottish and Irish Leagues in one season. Deciding to put the past behind him he went to chill out in Finland for a while, then Malta. Yet for all of Vic's antics, it was probably Mark Walters who made the biggest impact as a Black player in Scotland in the '80s. Signing for Rangers – 70 years after Walter Tull is reputed to have put his signature to a contract and 40 years after Mohammed Latif played against Hibernian – Mark became a marked man. Opposition fans sent him bananas. He never had so much fruit offered up. This 'hun on the run' was even nicknamed 'Jaffa', black on the outside, orange inside. It was a brave move by Walters and his manager Graeme Souness. The Ibrox club were renowned for symbolising far-right and loyalist causes. Signing a Black man, despite the ghosts of Tull and Latif, was not quite as bad as signing a Catholic, but near enough. Souness did that as well.

Over at the Irish club in Glasgow's East End, the Bhoys had signed centre-back Paul Elliot from Pisa. Celtic had often signed Protestants – Jock Stein being the most notable. They had Gil Heron in the early '50s. 'The racial abuse I've suffered in Scotland is far worse than anything I had to put up with in England or Italy,' said the tall one with the perm.'[6] Elliot had statistics to prove it. Apart from having a full fruit bowl, he was booked 16 times in his first season. He'd only been pencilled in once before, for upending Maradona. Stuart Cosgrove reckons the Parkhead people think most first-class refs are masons (therefore sympathetic to Rangers, hostile to Celtic). While it might be paranoia, is it coincidence that Heron also complained about what he felt was biased refereeing during his time?

By the time Thatcher had been shown the door by the Tories in November 1990, most big British clubs had opened their doors to players of colour. Liverpool paid around £1 million for John Barnes in July 1987, and Alex Ferguson did not like that, to paraphrase another manager. Rod and Ray Wallace had joined Leeds from Southampton which in 1987–8 had all three Wallace brothers on their books. Viv Anderson moved from the Arsenal of Paul Davis and Michael Thomas to Manchester United, where Remi Moses was bossing the midfield and Paul McGrath was timing his tackles to perfection. Paul was also honorary captain of the OTAHDC – the Old Trafford After-Hours Drinking Club – while Wright and Bright were the boys on Stevie Coppell's block in Thornton Heath. In fact Crystal Palace fielded eight Black players for the whole game against Leicester City on 8 December 1993: Richard Shaw, Dean Gordon, Eric Young, Chris Coleman, Bobby Bowry, Chris Armstrong, Paul Williams and John Salako. Aston Villa played seven in a 2–0 win against Everton at Goodison on 19 October 1991. Up to this date Everton had only employed two Black footballers, Mike Trebilcock and Cliff Marshall. Before the signing of Barnes, the professional clubs on Merseyside, an area with one of the oldest Black communities in Britain, had operated what looked suspiciously like a colour bar. Liverpudlian Howard Gayle was Anfield's first player of colour, signing professional in November 1977. Tranmere Rovers had Elkanah Onyeali in the early '60s and then decided to look only at White boys. Yet such clubs were now, at the turn of the decade, a small minority.

The final chapter will discuss the relationship contemporary players of colour have to the British game.

EIGHT

The Numbers Game

In the middle of January 1999, halfway through his 22nd season, the assistant player–manager of Mansfield Town, Tony Ford, set a record of 825 outfield appearances in the Football League, beating the previous best held by Terry Paine of Southampton. Ford, the Grimsby-born son of a Barbadian father – who died when he was eight years old – began his professional career when Harold Wilson was prime minister, Leeds had just lost the European Cup final and David Essex was top of the pops with 'Hold Me Close' (luckily punk was just hammering its way into the ears and minds of thinking youth). As the century closed, Ford's longevity record in the oldest professional league in the world – in October 1999 he was playing for Rochdale – is significant in that it flags up, symbolically, the consistent presence of generations of players of colour in the British game.

As a Black Briton, rather than a migrant player of colour having to adjust to a different and sometimes hostile culture, Tony Ford doesn't feel attitudes to his pigmentation held him back, though he does recognise that the professional game has changed for the better in its treatment of players such as himself. Young Black wingers today aren't called 'Black cunt' every time they nutmeg the full-back. Managers don't now pick 'Niggers *v.* Whites' five-a-side games to ease down the Friday-before-the-match training sessions that ex-pro Richie Moran had to fight against.

Yet while these cultural changes in football have made the experience of the Black professional less contradictory, economic developments in football and society in general have resulted in a decline in Black British players in the Premiership.

During the summer of 1997, BBC2's *Black Britain* commissioned a short survey of the entry of Black British players into professional football. This initiative was the outcome of concern about the social effects and consequences of changes to the structure of schoolboy football with the abolition of the English Schools Football Association and its replacement with a two-tier system of club-run Soccer Academies and Schools of Excellence. *Black Britain*'s brief was to analyse this revamp in the context of wider social and economic changes in British society that have widened the gap between rich and poor, leading to a greater number of children living in poverty and one parent families.

The survey *The Entry of Young Black British Players into Professional Football at Élite Level* was brief, superficial and crude. The research had two primary sources, a phone survey and an examination of *Rothmans Football Year Books*. However, for all its shortcomings – and there were many – the findings which were broadcast in the Autumn of '97 did provide some insights about the relationship of contemporary Black players to the professional game. They were as follows:

- The total number of Black players in all divisions of the Football League and the Premiership doubled between seasons 1985–1997.
- Approximately 15 per cent of all professional footballers are Black.
- Approximately 14 per cent of Premier League footballers are Black.
- Approximately 33 per cent of all Black professionals play in the Premier League.
- The rise in the number of Black players in the Premier League seems to have reached a plateau.
- Immediately prior to the creation of the Premier League in 1992–3 approximately 50 per cent of all Black professionals played in Division One.
- The proportion of Black players within Premier clubs has declined as average squad numbers have increased during the life of the Premier League.
- Between 1985–6 and 1997–8 there has been an approximate increase of 35 per cent in the number of Black players in the Premier League.
- Between 1985–6 and 1997–8 there has been an approximate increase of 200 per cent in the number of Black players in the Football League.
- 17 per cent of all professionals in Divisions One, Two and Three are Black.
- There are distinct regional variations in the presence of Black players.
- The educational profile of young players is changing.

What the findings suggest is that the recruitment of Black British footballers to Premier League clubs has reached a plateau and may even be in decline. And if this is the case, it could reflect fundamental changes going on beneath the surface of the game at élite level.

As the primary researcher in this survey I would argue that the decrease in competitive football at schools has detrimentally and disproportionately affected youngsters from disadvantaged backgrounds. Instead of having competitive football 'on tap' at school where if you were good enough you played, the alternative for most young footballers is junior/colts leagues. In these leagues the economic and social circumstances of the player have far greater significance in influencing the access of that youngster to competitive football. The difficulty of those players from poor, one-parent and deprived backgrounds to fully commit themselves to the team – to be taken and collected from training, to buy boots, boot bag, pads, to pay subs and other expenses – acts as a filter siphoning out players from disadvantaged backgrounds. And a greater proportion of African–Caribbean children live in deprived, inner-city areas than their White counterparts. To play for a team in junior/colts leagues requires support and resources from families and carers of players. This is not the case with school football.

Football Academies and Centres of Excellence, run by professional clubs, require an even greater commitment by boys and their parents or carers. These, for the reasons outlined above, may also act to unwittingly exclude players from poorer backgrounds. Additionally the scouting system may reinforce this filtering process by not looking at youngsters who play outside the 'normal' scouting territories of junior and representative football. (British footballers from South Asian backgrounds could tell a story or two here.) *Black Britain* telephoned all 92 League and Premiership clubs to find how many of its trainees were Black: seven per cent was the answer. And how many of these will become pros?

The locked-in wealth of the Premier League creates pressures to avoid relegation at all costs. This short-term thinking translates into using the transfer market as a provider of instant solutions. This creates a paradox. While all clubs are expanding their coaching programmes for young players, those at élite level are ever more reliant on buying the finished product in the transfer market. Players are bought to perform immediately. This paradox is most obvious at Chelsea where virtually all the first-team squad have been bought in, with Jody Morris just about the only exception.

Until recently a small number of teams, such as Tranmere Rovers, Everton and Hartlepool had a noted absence of players of colour. This isn't the case in the late-'90s but how do these clubs explain their past employment practices which led them in the opposite direction to demographic trends in and out of football? Howard Kendall, while manager of Sheffield United, argued that one of the reasons he left his previous job at Everton was that the board wouldn't agree to buy Dion Dublin. Was it the money for his colour that worried them? There may have been a culture of institutional racism prevalent in the boardrooms of some clubs that 'explains' their consistent non-employment of Black players.

Premiership football is becoming gentrified in a number of ways – all-ticket matches; all-seater stadia; executive boxes; matchday packages; family enclosures – in an effort both to leave behind 'undesirable' supporters and entice those with more money to spend. Culturally the game at this level is attracting professional, middle-class supporters who no longer dissuade their sons from careers in football. The potential to earn a lifetime's earnings in one year of Premiership football has demolished any residual middle-class snobbery about a career in the game. With the scholarship programme replacing the Youth Training Scheme there is an educational dimension to the two-year apprenticeship. Football is now a fashionable career.

The concentration of Black players in the lower divisions mirrors wider social trends. The problems they face in attempting to become footballers may be symptomatic of the problems faced by the more disadvantaged sections of the working class as a whole. In the future we may find that the Ian Wright career path – he entered the full-time game at 22 – becomes more common for those from such backgrounds. Significantly, the three strikers – Wright, Ferdinand and

Collymore – used by England against Moldova at Wembley on 10 September 1997 all came late into full-time professional football: Ferdinand and Collymore were both signed at 20 by QPR and Crystal Palace respectively. This circuitous route into the full-time game is not uncommon among Black players. Chris Freestone, signed by Hartlepool from Northampton Town in 1999, was 23 before being offered a professional contract which, according to a report by Dr Stefan Szymanski of the Management School Imperial College, London, tends to be less lucrative than those offered to their White counterparts. Interestingly, Szymanski's study also found that teams with an above-average number of Black players usually finished higher in the league than other teams with a similar wage bill.

If Black players were, on the surface, part and parcel of the game in '90s Britain, Szymanski's research has highlighted contradictions that the late entry into full-time professional of Wright, Ferdinand and Collymore confirms. Fings ain't wot they seem. At the beginning of the '95–'96 season the three most expensive transfers in England were Collymore's £8.5 million move to Liverpool; Newcastle's £6 million for Les Ferdinand and Ferguson's £7 million to the St James's Park club for Andy Cole. Yet England manager Terry Venables defied the market – nothing wrong in that – by naming a lily-white selection against Colombia at Wembley in September, and against Norway and Switzerland in October and November. *Guardian* sportswriter Richard Williams pointed out this contradiction (*Guardian*, 6 June 1995) after England had beaten Japan. With all the wealth of Black talent available, and two years after Paul Ince became England's first Black captain at senior level, why were so few making it on to Venables's team list?

The FA, Premier League and Football League need to recognise the social consequences of economic and structural changes being implemented in football. Other national institutions more sensitive to the welfare of the game in its entirety, the PFA, Kick It Out and community-based groups such as Football Unites, Racism Divides (FURD) and Show Racism the Red Card (SRRC) are working at grass-roots level to attack the disadvantages caused by the actions of those who wield power. Both FURD and SRRC were formed to combat racism in football and work generally to make the game inclusive rather than exclusive, an objective for which many Premier League chairmen couldn't give a toss. Fortunately not all clubs are as selfish and short-sighted. Sheffield United, through FURD, provide over 100 complimentary tickets for people in the Sharrow district of the city – in which the club is based – who have traditionally felt excluded from Bramall Lane, such as Asian women and the sizeable group of Somali refugees who live around the ground. Sheffield United and FURD also combine to run coaching schemes for local youngsters and Asian women, some held at United's training ground. Indeed on 2 May 1999 the club hosted a multi-cultural community day, organised by FURD, at which local youngsters played small-sided games on the pitch and the Anti-Racist World Cup final between the Somali Blades and the Abbeydale Asian Youth Project was replayed after a drawn match in the original tournament in Italy in July 1998.

Other professional clubs have also joined forces with local anti-racist groups to develop programmes and initiatives designed to create a welcoming environment within the stadium and take the club into the community. Charlton Athletic, building on the 'Red, White and Black at the Valley' anti-racist open days have been involved, with 27 other local groups, in the formation of Charlton Athletic Race Equality (CARE). The South Londoners have taken a progressive stance on racism with warning signs inside the ground against 'racial abuse' in order to ensure all supporters and players feel welcome. They have also developed a formal relationship with Guru Nanak FC of Gravesend, Kent, assisting Nanak to run a school of excellence aimed at local Asian youngsters. Exeter City also have an anti-racist day.

The momentum for this kind of work by clubs, in partnership with community groups and their local authorities, is growing. A survey by the Sir Norman Chester Centre for Football Research of season-ticket holders at Premier League clubs during the 1996–97 season revealed non-White fans to be a tiny minority. Arsenal, with 2.8 per cent, topped the table. The encouragement of supporters from ethnic minorities to attend matches is another major battle that has to be won. In the street celebrations over Sunday and Monday, 9–10 May 1999, marking Bradford City's promotion to the Premiership for the 1999–2000 season, the participants – in a city that has the largest South Asian population in Britain – were overwhelmingly White. Nevertheless the club have made an effort to reach out: in September 1995, they hosted and provided the opposition for a UK Asian All-Star XI; a former manager is ex-Black professional Chris Kamara. They still have a way to go in assuring Bradford Asians that Valley Parade really wants them.

Such club or community initiatives often have much to do with the drive and dedication of committed individuals. At Millwall, there's Ken Chapman. At Orient, Neil Watson. In the case of Sheffield United and FURD, Andy Pack and Howard Holmes. At Northampton Town FC on 11 July 1999, a sculpture commemorating Walter Tull was unveiled in the newly dedicated Memorial Garden. A former director elected by supporters, Brian Lomax, had been the driving force behind this initiative. He has been backed by a supportive board, town council – who own the ground – and community groups. Brian has also been instrumental in encouraging the club to implement an equal-opportunities programme, the first of its kind in football inspiring others to follow.

These initiatives and campaigns are proof of the enormous goodwill and energy that exists in football, at grass-roots level and within some clubs. Sheffield United, Bradford, Northampton Town, Charlton Athletic, Millwall, Exeter City, Orient, Leeds United and Leicester City are at the forefront of initiatives designed to bring themselves closer to the communities to which they owe their existence. Needless to say, there are also others within these clubs, such as the chief executive at Leicester, Pierpoint, and the chairman of Sheffield United, who are pulling in the opposite direction.

Even with anti-racist campaigns becoming co-ordinated at national level with the formation of KIO, the problem of institutional racism still remains. Though Chris Ramsey has been appointed manager of England Under-20s taking them to the world youth championships in Nigeria in April 1999, the struggle for employment as manager, coach or administrator for Black ex-players is still problematic. While the history of Black managers probably reaches back to Arthur Wharton as player/coach of Stalybridge Rovers in the 1890s the colour bar still persisted for much of the next century. Why did Frank Soo have to shout most of his managerial instructions to Scandanavian players? Despite the historic presence of players of colour in the British game it is still difficult for such professionals to continue employment in football once their playing days are numbered. And while this is true for all players, the ratio of Black managers, coaches and administrators is much smaller than 15 per cent, their proportion of playing staff at professional clubs. However this glass ceiling is true for society as a whole. The higher you look – in terms of money and power – the whiter, more grey, masculine and privileged the occupants. The success of Tony Collins in taking Fourth Division Rochdale to the League Cup final in 1962 did not open the door for other players of colour intent on passing on their knowledge. Sammy Chung's success at Ipswich and Wolves a decade later still failed to inspire club directors to think rationally when shortlisting. While it would be parochial not to recognise that prejudice within boardrooms is a legacy of attitudes and practices that are commonplace in society as a whole, it would also be short-sighted and dismissive of fan-led initiatives to eradicate racism to think that football cannot be at the forefront of attacking these problems. Players, fans, clubs and their representative bodies cannot destroy racism within football but they can diminish it. A racist at boardroom level has the power to affect a person's livelihood. It is prejudice plus power, a deadly combination.

To democratise power within football clubs (in the first instance), to bring it under the control of the majority, would entail making far-reaching structural changes such as opening up boardrooms to fans and players – in effect making clubs co-operative. In any analysis of the finances of football it is the fans who put most money into the game: they fork out for season tickets, gate entrance, programmes, refreshments, club lotteries, club merchandise, club travel and therefore dwarf – in total – the input of individual capitalists like (Rupert Murdoch), Jack Walker, David Dein, Alan Sugar, Ken Bates, Doug Ellis, Michael Edwards, John Hall – most of whom have, through the clubs they control, actually increased their wealth through share issues. Yet these names have far more influence over the form and nature of football than the millions of fans with their millions of pounds of expenditure.

The men named above see themselves as successful in their roles. A back-of-the-envelope list of chairmen who were, or are, quite obviously abject failures would be far longer: Robert Maxwell at Oxford, Michael Knighton at Carlisle, Owen Oyston at Blackpool, Anton Rogers at Rotherham and Southend, Reg Brealey at Sheffield United and Darlington, Ken Richardson who tried to burn down Doncaster Rovers, Peter Swales at Manchester City, Robert Chase at

Norwich and Bill Archer at Brighton just to begin with. To label some of these 'abject failures' would be missing the point. One manager I interviewed said he knew of a consortium that offered, through a front man, to invest in clubs with redevelopment potential. In effect they were property developers posing as club saviours, a scenario Brighton and former Maidstone fans would recognise.

At any level of society, allowing one individual power to influence the lives of the majority is dangerous. It usually results in airheads acting stupidly. In football there is the absurd co-existence of democratic fan-based groups, such as Blades Independent Fans Association (BIFA) at Sheffield United and Manchester United Independent Supporters Association (MUISA) to name just a couple, who want to dilute power and democratise decision-making within clubs. They are often battling against dictatorial régimes headed by autocratic figures such as Ken Bates who thinks fans should be kept behind electric fencing. Yet there are clubs, such as Northampton Town, Bournemouth and Chester City, that have emerged out of difficult times with a little more power to the people. Northampton's Sixfields Stadium is owned by the town and used as a community resource. The board of directors has an elected representative of the fans. It is no coincidence that the Cobblers were the first club to introduce an equal opportunities policy and dedicate a sculpture in memory of its first Black player, Walter Tull. Brian Lomax feels such initiatives are important in building an organic bond between the club and its community. After emerging from bankruptcy in the early '90s, a reorganised and reconstituted Northampton Town have become an organic part of the community through their ownership, administration and initiatives.

With the club going the same way as Aldershot, Newport County, Accrington Stanley and Third Lanark, Brian and three others met in the Brewer's Arms pub in 1992 to whinge and work out the way forward. They formed a trust and held a public meeting attended by over six hundred. Soon after, bankrupt Northampton was put into administration. The trust's hour had come earlier than expected. They raised £60,000 for an 8 per cent share. They also demanded that the reconstituted club, as part of its lease agreement with the council, have an elected supporter on its board. Since this period, argues Brian Lomax:

> . . . gates have risen from over 2,000 to 6,000. This is of course about playing success and the new stadium, but the increase exceeds comparable situations elsewhere and, in my view, is partly because supporters now know they are stakeholders and not just turnstile fodder . . . There is a feeling of everyone being on the same side in a common enterprise, rather than just 'us and them' . . . the chief benefits [of supporter involvement at board level] have been felt in the areas [of] anti-racism, equal opportunities and disability.
>
> The trust has helped make the club more accountable, to supporters and the whole community. I believe football clubs are collective endeavours, where people come together to experience a sense of

community, loyalty, passion. I have always believed clubs should embody
that ethos, not exploit it, and that is what we've tried to encourage here.

Bournemouth AFC, though a company, is run as a trust with power distributed
among a committee rather than one individual. The trust fund holds 51 per cent
of voting rights. The chairman Trevor Watkins pays for his own season ticket and
doesn't get paid. The new owners of Chester City, the Smiths, also believe those
that breathe life into it should have a say in looking after it. A father and son
team from Florida, USA, they have agreed to Chester Independent Supporters'
Association having a 35 per cent share and three elected directorships in return
for the £130,000 raised and donated to the club through a public appeal. Son
Gerald, a former gridiron footballer argues 'this club has been part of the city for
114 years. Ultimately it belongs to the people and supporters of Chester'.[1]

As a child I used to be sent off to the Co-op for a pint of milk or packet of razor
blades. 'Hurry up . . . go on, I'll time you!' Each registered customer was a
shareholder with voting rights. Each time you shopped your share number was
recorded with a dividend paid at the end of the accounting year. Couldn't a system
of similar principle operate in football whereby those who support and work for
the club at all levels comprise a collective ownership and are active in running it?
In the Premiership, matches are all-ticket. No money is taken at the turnstiles. It
wouldn't be too difficult, therefore, for clubs and fans to register personal
attendance at games. Those supporters who'd attended a requisite number of
games – say 50 per cent of matches – would then become members, vote at
shareholder meetings and be eligible to stand for office. In the Football League,
even with turnstile matches, a version of this system could still operate. Essentially
the argument here is that power should be distributed as widely as possible within
clubs. There are numerous ways this could be done other than the suggestions
outlined above. Clubs should be administered, on a day-to-day level, by those who
are formally representatives of the majority and committed to its best interests as
recognised by that majority. While football can never cocoon itself from the
pressures and prejudices of the society of which it is a part, it can act as a
progressive force at the vanguard of change. Those involved in anti-racism
campaigns in football know that the hardest door too open is the chairman's. This
is not a coincidence. Within is the man with the big stick, reflecting the power
structure of the world outside the stadium where, essentially, economic wealth
determines power. Those progressive forces inside football fighting racism,
property developer chairmen, gentrification and other issues recognise that the
unifying element in all these issues is the question of the allocation of power. If
wealthy individuals can buy clubs and use them as extensions of their ego, the
most important people in those clubs, the players and fans, will always be subject
to the arbitrary whim of an individual under little or no constraint. Chairmen
now fancy themselves as managers: Michael Knighton tried it at Carlisle with the
obvious consequence. Ron Noades has his own tracksuit at Brentford and guided
them to the 1998–99 Third Division Championship.

However the experiences of Knighton, who almost managed to lose Carlisle their Football League status, and Ken Richardson of Doncaster Rovers, who did what Knighton narrowly failed to do, are more typical. After Richardson had decided, in October 1997, to walk away from a team he'd made very poor with his transfers, signings, selection and tactics, he appointed another complete novice in football management, Mark Weaver, who responded by sticking his next door neighbour, a pub goalie, between the posts. Come May 1998 Doncaster had sunk out of the Football League and were waving their arms at the conference. The 'benefactor' of Rovers (Richardson was never registered as a director – a family company called Dinard operating out of the Isle of Man owned the majority of shares) had also put Bridlington Town out of business.

Chairman Ken tried to burn down Rovers in 1995 when a deal fell through with the council which he thought would net £1.6 million. Richardson's career as a scam artist could not have been scripted better by the writers of the Phil Silvers Show. In comparison, John Sullivan's archetypal ducker and diver 'Del Boy' is the consummate smooth operator. Unlike his Rovers, Ken had a bit of form. In 1984 he entered a ringer in a horse race and got caught: nine months suspended, £20,000 fine and £200,000 in legal costs. Having learnt from his mistakes his plan to torch Belle Vue was meticulous – by his standards. He hired a former SAS soldier Alan Kristiansen, who in turn hired two others, and agreed to pay them £10,000 (petrol and matches not included). Unfortunately this failure to pay attention to small detail and not front up exes for light and fuel was the achilles heel of the plot. In June 1995, Kristiansen filled up four cans from the pumps at a petrol station and paid with his credit card, all of which was filmed on video. At Belle Vue, inside the mainstand tearoom, they did the business. But, eager to make a quick getaway, they left behind the cans, the rucksack in which they were carried and Kristiansen's mobile phone. Like the team on the park, the trio hadn't set Belle Vue ablaze. If just one of them had genned up on the first principle of pyrotechnics – fire needs oxygen – and opened the tearoom door, the blaze would have left more than just a hole in the roof. And Kristiansen and his firm had had two goes at it, their first attempt in May 1995 failing completely!

Richardson took over Doncaster Rovers because he thought there was money to be made from a relocation of the ground. He had no interest in the welfare of the club. Fortunately, in this respect he is not typical of most chairmen. However a characteristic of his position that was shared by other chairmen is unrestrained power. Almost anyone who promises to pump money into a hard-up club will be offered a major shareholding by sycophantic directors and supported by fans. Doncaster Rovers have been in existence since 1879. Arthur Wharton chose Rovers as the opposition for his Rotherham Town benefit match in 1892. Yet because of the greedy imaginings of a wealthy scam artist attempting to use the club for his own gain, they nearly folded up. Richardson is not alone in envisaging a pot of gold at the end of the players' tunnel – many chairmen in the Premier League have enriched themselves through their clubs, whether by design or accident.

To play professionally a footballer has to be good. In Italy, to manage a Serie A club you have to have taken an accredited course in soccer management. Increasingly, professional coaches are taking their UEFA 'A' licences. But any chap who's made a fortune in the City, in property development – in anything – can take over a football club, lock, stock and barrel. How things turn out is down to luck and chance. And if the road travelled is bumpy, hard and barren, the major shareholder can bail out. Fortunately the supporters will still be there, although they'll still be relatively powerless unless they're prepared to take direct action. While fans have managed to chase a few idiots out – Robert Chase at Norwich and Bill Archer at Brighton spring to mind – they haven't been successful in the past in pushing their choice through the revolving door.

What has discussion of bent chairmen got to do with players of colour? We come back to the fundamental relationship that underpins many of the issues raised in this book: the allocation, distribution and utilisation of power. The term 'players of colour' is a descriptive umbrella, used to gather all those who face a common experience – racism – and the consequent real disadvantage that springs from it. Under this canopy stand people from different cultures and backgrounds, sometimes with little in common: Tony Whelan's experience as a Mancunian footballer playing in his home town will have been substantially different from Elkanah Onyeali's encounters up the East Lancs Road and across the Mersey in Tranmere. What unites both is the way they were publicly perceived and received – as Black players – by football fans and the public in general. Slowly the divisive weapon of racism is being blunted. But it is still painfully slow: the abuse aimed at Rotherham's Leo Fortune-West at Chester on the last weekend of the 1998–99 season; Newcastle United fans' racist cussing of Coventry's Youseff Chipo in the match at Highfield Road, 16 October 1999; and the neanderthal reaction by the *Daily Record* – 'Jamaica Mistake – Anger Over Scotland's Reggae Rescuer' – to Craig Brown's consideration of West Indian David Johnson for the national team, are an indication of just how slow it is.

While great strides have been made in the professional game, despite the Toon's racist Goons effectively ignoring their own players' condemnation of racism in abusing Chippo, some County FAs responsible for administrating grass-roots football are still celebrating England's 1966 World Cup win. Like South Asian amateur club Bari, FC Santos – an African–Caribbean team from west London – have been abused and attacked while playing. At a five-a-side tournament in Hertfordshire they had to fight against pitch invaders intent on chivvying a nigger. One of the attackers had a knife. The organisers of the competition and the Hertfordshire FA refused to take any responsibility. Another amateur footballer, Clint Eastman, also playing under the auspices of the Hertfordshire FA in the Olympian League, was slashed with a knife at a match. A few seasons back a Black Scot, Stephen Roberts, playing for Campsie Black Watch in the West of Scotland Golden Goals Under-21 Cup was hospitalised with a fractured skull he received from two opponents, Craig Pringle and Peter McGregor, while he was posing for a triumphant photograph with the cup.

Racism is still used to create inequalities between people – in employment, housing, education – whereby pigmentation determines life chances and experiences. The only thorough and systematic solution to eradicate such inequalities in life chances is to ensure that power is democratically controlled and fairly utilised by and for the benefit of all. At present, football is a plutocracy with monied people shouting the odds. It is not the aggregation of a little money in a lot of hands that carries weight, but a lot of money in one hand.

Democratic control of football would entail a radical restructuring that, if I were to be completely honest, I can't see happening in the near future. Clubs run by the community for the community may be a utopian idea, beset by all sorts of practical problems: the difficulties of decision-making by committee; incessant compromise; a plethora of visions; rival factions etc. But if mistakes were made they would be made by the majority, with responsibility for correction falling to the majority. Having access to power stimulates interest and involvement, and diminishes the fear of pitfalls and failure itself. And with participation by those in the community interested in benefiting from a community resource – in the widest sense of the term, as meeting place, leisure facility and public space – prejudice and racism would wither because, quite simply, it wouldn't be practical or useful. Nor would it be necessary to write a book such as this. Footballers would just be footballers . . . zzzzzz!!! Sorry, I was dreaming again.

Postscript: At the 1999 Labour Party Conference, Chris Smith, Minister for Culture, Media and Sport argued that professional football is in danger of losing touch with its roots. Some would argue that in the Premiership it already has. Criticising those who run the game he asked for a return to 'community values' and 'social responsibility'. To this end a unit would be established at the Football Trust with the aim of helping supporters get an economic and political foothold in their clubs. New Labour calls this idea of shared ownership New Mutualism. A limited amount of money and advice would be on offer from the Co-op Bank. It is a small step in the right direction. Hopefully it will give a further kick-start to the fan-power movement that will only halt when clubs are in the hands of the people who support and work for them – and not money-grabbing, power-hungry parasites like Rupert Murdoch who seem to miss the point of life at every turn.

Endnotes

ONE — THE PIONEERS 1883–1918

1. Much of the material on Wharton is taken from Phil Vasili *The First Black Footballer. Arthur Wharton, 1865–1930. An Absence of Memory* (London 1998).
2. T.H. Smith, 12 January 1942.
3. 29 October 1887. Quoted by E. Griffiths, director, Preston North End Football Club in correspondence with Dr Ray Jenkins 20 February 1985.
4. *Athletics Journal*, 26 June 1888, p.7.
5. 'The Referee' as reprinted in the *Darlington and Stockton Times*, 17 July 1886.
6. PRO, CO 96/238/2044, 2 November 1892.
7. PRO, CO 96/238/2044. Also in Jenkins, IJHS *op.cit.* p.50.
8. Odette Keun 'A Foreigner Looks at British Sudan' (1930) in Anthony Kirkham-Greene 'Imperial Administration and the Athletic Imperative: The Case of the District officer in Africa' in W.J. Baker and James Mangan (eds) *Sport in Africa* (London 1987).
9. 'Committee on the System of Appointment in the Civil Service' Cmnd. 3554, 23 in Kirkham-Greene, *op.cit.* p.92.
10. Kirkham-Greene, *op.cit.* p.93. See also Henrika Kuklick 'The Imperial Bureaucrat: The Colonial Administrative Service in the Gold Coast 1920–1939' (1979) in Kirkham-Greene *op.cit.*
11. *Sheffield Independent*, 11 September 1888.
12. Much of this information about Wharton's extended family history comes from Sheila Leeson, interview with the author, Rotherham, 24 April 1996.
13. Andrew Ritchie, *International Journal of the History of Sport*, vol.16 (March 1999) no.1 pp.189–192.
14. Charles A. Dana in Arthur Ashe Junior *A Hard Road To Glory* vol.1 (1993 edition) p.27.
15. Jeffrey P. Green 'Boxing and the "Colour Question" in Edwardian Britain: The "White Problem" of 1911' in *International Journal of the History of Sport* 5, 118, (1988).
16. Peter Lovesey *The Official Cenetary of the AAA* (London) p.75.

[17] Theophilus E. Samuel Scholes 'Glimpses of the Ages: or the superior and inferior races, so-called, discussed in the light of science and history' 176, 177, 179, 237 in Peter Fryer *Staying Power: The History of Black People in Britain* vol.II (1984) p.439.

[18] Mike Marqusee 'Sport and Stereotype: from role model to Muhammed Ali' in *Race and Class* 36, 4 (1995) p.10.

[19] *Ibid.*, p.20.

[20] George Breitman 'The Last Year of Malcolm X' (New York 1967) pp. 206–7 in Kevin Ovenden *Malcolm X. Socialism and Black Nationalism* (London 1992) p.41.

[21] C.L.R. James *Beyond A Boundary* (London 1996) p.124.

[22] C.L.R. James *Beyond A Boundary* (London 1963) p.110 in Peter Fryer *Staying Power: The History of Black People in Britain* (1984) p.364.

[23] *Sheffield Telegraph*, 16 December 1930.

[24] Liverpool University: the National Children's Home (NCO) Archive. Cause of death listed in Application for Walter and Edward to enter 'The Children's Home and Orphanage'. My thanks to Brian Parnell of the *NCO* for assisting my access to the Tull file.

[25] Butcher to Gregory, 11 October 1900 in NCO Archive.

[26] *Illustrated Sporting and Dramatic News*, 17 April 1909, p.234.

[27] Tull to Morgan, NCO Archive.

[28] John Harding *For the Good of the Game: The Official History of the Professional Footballers' Association* (London 1991) p.29.

[29] *BAH*, 8 June 1909.

[30] *BAH*, 6 June 1909, p.3. 'Wednesday next' refers to Liga Argentina *v.* Tottenham Hotspur. Spurs won 4–1, with Tull at centre-forward.

[31] *BAH*, 23 May 1909, p.9; See also 15, 17, 25, 26, 27, 29 June.

[32] *Ibid.*, 8 June.

[33] *Daily Chronicle*, 13 September 1909.

[34] *Daily Chronicle*, 4 October 1909.

[35] *Football Echo* (Northampton) March 15 and September 13, 1913.

[36] *Illustrated Sporting and Dramatic News,* 9 December 1899 pp.573–4.

[37] FC. The report of October 1909 carried the sub-heading 'Football and the Colour Prejudice'. Unfortunately the origin of the report is unknown.

[38] Fryer, *op. cit.* pp.1–2.

[39] David Killingray, 'All the King's Men? Blacks in the British Army in the First World War, 1914–1988', pp. 67–69, *Under the Imperial Carpet: Essays in Black History 1780–1950* (Crawley 1986).

[40] A.F. Pollard in a letter to the *Times*, 7 November 1914 in Mason, *Association Football and English Society 1863–1915* (Brighton 1980) p.251.

[41] T. Mason, *op.cit.* p.254.

[42] Everard Wyrall *The Die-Hards in the Great War,* vol.1, 1914–16 (London 1926) p.238.

[43] C.R.M.F. Crutwell, 'A History of the Great War' (Oxford University Press,

1934), p.154 in Marwick, *op.cit.* p.16.
44 War Diaries, *op.cit.* 26 January 1918.
45 Original letter in Finlayson Collection, *op.cit.* See also Glasgow *Evening Times,* 12 February 1940.
46 Letter from Major B.S. Poole, Middlesex Regiment, to Edward Tull, 12 April 1918 in Finlayson Collection, *op.cit.*
47 *Leith Observer,* 19 March 1898.
48 *Carrick Herald* (Girvan), 15 December 1950.
49 Obituary *Ayrshire Post,* 15 December 1950, p.8.

TWO — BATMAN AND THE BARROWBOY: THE SECOND GENERATION 1919–45

1 Andrew Ward *The Manchester City Story* (1984) p.22.
2 *Derbyshire Football Express,* 16 October 1920.

THREE — TOURING TEAMS 1888–1959

1 *Newcastle Evening Chronicle* 2 September 1899; *Sporting Man* (Newcastle) 5, 6 September 1899.
2 *ibid, African Review* 9 September, vol.xx no.355; *Sporting Man* (Newcastle) 7 September 1899.
3 *Football Echo and Sports Gazette,* 18 September 1899.
4 *Sporting Man,* (Newcastle) 6 September 1899.
5 Phillip, Viscount (later Lord) Swinton, 'Address to Achimota College Students', 30 June 1944. Swinton Papers, 174/15/5 Churchill College, Cambridge.
6 Peter Canham 'Africa in the Colonial Period. The Transfer of Power. The Colonial Administrator in the Age of Decolonisation' (Oxford 1978) in Photography Archive, Royal Commonwealth Society Library, Cambridge y304480.
7 See correspondence of Governor Richards in Catherine Thomas 'Colonial Government Propaganda and Public Relations and the Administration of Nigeria 1939–51' unpublished Ph.D, University of Cambridge, 1986 pp.149–50. And Richards to Swinton, 15 December 1945 where he argues a) that it 'is time to go for Zik' b) that the Zik press should be suppressed and c) that the previous governor Bourdillon 'encouraged every kind of wild cat trade union'. Swinton Papers, *op.cit.*
8 *West Africa* (*WA*) 17 September 1949, p.889.
9 See 6, 8, 9, 10 February 1945.
10 *WAP* 8 February 1945.
11 Terence Ranger, 'The Invention of Tradition in Colonial Africa' in *The Invention of Tradition,* Eric Hobsbawm and Terence Ranger (eds), (Cambridge

1983) p.228.
12 *WAP* 6 February 1945.
13 Namdi Azikiwe *My Odyssey* (London 1970) p.410.
14 'Hibernicus', in *WA* 8 October 1949, p.953.
15 *WAP* 8 February 1945.
16 Samuel Ekpe Akpabot, *Football in Nigeria* (London 1984), p.14, 21–22.
17 (London) *Times*, 30 August 1949, p.6.
18 Quoted in *WA* 15 October 1949, p.967.
19 *Ibid.* For an example of regional differences within West Africa on this matter see Phyllis M. Martin, 'Colonialism, Youth and Football in French Equatorial Africa' *IJHS8* (May 1991), 1. The author describes how boots were preferred by African players in Brazzaville, capital of French Congo. The European administrators, however, wanted them to play in bare feet! Again, it was a battle of wills and resources that held significance with consequences that went far beyond football.
20 Chief Anthony Enahoro *Fugitive Offender* (London 1965) pp.43–4.
21 'Will to Win', Channel 4, Autumn 1993.
22 *WAP*, 23 July 1949.
23 *Ibid.*, 17 August, 3 September 1949.
24 See *Liverpool Echo*, 1, 29 September, 1 October 1949. E. MacDonald Bailey was a leading African-Caribbean sprinter, holder of the (British) Amateur Athletics Association 100- and 200-yards record. This colour-coded humour reflected the degree to which 'racial' stereotyping was commonplace and acceptable. It was also found on BBC Radio – and no doubt elsewhere – with a programme in 1947 called *The Darkie Minstrel Show:The Coloured Coons*. With unconscious irony the 1 October edition also printed a feature on Dick Turpin, the Black middleweight boxing champion of Great Britain. He was allowed to fight for the belt, in 1948, under revised British Boxing Board of Control (BBBC) rules which scrapped an earlier decree that no Black boxer could fight for a British title. The ban was initiated because Jack Johnson preferred not to defend his heavyweight title in Britain.
25 *WA*, 17 September 1949.
26 *Ibid.*
27 *WAP*, 13 September 1949.
28 *WA* 24 September and *WAP* 22 September, 1949.
29 (London) *Times*, 26 September 1949; *Amateur Sport*, 17 September 1949.
30 *WA* 15 October 1949.
31 *Liverpool Echo*, 27 September 1949.
32 Akpabot, *op. cit.* pp.21–22.
33 *Ashanti Times*, 3 August 1951.
34 Canham, *op. cit.*
35 *Barnet Press and News*, September 15, 1951 p.7.
36 H.T.C. Weatherfield 'Uganda Notes' September 1903 p.43 in *Uganda Journal*, 11 (September 1947), 2 (London) p.120.

[37] W.E. Hoyle 'Early Days In Kampala' *Uganda Journal*, 21 (March 1957), 1 pp.94–95.

[38] 'Uganda Notes' in *Uganda Journal* 12, December 1905, 2 p.194.

[39] C.A.G. Wallis 'Report of an Inquiry into African Local Government in the Protectorate of Uganda' pp.13–15 in D. Wadada, *Imperialism and Revolution in Uganda* (London 1980) pp.147, 214.

[40] *UA* 24 August.

[41] *Peterborough Citizen and Advertiser*, 11 September 1956.

[42] (London) *Times*, 27 September 1956.

[43] *UA* 5, 10 October 1956.

[44] (Plymouth) *Western Morning News*, (*WMN*), 5 October 1953.

[45] (Trinidad) *Evening News*, 6 August 1953.

[46] *WMN*, 21 September 1953.

[47] *Ibid.*, 22 September 1953.

[48] (London) *Times*, 13 October 1958, p.6.

FOUR — NURSES, TUBEWORKERS AND FOOTBALLERS: TRAVELLING TO WORK 1945–70

[1] G.A.L. Thabe *It's a Goal: 50 Years of Sweat, Tears and Brama in Black Soccer* (Johannesburg 1983) p.5.

[2] *Ibid.*, p.55.

[3] *Ibid.*, p.57.

[4] *Ibid.*, p.24.

[5] Mokone & J.W. Ryan (Pretoria n.d.) p.34.

[6] Telephone interview, 13 November 1997.

[7] Mokone and J.W. Ryan, *op.cit* p.32.

[8] Speech given at the 'Tribute to the Pioneers of Black Football', Birmingham, 30 May 1998.

[9] Telephone interview, *op.cit.*

[10] Mokone and J.W. Ryan, *op.cit.* p.47.

[11] *Ibid.*, p.77.

[12] Mokone, in communication with the author, 7 July 1998.

[13] In E. Andrews and A. Mackay *Sports Report no.2* (London 1954) pp.163–4.

[14] *Sheffield Telegraph and Independent*, 13 January 1942 p.4.

[15] Jimmy Seed *The Jimmy Seed Story* (London 1957) p.53.

[16] M. Jarred and M. Macdonald *Leeds United: A Complete Record* (Derby 1996).

[17] Dan Wharters *Leeds United: The Official History of the Club* (1979) p.44.

[18] Johnny Giles in B. Bremner *You Get Nowt for Being Second* (London 1969) p.59.

[19] Giles in Jason Thomas *The Leeds United Story* (London 1971) p.33.

[20] Thomas (1971) *op.cit.* p.11.

[21] Giles in Bremner (1969) *op.cit.* pp.59–60.

22 Thomas (1971) *op.cit.* p.52.

23 Jack Charlton *For Leeds and England* (London 1967) p.88.

24 Howard Wilkinson to Richard Williams, *Guardian,* 3 October 1995.

25 Mark Rivlin 'Albert Memorial' *When Saturday Comes* November 1995 p.10.

26 *West Africa* 8 October 1949 (no.1702 vol. xxxiii) p.9403.

27 *Peterborough Citizen & Advertiser* 30 August 1955.

28 *Ibid.,* 2 September 1955.

29 *Ibid.,* 20 and 23 September 1955.

30 *Ibid.,* 27 September 1955.

31 *Ibid.,* p.23.

32 *Liverpool Echo* 3 September and 16 November 1960, *Birkenhead News* 3 September 1960.

33 *Liverpool Echo* 16 November 1960.

34 Rogan Taylor and Andy Ward *Three Sides of the Mersey. An Oral History of Everton, Liverpool and Tranmere Rovers* (London 1993) p.208. Thanks to Andy Ward for drawing this to my attention.

35 Phil Vasili 'The Entry of Young Black British Players into Professional Football at Elite Level', a report for *Black Britain* BBC2, broadcast October 1997.

36 *Cambridge Daily News,* 11 October 1961.

37 *Ibid.,* 7 October 1961.

38 *Ibid.,* 10 October.

39 *Ibid.,* 11, 17 October; 21, 27 November 1961. Thanks to Neil Harvey for information on Feyami.

40 *Ibid.,* 14 December 1961.

41 In Al Hamilton *Black Pearls of Soccer* (London 1982) p.69.

42 Richard Adamson *Bogota Bandit. The Outlaw Life of Charlie Mitten: Manchester United's Penalty King* (Edinburgh 1996) p.138.

43 James E. Handley *The Celtic Story: A History of Celtic FC* (London 1960) p.166.

44 G. Heron *As I See Celtic* (n.d.) article provided by Celtic FC.

45 G. Heron *I Shall Wish Just for You* (Detroit 1992).

46 G. Heron *As I See Celtic* p.13.

47 Stuart Cosgrove, *Hampden Babylon* (Edinburgh 1991) p.130.

48 Mitten in Adamson, *op.cit.* p.77.

49 Ron Greenwood in Hunter Davies *My Life in Football* (Edinburgh 1990) p.29.

50 *Marshall Cavendish Book of Football* (London 1972) p.554.

51 *Daily Mirror,* 11 February; 7 January 1974.

52 Hunter Davies, *op.cit.* p.32.

53 *Marshall Cavendish Book of Football op.cit.* p.555.

54 *Across the White Line,* BBC Radio, February–March 1995.

55 Peter Read *Charles Perkins: A Biography* (Australia 1990) p.xiii.

56 *Ibid,* p.43.

[57] *Ibid*, p.51.
[58] *Ibid*, p.54.
[59] *Ibid*, p53.
[60] John Pilger 'Fixed Race' in *Guardian Weekend*, 21 August 1999, p.21.
[61] *Ibid*, Sir Roland Wilson.
[62] Peter Read (Australia 1990) *op.cit.* p.171.

FIVE — '66, '68, FOOTBALL IN BLACK AND WHITE: BLACK BRITISH FOOTBALLERS 1945–70

[1] *Sporting Mirror*, 16 September 1949. The feature focused upon 'two star centre-forwards', the other being Ronnie Turnbull of Manchester City. Thanks to Barry Bendell for bringing this article to my attention.
[2] *Sporting Mirror*, *op.cit.*
[3] Keith Hall, *Bullseye. Hereford United FC* (match programme) *v.* Middlesbrough, 24 September 1996.
[4] Trefor Jones *The Watford Football Club Illustrated Who's Who* (Middlesex 1996) p.59.
[5] Alex Ferguson *Six Years at United* (Edinburgh 1992) pp.23, 27.
[6] Collins in *Watford Observer* 30 April 1993, *op.cit.*
[7] Charlie Williams in *'Charlie' The Charlie Williams Story* Stephen D. Smith (Barnsley 1998) p.49.
[8] Stacey in communication with Peter Jones, June 1996.
[9] From Hunter Davies *My Life in Football* (Edinburgh 1990) p.29.
[10] Tony Pawson, *100 years of the FA Cup. The Official Centenary History.* (London 1972) pp.259–60.
[11] Kenneth Chapman, *Black & Blue. Millwall FC* (match programme) *v.* Northampton Town, 21 February 1998.
[12] *Manchester Evening News Football Pink*, 17 March 1973.
[13] Interview with Tony Whelan, Old Trafford, 13 March 1996.
[14] *Ibid.*
[15] Anonymous newspaper report supplied by Ester Smith of the St Kitts and Nevis High Commission, London 18 November 1998.
[16] *Ibid.*

SIX — TOO SMALL, TOO SMELLY, TOO CLEVER AND NOT INTERESTED: PLAYERS WITH ASIAN ANTECEDENCE 1919–1970

[1] Ivan Sharpe *Forty Years in Football* (London 1952) p.84.
[2] Percy M. Young *Football Year* (London 1958) p.114.
[3] Alan Breck *Alan Breck's Book of Scottish Football* (Edinburgh 1937) p.12.
[4] Geron Swann and Andrew Ward *The Boys from the Hill: An Oral History of*

Oxford United (Oxford 1996) p.67.

5 *Ibid.*
6 *Ibid.*
7 Philip Webster *Keelan. The Story of a Goalkeeper.* (Norwich 1979) p.13.
8 *Ibid*, p.16.
9 Eamon Dunphy *Sir Matt Busby & Manchester United. A Strange Kind of Glory* (London 1991) p.277.
10 *Ibid*, p.276.
11 Paul Daw *United in Endeavour. A History of Abbey United/Cambridge United FC 1912–1988* (Cambridge 1988) p.118. Thanks to Brian Lorimer for bringing this book to my attention.
12 *Cambridge News*, 1 July 1968.
13 *Ibid.*
14 Interview with Leivers, *op.cit.*
15 *Scottish Sunday Express*, 12 May 1975.
16 *Scotland on Sunday*, 24 November 1996.
17 *Match of the Day Magazine*, September 1997, pp.16–17.
18 *Independent* 4 October, 1999, p.4.
19 *Independent* 27 September, 1999, p.4.

SEVEN — EXPLODING INTO MATURITY: THE '70s AND '80s

1 Ernest Cashmore *Black Sportsmen* (London 1982), pp.57–59.
2 *Times*, 2 January 1981.
3 Brian Woolnough *Black Magic* (London 1983) p.3.
4 *Sunday Times*, 14 December 1975 p.27.
5 *Guardian*, 26 July 1982.
6 Stuart Cosgrove *Hampden Babylon* (Edinburgh 1991) p.130.

EIGHT — THE NUMBERS GAME

1 *Independent*, 7 October 1999.